PIOUS PRACTICE AND
SECULAR CONSTRAINTS

PIOUS PRACTICE AND SECULAR CONSTRAINTS

Women in the Islamic Revival in Europe

JEANETTE S. JOUILI

STANFORD UNIVERSITY PRESS
STANFORD, CALIFORNIA

Stanford University Press
Stanford, California

Printed in the United States of America

Library of Congress Cataloging-in-Publication Data

Jouili, Jeanette Selma, author.
Pious practice and secular constraints : women in the Islamic revival in Europe /
Jeanette Selma Jouili.
    pages cm
Includes bibliographical references and index.
ISBN 978-0-8047-9287-5 (cloth)—ISBN 978-0-8047-9466-4 (pbk.)
1. Muslim women—Religious life—Europe. 2. Muslim women—Europe—Conduct of
life. 3. Islam and secularism—Europe. 4. Islamic renewal—Europe. I. Title.
BP188.18.W65J68 2015
297.082'094—dc23
          2014038922

ISBN 978-0-8047-9489-3 (electronic)

Typeset by Bruce Lundquist in 10/14 Minion

To my parents

CONTENTS

ACKNOWLEDGMENTS

This book is the outcome of a long journey—longer than I imagined when I began. The book traveled under the auspices of many individuals, and the journey has taken me to numerous institutions in several countries, to all of whom I owe my deep gratitude.

I extend my thankfulness to Nilüfer Göle at the École des Hautes Études en Sciences Sociales, Werner Schiffauer at the European University Viadrina Frankfurt (Oder), and Annelies Moors at the International Institute for the Study of Islam in the Modern World and the University of Amsterdam for being significant mentors at various stages of my academic career and for being encouraging and supportive in so many ways.

My participation in the research group Configurations of Muslim Traditions in European Secular Public Spheres, sponsored by the Research Institute for Theology and Religious Studies at Utrecht University and funded by the Netherlands Organisation for Scientific Research, from 2008 to 2011 provided a wonderful environment in which to develop collaboratively our reflections about Islam and secularism in a European context. This period of collaboration was an extremely stimulating time for me, and my work benefited enormously from these meetings and conversations. My gratitude goes most notably to Schirin Amir-Moazami, Sarah Bracke, Alexandre Caiero, Nadia Fadil, Christine Jacobsen, and Frank Peter.

The research on which this book was built was supported by the German Academic Exchange Service (DAAD). During the writing phase I was also supported by postdoctoral research positions in the Netherlands, at the International Institute for the Study of Islam in the Modern World and at the University of Amsterdam where the position was funded by the Dutch Research Council (NWO); by a fellowship at the Society for the Humanities at Cornell University; and by a postdoctoral research position in women's studies at Duke University. At both Cornell and Duke I benefited tremendously from a number of colleagues and friends. At Cornell I most notably thank Timothy Murray for guiding me through my first steps in U.S. academia and for pushing me to continue working on this project even though it was not related to my fellowship. I also acknowledge Iftikhar Dadi, Salah Hassan, Viranjini Munasinghe, and Jennifer Stoever for their help in so many ways. At Duke University, my gratefulness goes to Frances Hasso, Anne Allison, Claudia Koonz, Miriam Cooke, Ebrahim Moosa, Ellen McLarney, Clare Counihan, and Alyssa Miller, who commented on different chapters of this book and provided other kinds of significant support.

Additionally, numerous colleagues and friends in various institutions have provided generous support over the years. I especially want to mention here Nikola Tietze, Armando Salvatore, Martin van Bruinessen, Riva Kastoryano, Georg Stauth, Maleiha Malik, Mbaye Bashir Lo, Carina Ray, Asma Barlas, Lisa Samuel, and Christine Moliner. The International Studies Program at the College of Charleston provided a home during the final stage of this book's preparation. At Stanford University Press, I have had the chance to work with Kate Wahl and Anne Fuzellier Jain, who made the experience of the "first book" truly satisfying. Their professionalism and competence were precious. I am also grateful for the helpful questions, suggestions, and remarks made by the anonymous reviewers for Stanford University Press.

Furthermore, I acknowledge all those who provided significant help throughout the fieldwork I conducted in several stints between 2002 and 2010. I thank especially a number of people who considerably facilitated my entry into the scene I have studied: in Paris, Noura Jaballah, Mehrezia Maiza, Dora Mabrouk, and Hichème El-Arafa; in Cologne, Amina Theissen, Hanim Ezder, and Birsen Uerek. Moreover, I am deeply grateful to all the women I worked with, whose names I cannot list here for the sake of confidentiality. Without their willingness to sacrifice their time, share their life stories, and invite me into their everyday life, this work would not have been possible. I am also thankful to Elodie Bouigues and Christina Guttuso, and again to Nikola Tietze, who contributed much to making me feel at home in Paris; and to Eritrea Berhane and Ute Wotsch for ensuring that Cologne wouldn't lose the feeling of home. Their presence during the fieldwork was priceless.

Without the love and support of my family, the journey that this book represents would never have been possible. My partner in life, Idrissou Mora-Kpai, has stood by me through it all. He has brought me back to calm whenever work-related doubts have seemed to overburden me; our conversations and his critical mind have constantly pushed me to see the big picture. I am grateful to our children, Mounir and Aqeel, for putting up with a mother who was often unavailable and usually stressed out and for remaining so cheerful about my work. I thank my uncle Khmaies and aunt Khadija Jouili in Tunisia, and their children, for providing me with a wonderful "roof-top office," baby-sitting included, so that I could continue writing during so many summer breaks. Finally, my gratitude to my parents, Abdelaziz and Gunthild Jouili, cannot be put into words. They have supported me unconditionally, encouraging me in all my life choices and never losing faith in me. Their spirits have accompanied me wherever life has taken me. It is to them that I dedicate this book.

NOTE ON TRANSCRIPTION
AND TRANSLATION

I have adopted a highly simplified system for transcribing words and phrases in Modern Standard Arabic. With the exception of proper names, all diacritical marks have been omitted except for the ayn and hamza.

All the quotations from secondary sources published in French and German as well as the quotes from my interlocutors are my translations.

1 PRACTICING ISLAM IN INHOSPITABLE ENVIRONMENTS

ONE SATURDAY A MONTH, women gathered for a potluck brunch at the Centre d'Études et de Recherche sur l'Islam (CERSI) in St. Denis, a *banlieue* (suburb) in the north of Paris. When I arrived, many women were already present in the classroom where the meeting took place. The tables were filled with food and beverages: tarts, quiches, baguettes, cheese, and Arabic pastry, along with a range of soft drinks and juices, tea and coffee. Everyone was busily reaching out for snacks and drinks while chatting and laughing with one another. Gradually the women sat down and the chatter slowly decreased. Olfa, teacher of the "Islamic morals" class at the center and main organizer of the brunch, stood up. A thirty-year-old woman with friendly eyes, she was dressed in a *djellaba* and a long headscarf. After greeting the other women with a warm "*Salam 'alaykum,* sisters," she sketched out the theme of the day: "How can we reconcile Islamic practice and worship with an active life in a secular [*laïque*] society?" While we were still eating, Olfa briefly outlined some of the central challenges that practicing Muslims can face in French society, provided some general advice, then invited the participants to share their personal experiences on the issue, both the difficulties they had encountered and their personal achievements.

Aliya, a woman in her early thirties, raised her hand and was the first to speak. She acknowledged that her turn to Islamic practice, in itself already a thorny and lingering process, had furthermore complicated her daily social life, especially on the professional level. An employee in a center for the socioprofessional insertion of migrant women, Aliya also recognized that she had been exceptionally lucky to be allowed to introduce her *hijab* (headscarf)—discreetly tied in the back—into her workplace. And after having hesitated for a long time, she had recently started to pray in her office, because making up the missed prayers in the evening had turned this act of worship into a burden. Generally she would do everything to hide her prayer, even interrupt it in order not to risk being discovered by her colleagues. The preceding week, however, she had not hidden it, and it was the resulting incident that Aliya wanted to share with the group.

> Usually, I stop when I hear someone approaching, but that day something pushed me not to do so. During my prayer, I heard steps and could see out of the corner of my eyes a silhouette appearing at my office door. Instinctively I wanted to stand up, but something forced me to resist this impulse and I continued praying. My colleague left immediately when he saw me. I was extremely scared of his reaction afterward. But when he came in a while later, he did not mention anything at all. Only after we had finished our professional conversation and as he was about to leave the room did he turn around and say, "Mecca is over there; you prayed in the wrong direction." Can you imagine that? I was speechless. I couldn't believe what I had just heard. This guy was a Catholic though, the only religious person among my colleagues. You see, we face a lot of setbacks, but at times you encounter goodness and sympathy. We have to acknowledge that. And we need to be steadfast in our practice and pray to *Allah subhanu wa ta'ala* to facilitate things for Muslims who live in a non-Muslim country.

As Aliya described her colleague's reaction, the women paused eating, and exclamations such as such *Masha'Allah* and *Subhan'Allah* went through the room; those in attendance were visibly touched by that unexpected gesture of kindness. After Aliya's concluding remarks, a vibrant discussion emerged. Some participants emphasized the duty to endure patiently the discriminations they encountered. One woman insisted on the importance of tactfully but persistently trying to make space for their religious practice, because that should be part of one's religious freedom anyway. Another woman, again inspired by Aliya's experience, raised the issue of building solidarities with religious people from other faiths. And all present agreed that no matter what approach they pursued, it was their essential duty to teach their non-Muslim peers about the misconceptions they held in regard to Islam and to try to represent Islam in the best way possible.

religious discrim.

intro

That Saturday morning discussion crystallizes in a lucid way the struggles that pious Muslim women face in their quest to live according to their religious principles within European secular societies. It is the task of this book to examine these everyday struggles closely. First, it explores how young European-born Muslim women cultivate (orthodox) Islamic subjectivities in a context that has increasingly stigmatized and politicized the practices that go along with these kinds of subjectivities. Like Aliya, many young European-born Muslim women did not rigorously practice their religion while growing up and frequently identified many internal resistances to their efforts to become more pious. Many of the challenges they faced in adopting (socially conservative) Islamic lifestyles can be explained by the fact that these women had been fashioned not only by European discourses and ideals, but also by various nonorthodox approaches to Islam, which, if not outright critical, are at least skeptical toward these very lifestyles. Second, the book investigates how these women cope on a practical level with the everyday difficulties of living a religious life in a society ever more hostile to visible forms of Islamic piety. The discussion that followed Aliya's story revealed the various modes of reasoning that accompany individual responses to that challenge. And most significantly, the debate exposed that the individual's response is rarely only about the practitioner's effort to pursue her individual practice, but also about the overarching duty to represent the Muslim community properly within European society.

What intrigued me in listening to these kinds of debates was the constant, underlying concern to do the *right* thing. For these women, carefully adhering to one's religious duty was certainly important, but it alone was never enough, because one always had to consider the social consequences of one's individual acts. The women would point to an ethical-political commitment that does not disconnect the individual striving for pious self-cultivation from an understanding that the rituals and other practices that are part of that self-cultivation exist within a web of human relationships and therefore might impact these relationships too.

Ethics and its political consequentiality has become an increasingly important topic within the discipline of anthropology.[1] A now burgeoning literature acknowledges the centrality of ethics in the shaping of human communities and the "moral making of the world" (Fassin 2012: 4). Depending on their authors' respective philosophical inclinations or affiliations, different domains within the vast field of ethical practices are described and theorized—modes of ethical (self-)cultivation, moral dilemmas and choices, or forms of ethical judgment and reasoning that already point to care for and obligation to others. These modes of ethical action can be either tacit and commonsensical or rationalized and intellectualized.[2]

My work contributes to the discussions initiated in this body of work and offers a number of interventions. It especially aims to bring into conversation perspectives with distinct intellectual lineages that are not commonly discussed together, in order to account for the complexity of the ethical struggles that these Muslim women face. Not only have my interlocutors learned to accept, comprehend, and internalize a range of pious practices and modes of conduct, but they also have to enact them in specific social contexts, in various moments of their everyday life, which raises questions about how each practice can or should be implemented in each context. By examining the various deliberations around these practices, I argue that Islamic ethical life quests are not merely hampered or disrupted by a context that stigmatizes and increasingly restrictively regulates, in the name of secularism, Islamic practice. Nor are these quests weakened by inconsistencies that might result from being confronted with and shaped by competing sets of moral codes. Rather, as I show throughout this book, these complicated and restrictive settings produce experiences of ambiguity, suffering, and injustice, thereby simultaneously creating conditions for the intensification of ethical labor. Before returning to this issue, I want to briefly address the specific nature of French and German secularities that contextualize my fieldwork and pose a wide range of challenges to everyday female Islamic piety and, more broadly, to the thriving of the Islamic tradition in Europe.

Situating French and German Secularities

The Islamic revival movement in Europe emerged in the 1980s but gained visibility in the 1990s, not only through the proliferation of headscarves in the streets but also through requests for the construction of mosques, for dietary adjustments in cafeterias, and for prayer spaces in workplaces.[3] If the revival movement appeared in the public sphere mainly through these types of claims to public authorities, its activities were first and foremost geared to Muslim immigrant communities, whose members had arrived from the 1950s onward, to a large extent as part of post-WWII labor migration. By providing these immigrant communities with religious education, the revival activists sought to enable Muslims to maintain their Islamic ways of life, which were perceived to be endangered by a gradual secularization of Muslims in Europe. Through their participation in these new educational facilities, first in and around the mosques, then in separate institutional structures, Muslim men and women who previously had not practiced started to pursue their prayers more regularly, to fast, and, for women, to don the veil.[4]

This new public visibility of the religious difference of an ethnic and racialized minority group posed new challenges to the self-definition of European nation-states (see, for instance, Göle 2002). This holds especially true for France and Germany. While comparative literature on the politics of race and immigration, and on secularism has, in the past, often presented both countries as two (almost) opposed ideal-typical models[5], they were nonetheless considered to be less accommodating to immigrant-descendent minorities than other European countries. The French model of integration, defined as "universalist" and "egalitarian," builds on a type of republican individualism, which seeks to assimilate individuals who become citizens through a "political choice" (Kastoryano 1996: 9). All other collective identities beyond the national one are here defined as "particularistic" and appear in this model as obstacles to social progress that need to be transcended.[6] Opposed to France's model of the nation stands Germany's model of *Volk*. This notion of a "pre-political" (Brubaker 1997: 19) German nation was not linked, initially, to the abstract idea of citizenship but instead tried to capture the organic and highly particular nature of Germany as a community of culture, language, and race. In spite of the opprobrium under which the *völkisch* ideology has fallen since the end of National Socialism, the young Federal Republic's definition of nationality maintained this understanding of the German people. Accordingly, nationality was based on the *ius sanguinis* (law of blood). The Federal Republic withheld citizenship from immigrants for a very long time, and populations present in Germany for three generations still held the status of *Ausländer* (foreigners; Kastoryano 1996; Chin 2007; Mandel 2008). After this idea was partially revised by the 2000 reform of the citizenship law (that dated back to 1913), successive debates about German *Leitkultur* (literally *leading culture*) tried to grapple (without much success) with the elusive nature of Germanness (see, for instance, Ewing 2008).

At least since the now-infamous headscarf affairs in France, the French concept of *laïcité* has in many ways become the paradigmatic example of a strict or radical secularism. *Laïcité* was established through the 1905 law on the separation of church and state, defining the relation between these entities as one of "neutrality" and "reciprocal incompetence" (Tietze 2002: 152). On an ideological level, *laïcité* expands on the republican norm, as its seeks to ban religion from the public sphere, thereby relegating it purely to the domain of the private. In the French collective imaginary, *laïcité* continues to be a social and moral ideal, founded on the "providential trinity reason–science–progress," which emerged victorious out of a long struggle between clerical and anticlerical forces (Morin 1990: 38). The concrete and pivotal achievement—literally its sanctuary—of *laïcité* was the establishment of the French republican school, which was designed to teach students a "secular morality" that is universal, rational, and progressive (see Baubérot 1990: 136). The passionate character of the debates about the wearing of headscarves in schools from 1989 until the passing of the 2004 law banning conspicuous religious symbols in public schools can be grasped only if one takes into account the place of French public schools in the collective imaginary around *laïcité*. But in spite of the 1905 law and its powerful symbolic status, in practice, the state continues to carry out certain tasks on behalf of the officially recognized religions. Among other things, it maintains the religious buildings constructed before 1905, and pays the salaries of teachers in those private confessional schools that have received state accreditation.[7]

German society has not known comparable conflicts over the relation between church and state. Traces of institutional cooperation are generally dated back to the Peace of Westphalia in 1648, which established confessional (protestant and catholic) states. From then on, the two churches were increasingly brought under the tutelage of the state. German secularism in the 20th century was built on this confessional dualism of the public space, resulting in an "interpenetration of ecclesiastical, social, and political structures." The principles of religious liberty and freedom of conscience materialized in the right of any religious community to constitute itself as a "religious society" (*Religionsgesellschaft*), which can receive the status of "corporation of public law" (*Körperschaft des öffentlichen Rechts*). This status, which was initially conceived for the Catholic and Protestant churches, defined the churches' relation to the state as a partnership and allowed for its internal autonomy.

The respective institutional arrangements constituting the relationship between state and religion have determined to a certain degree the ways in which both countries have set out to integrate Islam as a "newcomer" religion. However, at least as important as the institutional arrangements of secularism in each country are the representations of Islam that dwell in the respective national imaginaries. For France, which has an intensive colonial history with many parts of the Muslim world—a history that produced a traumatic memory through the decolonization of Algeria—Islam is considered the racial and religious Other *par excellence.* This perception is perpetuated in mainstream discourses that question Islam's compatibility with the principle of *laïcité.* Here, it is the minority religion of post-colonial Muslim populations (rather than the once dominant Catholic church) that emerges at laïcité's main antagonist.[8] The nationwide headscarf debates between 1989 and 2004 repeatedly posed the question of Islam's capacity to integrate into a French secular environment.[9]

As the Islamic revival movement grew in France and as anxiety increased about the possibility of Islamic extremism spilling over from Algeria into France in the 1990s, the state began to put more sustained effort into initiatives that aimed to better integrate the Muslim community and to produce a form of Islam that would be able to become "French." State actors sought to establish a national representative authority capable of serving as an interlocutor vis-à-vis the French state and its institutions as well as of regulating the Muslim community (Ferrari 2006; Caeiro 2006). These initiatives aimed to domesticate Islam, especially by stripping foreign sources of any influence on French Islam and by encouraging a "moderate" version of Islam. They resulted in the establishment of the Conseil Français du Culte Musulman (French Islamic Council) in 2003 (see Bowen 2007).

Mosque construction was one instance in which the state tried to regulate Islamic life. Muslims in France had commonly worshipped in makeshift prayer halls (often in the basements of housing projects in the *banlieues,* densely populated with immigrants and their descendants), which became the imagined spaces of the new wave of Islamism. From the 1990s onward, French authorities called for Muslims to be brought "out of the basements" and helped them to build proper houses of worship. Initially the idea was to build "Cathedral Mosques" that were highly visible in central locations and of prestigious architectural design. Nowadays, the initiatives have shifted to respond to the realities of "neighborhood Islam" (Maussen 2007). Although many municipalities continue to prevent Muslim associations from building mosques, others have shown willingness to facilitate the building of mosques or cultural centers in densely populated Muslim neighborhoods. That willingness was connected to the effort to have some control over these spaces (Bowen 2010; Césari 2005; Maussen 2007). If one sees among these local authorities a wide range of attitudes in terms of their readiness to cooperate with Muslims on this issue, the situation is much bleaker in regard to Muslim private schools. As of yet, none of the very few existing schools has been accredited by French authorities (Bowen 2010).

Germany's political system, which generally is more accommodating toward religious institutions than the French system, has nonetheless not allowed for easier recognition of "immigrated" religions. The German state and society have long considered the religion of Turkish *Ausländer* to be ethnically and culturally alien and, especially, as a temporary element in German society (Adelson 2005; Chin 2007). Given many immigrants' similar perception of their stay as temporary, as well as their lack of financial means, Islamic collective worship took place in cheap, makeshift places, mostly transformed commercial buildings at the edge of town (and thus the situation was quite similar to that of France). After citizenship laws were changed in 2000 to acknowledge that the immigrant Muslim community was in Germany to stay, and as a new generation emerged that was more self-confident about addressing their claims to the state, the demand for functional and publicly recognizable mosques was increasingly voiced. These initiatives, which took place mostly in situations where relations between Muslim communities and municipalities were not yet established, have regularly been met with a clear unwillingness to cooperate, whether on the part of the municipality, the local residents, the churches, or the media, and with an organized effort to block them (Jonker 2005; Leggewie, Joost, and Rech, 2002).

Most conflicts over the integration of Islam and Muslim practices into German society are addressed at the *Länder* (state) level of Germany's federal system. Some state-operated schools provide instruction on Islam. And in response to Germany's own headscarf debates (far less passionate than those in France) over a Muslim teacher's claim that she had the right to wear her headscarf in school, a number of *Länder,* among them North Rhine-Westphalia (the site of my fieldwork), forbid civil servants (including teachers) to wear the headscarf (Amir-Moazami 2007; Beverly Weber 2004).

Islam has been propelled onto Germany's national political scene, if not since the reform of the citizenship law in 2000, then definitely since the events of 9/11, when Germany discovered that hidden Al-Qa'ida "cells" had participated in the World Trade Center attack. And despite the lack of involvement of Muslims of Turkish background in 9/11, much of the antiterrorism legislation and many antiterrorism policies have nonetheless been geared toward that community (Ewing 2008; Schiffauer 2006). Another consequence of Islam's enhanced political presence was an increase in the number of political voices arguing in favor of the institutionalization of Islam in Germany, with the desired result being the recognition of Islam as a corporation of public law

(Galembert 2005; Jonker 2002; Tietze 2002), and the transformation of Muslims in Germany into "German Muslims" (Amir-Moazami 2011: 12). Toward this goal, in 2006, then Minister of the Interior Wolfgang Schäuble inaugurated the Deutsche Islamkonferenz, a forum for dialogue between the German state and select members of the Muslim community, with the immediate aim to "ameliorate the religious and social integration of the Muslim population" (Peter 2010a: 120), and the longtime goal to grant Muslim associations the corporation of public law status.[10]

In spite of the legal settlement of the headscarf "affairs" and the initiation in both countries of a process of institutionalizing Islam, relations between the French and German publics and their Muslim communities have not shown a marked improvement in the ensuing years. Rather, public controversies over a range of Muslim (supposed or real) practices, reactions, and beliefs have proliferated rather than declined (Göle 2013a, 2013b). One of the striking aspects in these controversies is that—in continuation with the headscarf affairs—Muslim woman emerged as key figures in the definition of Islamic cultural differences. Debates over what were quickly labeled "honor killings" brought to the fore in both countries a number of secular feminists of Muslim background who had gained enormous media attention and subsequently became the essential interlocutors in the public sphere on all issues linked to Muslim women's perceived oppression (Amir-Moazami 2011; Chin 2010; Ewing 2008; Fernando 2009; Rostock and Berghahn 2008; El-Tayeb 2011).[11] They thereby effectively stirred rather than soothed these debates. The "Burka ban"[12] that became law in France in 2010 and, in the previous year in Germany, the scandal provoked by a polemical anti-Muslim book written by politician Thilo Sarrazin[13] as well as the public outcry against then President, Christian Wulff, for declaring that Islam now belonged to German history were further instances in the series of now seemingly nonstop public agitations.[14] Although the controversies in both countries were framed in idiosyncratic national idioms, they nonetheless reveal many similarities. These debates were all meant to defend liberal values and human rights, but they exposed a striking incapacity to take questions of race and racism into account.[15] In statements made by French president Nicolas Sarkozy in late 2010 and German chancellor Angela Merkel in early 2011 about the failure of multiculturalism (an agenda that pays at least lip service to policies of antiracism), both countries confirmed and reiterated the political goal of assimilation rather than arguing for the accommodation and protection of their (Muslim) minorities.[16]

The German and French political cultures are strongly marked by their specific institutional arrangements—the French by *laïcité* and universalism, the paradigm of the French model of integration; the German by the long-lasting refusal to be an immigrant society and by specific ideas about Germanness. These national specificities map out "horizons of meaning in which the actors find benchmarks for understanding and action," and they function as "publicly available grammars" (Galembert 2005: 190). Although these particular grammars produce differences in how Islam is debated, contested, and institutionalized in each country, there are nonetheless some overarching convergences: both countries express an anxiety over (and are reluctant to accommodate) visible Islamic religiosity in the secular public sphere. Concern about the Otherness of Islam, exacerbated by the post-9/11 climate, also fostered in both countries a sense of urgency to domesticate Islam, with the goal of better regulating and controlling it. In both countries, the aspiration emerged to turn this "foreign" religion into a national religion that, in the process, would adopt the characteristics of French or German ways of believing: develop into an interiorized and privatized faith and thereby, presumably, better equipped to acquire a tolerant and moderate mind-set.[17]

In the early 2000s—when I began my fieldwork—these two countries were often contrasted in the literature as quite distinct from countries such as the Netherlands, Great Britain, or Sweden, which were then considered to follow "multicultural" policies and therefore to be more hospitable to Muslim difference.[18] More recent developments in these various Western European countries, of course, have brought them much closer to France and Germany in regard to their treatment of the so-called Muslim problem. This now shared concern about Muslim Otherness has given rise to similar rearticulations of the notion of citizenship, increasingly viewed through a more clearly delineated cultural lens. In this process citizenship appears not merely as a legal status that enables political and economic participation, but rather as a requirement to accept certain proclaimed national norms and values.[19]

In their effort to institutionalize and reshape Islam, France and Germany very much do what every so-called secular nation-state does: they intervene in and regulate religious life by juridicial and legislative means in order to circumscribe the religious domain in ways considered appropriate for a secular state, even if the concrete institutional intervention takes place according to historically specific national rationalities. Critical scholars of secularity have pointed out that this interference is more far-reaching: the secular state relentlessly seeks to delineate and contain religion itself (understood here as an abstract and universal category), to define "the spaces it should inhabit" and "to discipline actual religious traditions so as to … fit into those spaces" (Agrama 2010:503), thereby also reshaping its underlying "subjectivities" and "epistemological claims" (Mahmood 2005). Thus, beneath local (national) secularisms, lies a conceptually prior "secular" (Asad 2003: 16). Such an approach is important in that it does not measure the degree of secularity or, to use Hussein Agrama's (2010: 500) words, define a "scale of secularity" on which France, in our case, would appear as the "paradigm secular state" and Germany, with its complicated church-state relations, would appear as the less completed secular entity. By producing an ethnography that seeks to understand how religious Muslims live out their religion within more than one specific national secular regime, I also seek to pay attention to the conceptually prior secular.

Nevertheless, the particular national political cultures, the specific memories, and the (evolving) imaginaries that underpin them mattered. They determined how Islam is discursively articulated in both countries, and they explained the tangibly changing institutional landscapes of Islam in the two contexts, which constituted an important background for my fieldwork. These national specificities had an impact on the particular ways in which my interlocutors perceived and critiqued their own Otherization. The specific publicly available grammars shaped how my interlocutors articulated and practiced (in "very German" or "very French" ways) their piety in their respective environments, which had concrete consequences for their ability to dwell, or not dwell, in certain places. Although the book is not defined by a comparative approach, the specific national backgrounds it presents help to situate and contextualize further the day-to-day struggles of my interlocutors, who were set off by their quest to lead a pious life as promoted in the Islamic circles they attended.

Europe, Islamophobia, and the Reconfiguration of Tradition

Today, not only is Islamophobia reflected in violent acts or populist discourses, but also its underlying assumptions are echoed, as already discussed, in national governmental policies and in law proposals and regulations, justified as defenses of the supposedly threatened secular state.[20] In the process, the qualifier *Muslim* has increasingly been naturalized and thereby racialized (Rana 2011). A range of scholars have exposed that in the current reconstruction of European national identities, Muslims appear not only as those who do not belong but also as those who represent a threat to Europe's particular identity, that is, Muslims' mode of life is seen as detrimental to Europeans' sense of self (Bracke 2013; Ewing 2008; El-Tayeb 2011; Guénif-Souilamas 2006; Moors 2009; Joan W. Scott 2010; see also Göle 2013b). Consequently, Muslims become the "abjected" Other, because they occupy a zone that is considered "uninhabitable" (Butler 1993).

In this discursive context, where Islam and Muslims are continuously presented as key challenges to national cohesion and identity, one could argue that Islam itself has come to function as a particular "problem-space" (David Scott 1999, 2004); that is, Islam in Europe delineates an ensemble of questions and answers with assigned ideological-political stakes that require intervention. The participants in the Islamic revival in Europe cannot avoid positioning themselves in relation to that problem-space, but their own arguments are responses partly fashioned by this discursive field. And because any argument about producing the correct answers (and thus truths) alludes to the nexus of knowledge and power, the Muslim community feels compelled to produce a "counterknowledge" (Foucault 2003) that challenges the mostly stereotypical knowledge *on* Muslims articulated in public discourses, from media accounts to political debates. This is why, for instance, activists in the revival movement persistently try to define an Islamic modernity, in order to challenge the dominant European representation of Muslims as premodern. The critique of these stigmatizing discourses and the elaboration of a counterdiscourse have thus become part of the important occupations of Islamic revival institutions.

Because public discourses so often focus on specific Muslim practices, part of the effort to produce counterknowledge passes, for religious Muslims, through a contestation of the negative meanings attached to these (religious) practices. That is, because these practices are being *read* in delegitimizing ways, religious Muslims are propelled into struggles over the correct *meanings* attached to them. Thus, whenever practicing Muslims find themselves outside the safe sphere of the private home or Islamic environments, they are aware of the performative and readable character of their bodies, rituals, and modes of conduct. In the struggle over (symbolic) meanings, they might consciously deploy the performative and readable character of their practices to convey oppositional messages that contest their exclusion and demonstrate, in a language accessible to the outsider, that they belong to the space from which they are excluded. Inevitably, practices might thus acquire meanings they did not priorly have.

Comparable kinds of embodied and discursive performances by certain stigmatized or marginalized minority groups in their effort to obtain recognition within a redefined pluralist political community have often been described in terms of identity politics. Though celebrated by many, the idea of identity politics has also raised important critiques that pinpoint its various analytical shortcomings.[21] These discussions have especially highlighted that identities constructed through exclusion have also been naturalized by that process—whether on the basis of race or ethnicity, gender, or sexual orientation—which identity politics did not deconstruct. But how do we approach embodied struggles over recognition if the identities as well as the practices employed in that struggle have a history that precedes the processes of exclusion and politicization? The now stigmatized mode of living of my Muslim interlocutors is embedded within long-standing religious traditions and is therefore at least partially anterior to any process of politicization. To employ Wendy Brown's (1993: 407) terms, these traditions are not constituted by "injury" but rather exist "prior to its wounding and thus prior to the formation of identity at the site of the wound."[22] Scholars who have employed the trope of Muslim "identity politics" to explain the public visibility of the revival movement's practices (Haenni 2002; Ismael 2004; Nökel 2002) have neglected to investigate that significant difference further. They have therefore failed to examine the complicated connections between these practices as communicable identity markers and their embeddedness in long-standing traditions of self-cultivation (Mahmood 2005).

In this context, it is helpful to approach the notion of an Islamic discursive tradition (Asad 1986) as one that has been significantly reconfigured by the diasporic context in which Islam is defined as a problem-space.[23] Noteworthy in this regard is David Scott's (1999) rearticulation of that concept for a diasporic framework (he discusses the African diaspora) that allows thinking about "tradition" in the context of (discursive, ideological, and political) domination. Following Scott, one can define the diasporic Muslim subject in Europe as a subject whose "historical fate" (1999: 125) as to be "Muslim," whatever his personal religious orientation, has been produced through (post)colonial racialized social relations, ideological apparatuses, and political regimes that have been exacerbated by the post-9/11 global war on terror. As a consequence, it is necessary to investigate the impact that these institutions and technologies have on the rearticulation of the Islamic tradition, even if it can never be reduced to these technologies. Importantly, one of the effects of this rearticulation is the redeployment of this tradition in new ways that correspond to the stakes by which it is now defined—stakes also centered on questions of identity and difference (see Scott 1999: 118).

Thus, in this book I trace the various ways in which this novel context acts on the tradition's possibilities to reflect upon and articulate itself. One most obvious aspect here is how European Muslims' arguments about virtues and excellence, duties, obligations and rights within the Islamic tradition are, whether willed or not, embedded in *moral struggles over representation*. "Apt performance" (Asad 1993: 62) of the rituals and embodied practices that constitute the tradition might therefore, in certain contexts, also involve considering to what extent the performance will deconstruct the negative representations that are prevalent in mainstream society. Certain embodied practices, languages, and modes of self-presentation that other minority groups have articulated in response to their oppression might resonate with Muslim diasporic subjects and impact how they redeploy their various practices in critical relation to dominant representations and institutional exclusions.[24] However, in relation to the pious Muslims I study here, this "representational politics" does not exist on its own but, crucially, is part and parcel of the struggle to lead an ethical life as defined by the Islamic tradition. It is thereby embedded in the dispute over what constitutes the goods of the tradition, which always requires some form of authorization from the tradition itself.

The Anthropology of Ethics

The pursuit of an ethical life is an inherently multifaceted and thorny endeavor. Living an ethical life defined by a tradition that is regarded by the mainstream society with a hostile eye—which is the topic of this book—makes it even more challenging. And it becomes even more so if living that kind of ethical life involves unmaking earlier habits and modes of perception. In my effort to grasp the numerous ethical struggles in which the pious practitioners I studied engage, I was inspired by Aristotelian ethics and by those scholars who have made Aristotelian ethics fruitful for a contemporary, more anthropologically grounded inquiry.

One of the major insights that renders Aristotelian virtue ethics so relevant for anthropological research is its insistence on ethics as practice (rather than on reason) within a specific mode of life (*ethos*). His approach has been recently used to criticize post-Enlightenment moral thought (influenced by Descartes and Kant), which defined morality as separate from action, from disciplines, and from the body.[25] One reworking of his ethics focuses on ethical self-cultivation. Building on the work of Talal Asad (1993, 2003), Saba Mahmood (2005) and Charles Hirschkind (2006) elaborate on this tradition of ethics from a poststructuralist vantage point, especially by reading it through a Foucaultian lens, in order to highlight that the ethical self-disciplines enacted by Muslim practitioners in the Egyptian Islamic revival movement are thoroughly embedded in power relations. In this theory, ethics is a "modality of power" (Mahmood 2005: 28) that "permits individuals . . . a certain number of operations on their own bodies and souls, thought, conduct, and way of being" (Foucault 1997c: 225, quoted in Mahmood 2005: 28), and that is defined by a historically specific moral discourse and set of moral codes. My work has been deeply stimulated by this scholarship, and the present study is likewise interested in analyzing the observed practices of self-cultivation, with attention to how various forms of power do not disable but instead cooperate in the constitution of ethical subjects.

At the same time, however, I am led to make a slightly different argument, because the practices of self-cultivation I have studied generally appear considerably less linear, less completed, and the set of moral codes that nourish them seem less unequivocal and self-evident. First, the moral codes are often not so clear; many revival circles in Europe, with their various intellectual lineages, are still involved in defining and outlining a set of principles that corresponds to the diasporic European condition while being not impervious to a range of principles and values hailed in liberal democracies. Second, having often started their religious practices only during late adolescence or early adulthood, the women I discuss in this book problematized, in quite explicit ways, the numerous obstacles implied in the work of ethical self-cultivation according to an orthodox Islamic framework. The pious practitioners grasped this work in terms of a constant, never-ending *jihad al-nafs* (struggle against the lower self), in which the formation of a stable disposition could never be taken for granted. My fieldwork provided me with many stories and examples of practitioners being drawn back into old habits and doubts. Frequently they were frustrated by their own incapacity to implement this pious self-reform and by the influence that secular modes of life that were endorsed and promoted by the mainstream society continued to have over them. Thus the individual's work on herself was significantly and long-lastingly complicated by prior habits and by the availability of other sets of moral codes.

Although Foucault did not pay too much attention to this dimension, Aristotle was clearly aware of the difficulties involved in reshaping character after a youthful age.[26] Aristotle certainly claims that "none of the moral virtues is engendered in us by nature" (2001: 1103a14–b1), but he also asserts that "even habit is hard to change just because it is like nature, as Evenus says: I say that habit's but a long practice, friend, And this becomes men's nature in the end" (Aristotle [1941] 2001: 1052). This apparent inconsistency becomes clearer when one recognizes that much of Aristotle's pedagogy is actually concerned with the education of youth rather than with adults. Aristotle, who was himself an educator, alludes throughout his *Nicomachean Ethics* to the fundamental necessity of a good education at a young age. It is probably this skepticism about the possibility of altering a fully shaped character that Bourdieu (1977) elaborates on when he demonstrates the difficulty of altering the internalized experiences of one's outward social relations—the socialized norms that guide one's thought and conduct—which he has captured with the term *habitus*. If we do not reproduce Bourdieu's socioeconomic determinism, of which he has often been (rightly) accused, his rich account of the deep embeddedness of habitus as physiological and psychological dispositions can help us expose how onerous, though not impossible, any willed transformation is—which is the case precisely because such a transformation has to go against deeply embedded bodily structures and affective sense perceptions, which first have to be made reflexive and then have to be worked against.[27]

Thus, although I acknowledge and take seriously the ethical work that my interlocutors have undertaken in their efforts to cultivate Islamic dispositions within themselves, I do not want to play down the many impediments they encounter in that process, which I will elaborate in the first half of the book. At one point in their life, most often during adolescence or early adulthood, the women I worked with renewed their encounter with their inherited religious tradition, aiming to get a better grasp of it. An important moment in this process was their participation in Islamic institutions of learning and their attendance at Islamic conferences. Learning, as Chapter 2 discusses, is the most basic technique for cultivating an Islamic habitus. As both a cognitive and an emotional activity, it provides the believer with important information that allows her to lead her life in an Islamic way, but it also creates an affective environment that fosters and sustains the underlying dispositions that let faith grow. At the same time, "studying Islam" requires a continuous discipline, which these women active in the French and German societies do not always bring with them. The institutional structures that seek to respond to the needs and expectations of young Muslims who were born and raised in Europe provide learning communities and pedagogies designed precisely to counter the possible weakening of the participants' motivation.

As they learned how the normative subject of Islamic piety is defined and understood, these women were confronted with the discrepancy or mismatch between that norm and their own dispositions and modes of conduct (which were also impacted by various secular ideals). Consequently, they came to question their pre-reflexive habits—their embodied orientations toward thought and action—which then became objects for corrective self-practices, though without a guarantee of success. Interestingly, the pedagogies enacted in the centers I researched sought to account for these manifold difficulties by developing a methodology that focused more on the effort implied in working on the self rather than on the result. Chapter 3 documents the meticulous efforts of my interlocutors to improve, especially with the help of Islamic classes, their mastery of the ritual prayers (*salat*) and their implementation of feminine modesty through dress and conduct. The women addressed freely the various obstacles they faced, which often exposed a general difficulty in finding a balance between competing normative claims coming from, on the one hand, dominant secular liberal discourses and, on the other hand, from the religious tradition transmitted in the Islamic circles. Chapter 3 also argues that Aristotle's contempt for these less linear and incomplete ethical struggles exposes an important weakness in his model of ethics.

Chapter 4 continues the conversation by examining the women's attempts to produce an Islamic language for women's dignity and self-realization that could provide an alternative to the dominant secular languages of equality, individual rights, and autonomy. Although they considered female empowerment to be *intrinsically related to* the endeavor to live Islam authentically, learning to submit to orthodox Islamic principles (including gendered and nonegalitarian ones) became equally decisive in the struggle for virtuousness and piety. Feelings of ambiguity and even doubt could also result and had to be tackled and worked against. Interestingly, this work upon the self was enabled by a specific social ethics the women progressively came to adopt, which emphasized notions of duty and obligation rather than individual rights and autonomy.

Becoming a virtuous Islamic subject was a major issue for my interlocutors. Another, at times more intricate, concern was how to become and be that kind of subject in a non-Muslim society and in a secular state that seeks to regulate and circumscribe the practices that sustain this very subject. When they stepped out of their (protected) Islamic or private spaces into a (hostile) secular public sphere in which they had to negotiate their various (often publicly discernable) pious norms and practices, these practitioners faced a range of dilemmas. The second part of the book investigates these dilemmas, which quite often required from the women to make hard, at times very painful compromises regarding these norms and practices. And, as mentioned earlier in this chapter, the possible implications of each decision for the women's broader ambition to represent Muslims to the mainstream society as active members always weighed heavily in their deliberations. By connecting their individual practices to the question of how they represented their community, the women exposed their deep concern for the social and moral ramifications of their individual actions. The reasoning employed to solve these dilemmas amounts, therefore, to a different kind of ethical work that is neither reducible to self-cultivation nor subject-centered but instead is inherently relational and gestures toward an ethics of intersubjectivity.[28] It is an ethical work made out of feelings of responsibility, obligation, and care for others that are (as discussed in Chapter 4) so decisive for the revival participants' piety.

Here Aristotle ([1941] 2001) again provides a useful conceptual framework, one in which an important domain of ethical action is "moral reasoning," or *phronesis*. Phronesis is the virtuous capacity of "do[ing] the right thing in the right place at the right time in the right way" (MacIntyre [1981] 2007: 150), and the right way is not what is right for the individual alone but what is right for human flourishing, for the *polis*.[29] Akin to other Aristotelian ethical concepts, this type of moral reasoning or practical knowledge is praxeological. As such, it is distinct from the type of reasoning that makes up the Cartesian legacy, which functions as an instrument for determining the most effective means to a determinate end. Neither contemplative nor theoretical, moral reasoning or phronesis alludes to an ethical know-how that transcends the subjective-objective distinction by positing a knowledge linked to being and becoming (see Lambek 2002a: 16). Michael Lambek's (2000; 2002a, 2011) hermeneutic anthropology, for instance, which introduced Aristotle's notion of phronetic reasoning as a dimension of ethical practice into the anthropological debate on ethics, employs phronesis to expose how people make ethical sense of a complex and complicated world not merely by strategically pursing their own interests but instead by striving for human flourishing more broadly.

Phronesis in the sense of caring for the common good thus obliges us never to reduce ethics to merely caring for the self *for the sake of* the self.[30] At the same time, however, it should not be opposed to caring for the self. Aristotle ([1941] 2001: 1035) speaks of phronesis as requiring, like any other ethical disposition, instruction and habituation (*ethismos*) in order to form character (*ethos*) and refine emotions (*pathos*). In the case of phronesis, the capacity to feel connected with and obliged to others has to be learned. Interestingly, certain Islamic legal and ethical traditions have developed their own version of phronesis called *istislah*—a highly flexible mode of reasoning that seeks to realize the public good (*maslaha*), as Armando Salvatore (2007) has shown. Even more important is that this tradition of reasoning was not only promulgated as a central method for use by Islamic legal scholars in thinking about the law, but has also been expanded to enable the commoner to deal with the intricacies of everyday life while pursuing a higher good.

As an intersubjective and relational form of reasoning, phronesis allows us to extend this inquiry into Muslim ethical striving from religious intracommunal life to more complex and difficult social contexts—contexts characterized by the coexistence of heterogeneous modes of being often perceived to be incommensurable and which do not accommodate all religious traditions equally. The term *moral reasoning* intrinsically refers to situations of dilemma, uncertainty, and conflict. The use of moral reasoning can therefore help to address the difficulties, struggles, ambiguities, and doubts that are involved in the implementation of (Islamic) ethical practices in a context defined not only by a constraining secularity and growing Islamophobia but also by competing norms that impact the practitioners in complicated ways.

Such a mode of reasoning was at play in the decisions that women like Aliya constantly had to make about if and how to participate in the public spaces of the mainstream society and about whether to appear there as a visibly practicing Muslim. Chapter 5 discusses these questions as manifested in my interlocutors' continual reflection on whether to opt for a professional life while also being dedicated to motherhood, the latter of which is promoted by the revival movement. They thereby have to deliberate over the revival circles' ideals of a gendered division of labor and the fulfillment of other social obligations of the believer that make them useful to the Muslim diasporic community as well as to the broader society. These deliberations are complicated—but not obliterated—by personal ambition, aspiration, and desire.

Chapter Six investigates how Islamic practices such as prayer, modest dress, and embodied modesty are enacted in the everyday living spaces of the pious practitioners who, as students, professionals, activists, and so on, participate in the public sphere. In the process of negotiating these contested practices, their very meanings quite often transform in not always predictable ways. But beyond a mere politics of visibility, and never limited to the notion of "*my* religious freedom" or "*my* religious duty," these negotiations are the outcome of a moral reasoning that crucially considers the larger social consequences of these particular acts. Approaching these deliberations in terms of a phronetic type of reasoning furthermore permits a better understanding of the internal moral conflicts that are triggered by the transformation of the Islamic discursive tradition, which must reposition itself in regard to modern ideals such as self-realization, authenticity, and individual choice.

Finally, Chapter 7 argues that the intricate commitment of my interlocutors' moral reasoning to questions of mutual responsibility and the common good have important implications for the women's understandings of citizenship and civic virtues.[31] This ethical mode of reasoning becomes directly political as it makes clear statements about how to live with Others. In this sense, my ethnographic material also resonates/echoes with those thinkers who attempt to bring politics and ethics together in ways that foreground the responsibility to the Other—as a commitment to "men, not Man" (Arendt [1958] 1998), to "being-with" (Nancy 2000) rather than to "being."

Two points of caution regarding the theoretical framing need to be elaborated here. First, by deploying *phronesis* in a way that seeks to go beyond subject-centeredness and subject-centered agency, my approach departs clearly from some of those philosophical strands, which have granted that concept a recent revival. *Phronesis* had been lauded for its capacity to mediate not only between the universal and the particular, but, furthermore between the agent and society, as well as for its capacity to grasp modes of deliberation and choice that go beyond the strict application of rules. In this sense, it is taken to account in a stronger fashion for individual creativity and singularity, something which a focus on ethics in terms of technologies of the self provided by authoritative moral norms supposedly can not do (see, for instance, Mattingly 2012). The recovery of *phronesis,* especially in humanist circles (see Gadamer [1975] 2004 and Nussbaum 1986), has therefore to be situated within a larger epistemological project that aims at recuperating "some locus of human self-creation not reducible to external determinations" (Keane 2003: 241–242). While not denying the effects of structure and power, such a rendering nonetheless appears to understand power (as, for instance, embodied in religious institutions or moral codes) as imposing itself externally on the actor, which is why phronesis is welcomed as a way to mediate between power on the one side and agency on the other. However, if one wants to consider power as an "internal relationship," as a "potentiality" to act, and therefore as *internal* to agency (Asad 2006a: 271), it does not make sense to conceptualize phronesis as a type of mediation between these two givens. Such an understanding reflects a very specific conception of freedom and agency, as if the application of rules would generally imply mechanical, nonreflexive, and therefore inhibited and passive conduct.[32]

Thus, as I see it, phronesis must also be understood as a capacity for action enabled by historically specific power relations. The situations that require phronetic reasoning, as well as the capacity for it, cannot be disconnected from the question of how various discursive regimes and "semiotic ideologies" (to use Webb Keane's [(2007)] locution; see Chapter 2) determine perception, or from cultivated and produced capacities to judge and to weigh different goods. But an understanding of the relation between phronetic reasoning and structural factors cannot be reduced to Bourdieu's (2000) insight on how perception of the "existing probabilities" is shaped by power relations. A discussion of phronetic reasoning—which is similar to ethical cultivation, and here I follow a basic Aristotelian insight—requires asking how perception and sensing are informed by prior cultivation of body and mind. Thus, if phronesis can tell us something about how subjects construct their lives, their choices, and their struggles as meaningful, it also obliges us to ask what the conditions are that enable the production of these specific meanings.

Second, though this book draws on the work of philosophical thinkers, it is obviously not a philosophical study. My ethnographic analysis is informed by philosophical reflections built with the previously mentioned Aristotelian ethical terminology (terminology that is discussed and elaborated on in various anthropological studies with very distinct intellectual lineages) because of the capacity of that terminology to illuminate and make intelligible the more complex and complicated aspects of the type of Islamic piety with which I am concerned here. The suitability of Aristotelian ethical concepts for the study of Islamic ethical practice is strengthened by the fact that many aspects of Aristotle's work on ethics and practice were adopted by the classical Muslim theologians of the seventh to thirteenth centuries (Moosa 2005; Fakhry 1994). Nonetheless, this book does not aspire to give a complete account of Aristotelian ethics, and obviously it does not subscribe to his metaphysical assumptions. I frankly acknowledge a nonconformist, pragmatic, selective, and at times critical use of Aristotle's ethical concepts. And rather than follow Aristotle's elitist account of ethics and ethical *praxis* (which Gadamer, MacIntyre, and even Foucault could be accused of doing), I take these concepts into the domain of everyday practices among pious Muslim practitioners.[33]

In my admittedly eclectic and partial use of different theoretical strands and approaches, I follow the plea of Yael Navaro-Yashin (2002: 17) for an "anti-, trans-, or multi-paradigmatic" way of applying theory that has to be led and determined overall by one's own ethnographic material. As such, it is necessarily unorthodox.

An Ethnography of Islamic Practices
Inside and Outside Religious Institutions

The number of Islamic centers in the major urban areas of Europe has mushroomed since the 1990s and they have played a significant part in the Islamic revival project, leaving a strong mark on Europe's migrant communities of Muslim background. The women I discuss in this book participated in these revival scenes. More particularly, in both France and Germany they attended those centers that reflect what John Bowen (2004) has called an Islam "beyond migration," that is, centers that are actively involved in transcending especially the cleavages of ethnicity, and to a lesser extent those of particular religious affiliations or lineages, and in forging an orthodox *French* or *German* Islam. This phenomenon is much more developed in France than in Germany, but it is a growing trend in the German Islamic landscape, too, although it does not displace the still dominant Turkish Islam.

My entry into the field in 2002 in the Paris region, where I had only recently settled to pursue my research, was significantly facilitated by a friend who connected me with women who were active in the local institutional structures of the Islamic revival scene. Gradually I discovered its many localities, spread mainly throughout the *banlieues,* such as the CERSI, the Institut Européen des Sciences Humaines (IESH), the Mosquée de la rue de Tanger, and the Institute Supérieur des Sciences Islamiques (ISSI) in Aubervillier. The mosque at the rue de Tanger was popular for its monthly conferences organized between 1994 and 2006 through the association Présence musulmane under the direction of Algerian-born Larbi Kechat. These conferences attracted many young Muslims from the entire region.[34] The ISSI, in Aubervilliers, was led by the Tunisian Dhaou Meskine, who also founded the first Muslim private school, École La Réussite (an institution that gave many women hope of finding employment in future Muslim private schools). The CERSI, run by Hichème El-Arafa, and the IESH, headed by Ahmad Jaballah (both of whom were also Tunisian-born), are connected to the French Muslim umbrella organization Union des Organisations Islamiques de France (UOIF), which stands in complex relationship with the tradition of the Muslim Brotherhood (Peter 2010b). Both the CERSI and the IESH offer sustained evening and weekend classes and dispense internal degrees at the end of the established curriculum, which takes up to three years.[35] Both centers—situated within walking distance of each other in St. Denis, just north of Paris also organize plenty of additional activities for their students from nightly prayer sessions (*qiyam al-layl*)—to cultural evenings with cinema screenings and presentations by Muslim performing arts troupes and summer camps. When I began my research, these centers were clearly dominated by Muslims of Maghrebi background, but since then young Muslims with roots in West Africa (Mali and Senegal especially) and East Africa (the Comoro Islands, in particular) as well as white French and French Antillean converts have increasingly been present in these centers.

After initially investigating various sites, I became more and more present at the CERSI and restricted my visits to the other institutes for conferences and other special events. CERSI was the institute least bound to one school of thought and among its faculty were individuals from various tendencies. In general, emphasis was laid on providing knowledge that was accessible to and practically useful for French Muslims, an approach that also guided the institute's pedagogical strategies.[36] While visiting a range of classes there, I followed most consistently the course "Islamic Morals," taught by Olfa (whom I introduced in the opening section of this chapter), which was explicitly intended to provide "applicable" knowledge. I also regularly attended her monthly Saturday morning potluck brunches. These brunches initially helped me to establish closer relationships with the women of the center, and it was here that I came to know their social and spiritual preoccupations. The relative ease with which I established contact with these women might have been also partly due to my own German-Tunisian background. This combination sparked quite some curiosity (for many of my interlocutors, a Maghrebi-looking person with a German accent seemed quite exotic), but it also played a role in my quickly gaining the trust of my interlocutors and in their willingness to share with me their life stories and their struggles related to becoming and being committed Muslim women (*musulmanes engagées*) in an immediately post-9/11 world.

In Germany my fieldwork was carried out in the city of Cologne, situated only about three hundred miles northeast of Paris. Although it is definitely not comparable to the metropolis Paris and its immense suburbs, Cologne nonetheless accommodates a quite significant and diverse Muslim population. It is the fourth largest city in Germany and proximate to several industrial areas as well to the former West German capital, Bonn. The greater Cologne area is an important hub for immigration in the state of North Rhine-Westphalia. Cologne is my hometown and therefore a city I know fairly well. Yet, doing research in an environment with which I was not familiar made me rediscover the city in a new way. It was again an acquaintance who provided me with the contact information for the Begegnungs- und Fortbildungszentrum muslimischer Frauen (BFmF), a center established in 1996 by Muslim women, some of Turkish background and some German converts. Women of North African and Middle Eastern backgrounds also worked there. The women who regularly attended the center's diverse Islamic activities were from equally diverse backgrounds in terms of religious affiliation, belonging to various schools of Islamic law (Maliki, Hanafi, and Shafi'i). Some were from families affiliated with various Turkish Islamic organizations (especially DITIP and Milli Görüş, and less frequently Suleymanli and Nurcu)[37] or with institutions dominated by Arabic speakers,[38] affiliations they frequently maintained in addition to their involvement in the BFmF. This center reflects a trend noticed in the literature: the feminization of the Islamic institutional landscape, by which women become more and more important in the work of knowledge dissemination (Jonker 2003; Werbner 1999). Headed by President Amina Theissen, this center not only offers a variety of classes in Islamic education but also has a school branch geared toward integrating migrant women and their daughters by providing language, computer, and other skills classes. The main activity of this branch is its secondary school, which offers young women—mainly girls raised in Germany who dropped out of school or had other difficulties—the opportunity to return to school and graduate from, *Hauptschule* and *Realschule,* the two lower levels of the German high school system. Diplomas from these schools allow women either to start professional training or to continue at the *Gymnasium,* which provides advanced secondary education and prepares students for admission to university.

My first visit to the center offered a welcome surprise. I met several women whom I had known as an undergraduate student at the University of Cologne. I had taken classes with some of them. This happy reunion assisted me tremendously in my research project. I found everyone at the center extremely helpful from the first day onward and established (and reestablished) amicable relations with many of them. I thus quickly became a regular at that center, attending the Islamic classes for adult women that were conducted in German (the center also offered a range of religious instruction classes in the Turkish language). Most notably, I attended the course "*Tafsir* [exegesis] and *Fiqh* [Islamic jurisprudence]: The Signification of the Islamic Sources for the Daily Life of Muslim Women," which back then took place twice weekly, on Tuesdays and Thursdays, and as the title indicates, was concerned, like Olfa's Islamic Morals class, with "applicable" knowledge. This class was taught by Salwa, a woman of Syrian origin in her early thirties who also worked at the center half-time as a social worker offering counseling to Muslim families. During my research stays in Germany I furthermore participated in the center's monthly Sunday seminars, at which invited speakers discussed a topic related to Muslim practice and life in Germany. Beyond attending these specific events, I also spent a lot of time in the center's cafeteria, the favorite hangout place for visitors and employees alike, appreciated for its daily freshly cooked food and delicious cakes. It was there that I had many of my most interesting conversations, with Salwa and other employees, as well as with the women who participated in the various classes.

These women also introduced me into the large, diverse Islamic scene in Cologne. In addition to the dominant Turkish Islamic organizations such as DITIP and Milli Görüş, there is the program of the Institute for Islamology, a "mobile" institute for Islamic theological studies. Its head office in Vienna, Austria, sends teachers to various cities in German-speaking countries, including Cologne. The instruction they dispense lasts two years and is comparable to the courses offered at the CERSI. The daylong classes take place once a month in the spaces of the BFmF. Several of the participants in Salwa's class were also enrolled in this institute.

Some of the women I met at the BFmF who studied at the local university additionally introduced me to the Islamic Student Union, Islamische Hochschulvereinigung (IHV), which organized meetings twice a month, in the format of a religion class. Its participants came from a variety of backgrounds and included Muslims who did not attend any other Islamic circles. It was in these different spaces that I circulated during my fieldwork, moving frequently between the buildings of the BFmF and the University of Cologne.

What stood out in both countries' Islamic circles was the participants' openness to go beyond their own specific doctrinal lineages. Even while acknowledging, for instance, their affiliation with a specific school of law—such as Maliki for those of Maghrebi background and Hanafi for those of Turkish background—they easily attended various Islamic institutions that followed a different lineage or scholarly approach, and admired a variety of Islamic scholars, thinkers, and preachers without necessarily being aware of possible conflicts between these individuals. Similarly, the classes I attended most—those taught by Olfa and Salwa, which were concerned with applicable knowledge, that is, knowledge useful in everyday life—drew on a relatively large body of sources, beyond one specific lineage, even while maintaining a certain coherence.

Notwithstanding the significant amount of time I spent within these various institutions and centers, this book is not an ethnography of Islamic institutions. I attended these institutions and their courses because I was interested in bettering my understanding of my interlocutors' efforts to adopt the practices promoted by these institutions, and particularly in how these practices were carried into the various spheres of the mainstream (secular) society. I therefore invested much time, in both cities, in following my interlocutors in their many other activities throughout town. I sat with them in university cafeterias, cafés, and mosque backyards, drinking tea, and eating cakes, and accompanied them on the subway or bus, in their cars, from universities to hair salons, from department stores to Islamic libraries. We went together to movie theatres and various sports activities. I thereby discovered their various ways of inhabiting their respective towns, how they moved around them, how they interacted with people they met on their paths, how they socialized with or confronted them. It was in these settings that I could see how their public personas responded in manifold ways to the pressures they felt as Muslim women living in a non-Muslim society—more or less visible, more or less outspoken, and more or less comfortable in the various spaces of the secular mainstream society.

Then I followed them back into the safer zones of their private homes, invited numerous times for *iftar* dinners (the breaking of the fast during the month of Ramadan), *Eid* meals, wedding ceremonies, and other casual gatherings. My interlocutors—whose names I have changed for the sake of confidentiality—welcomed me into their lives, and on that journey I undertook with them I laughed with them, shared their fears and sadnesses, saw marital relationships forged and ended, witnessed the beginning of promising careers and the end of professional dreams. It is these daily struggles, but also the pleasures, entailed in living as a pious Muslim woman in the French and German societies that I document in this book and that instigated its specific analytical and theoretical ventures.

2 "I WANT TO INSTRUCT MYSELF TO STRENGTHEN MY FAITH"
Learning in Islamic Institutions

My parents are Turkish and I was born here. We were a very typical Turkish family, more traditional than Islamic. We celebrated Turkish holidays, where *Turkish* also meant *Islamic*. This was very important to us. But I wouldn't say we were practicing Muslims. My dad went to the mosque on Fridays, and we prayed every now and then. In our village we were the only Turkish family; we were different because of our skin color, but not because of our religion. Religion only took place at home. My mom did not wear the veil, neither did my sister or I. We fit in quite well. The only thing was that we did not eat pork and there was no alcohol. Everything was a bit traditional at home, but we did not know why. My mom tried to explain it to us as well as she could, and we respected that, but we did not receive a real Islamic education. Later on, my brother started to question things on his own, and he started to read. Through my brother, my whole family began to wake up a bit. . . . My parents could not answer our questions. They were simple people—I would not say that now, but back then they were simple people. They could not answer our questions, but my brother could. He showed us a lot of things, prayed with us, and talked to us a lot about Islam. This is how it started with me too. . . . At university I said, OK, now I want to lead an Islamic life. And at the IHV [Islamic Student Union] I found a community of people like myself, who converted or who found Islam themselves, and we learned together there.

—Sevim, translator and language teacher at the BFmF

My parents were practicing Muslims; I saw them praying. But we didn't talk a lot. We returned to Algeria for four years; I prayed there, but when we came back, I stopped. Afterward, I didn't receive my high school diploma and started working at McDonald's. I met my friend Lamia there, as well as other practicing Muslims. We talked together a lot and this motivated me. I started to pray again. It's true: working at this fast-food place gave me a lot in regard to *din* [spirituality]. It was like a click in my mind; I started reading books. And then I started to go to this institute [CERSI]. I want to learn a lot of things because I realized that we are really ignorant, we don't know anything [*laughter*]. I want to instruct myself and especially to strengthen my faith.

—Saida, unemployed, studies at CERSI

THESE SNAPSHOTS are from my earliest conversations with Muslim women in France and Germany. Many women told me some version of these narratives to describe their own pious trajectories: a rather simple storyline that developed in a linear fashion toward a clear outcome—a journey from unawareness to a spiritual awakening and quest for knowledge. Of course this was only part of the story. In the years that followed I would learn that the process was far more complicated. But even if these narrations reduce a highly complex story of pious struggle into a neat package, they do have something important to tell us. They illustrate clearly that pious practitioners experience their trajectory as somehow distinct from the religious upbringing they received at home. Having embarked on a quest for Islamic knowledge during adolescence or young adulthood, my interlocutors expressed an ambiguous attitude toward the religious education they obtained from their parents (and in some cases from Qur'an school). Although they considered their early education to be insufficient, they still acknowledged that something had been passed down to them. Their parents had instilled in them a certain consciousness of their Islamic affiliation—a religious sensitivity, normative values, and certain habits and modes of conduct. Nonetheless, their parents' generation was seen as unqualified to transmit "real" Islamic knowledge. Over the months and years subsequent to my introduction to these women, especially while attending classes with them at the Islamic centers, I came to realize that this assessment of their parents' religious education reflected their concern with a particular kind of knowledge, as well as with the state of mind that such a knowledge (or the lack thereof) might enable. The terms they consistently employed in their narratives—such as *education, instruction, reflecting, understanding, researching,* and *ignorance*—index rather specific assumptions about what constitutes "real" knowledge.

All the women emphasized that their "deliberate" and "conscious" quest for Islamic knowledge began during adolescence or young adulthood and represented a decisive turning point. Their narratives often evoke a perceived transition from a former (nonorthodox) mode of belonging to and living Islam—often referred to as "Muslim by tradition"—to a new (orthodox) mode, which they describe as "becoming Islamic" (*Islamisch werden*) or as "entering Islam" (*rentrer dans l'Islam*). These locutions were also connected to the idea of taking this step *independently* from their parents. The distinction here was based on two different yet interrelated sets of assumptions. An Islam practiced implicitly, not rationalized, oral rather than scriptural, and lived in a more or less private manner within the family or the Islamic community was opposed to an Islam that was text-based, discursive, consciously reflected upon—and therefore "understood"—and put into practice by adopting a comprehensive and visible Islamic lifestyle in all domains of life. Related to this distinction was a second assumption that opposed Islam as a taken-for-granted family inheritance to an Islam reaffirmed as both identity and lifestyle through a *conscious* decision.

This conception of what counts as "true" Islamic education and knowledge was often closely intertwined with the valorization of personal understanding, and choice. By associating their parents' generation with "traditionalism," these women intersected in complex ways with common representations of the migrant figure in French and German societies.[1] In these discourses the migrant is criticized as "too traditional" because overly possessed by an Islamic worldview, and therefore passive and nonreflexive. These women, however, criticized the "traditionalism" of their parents for being not Islamic enough, which according to them also requires a heightened degree of reflexivity and self-consciousness.

Even when they recognized Islam as an inherited identity and tradition, the women persistently articulated a desire to understand their faith through particular cognitive means in order to arrive at conviction. Such an understanding of religion—one not reduced to tacit pre-discursive knowledge and practice but given an object-like quality through its inscription into language—is connected to specific assumptions about the self. The critique that these women put forward reflected the extent to which their understanding of religion and its exigencies was shaped by notions of the modern knowing subject. These notions, which lie at the heart of the "moral narrative of modernity" (Keane 2007), serve as the background against which my interlocutors' own pious trajectories were set. In their willed distinction of their own religious practice from their parents' "traditional" Islam, my interlocutors' stance pays tribute to the idea of the knowing subject who possesses *libre arbitre* (free will), refuses blind submission to authority, and is able to reflect intelligently and take self-responsibility (Taylor 1989).[2]

This chapter focuses on the practices of *learning* Islam that were asserted by participants in the Islamic circles I studied—practices that were experienced as sharply distinguished from the "traditional approach" of their parents. The generational discourse employed by young European-born Muslims who discard the religious modes of life and practices of the older generation as "traditional" and valorize a certain kind of "knowledgeable Islam" is now well documented.[3] Less examined are the new kinds of learning experiences and pedagogical approaches that have been instituted in the European revival structures that seek to transmit knowledgeable Islam. These structures respond to but also model young European Muslims' understandings of what "learning about Islam" should entail, the kind of sociability in which it should be embedded, and the intrinsic connections that exist between novel forms of knowledge transmission and the fashioning of a new kind of pious subjectivity. By tracing the "learning" stories" of my interlocutors, I seek to unearth not only the particular epistemological status that Islamic knowledge has acquired through its rearticulation with modern ideals about selfhood, but also its attendant affective status in that learning was expected to convey a specific emotional experience.

In Pursuit of Authentic Islamic Knowledge

Initially, when I asked the women in the Islamic circles in which I participated about their religious journeys, they cited a variety of incidents as triggers. They could point to particularly difficult moments, starting in adolescence, such as encounters with death, societal problems, teenage crises, and experiences of difference, discrimination, and racialization.[4] The experience of difference and Otherness was frequently invoked and often intersected with one or several other critical moments in life. These experiences regularly provoked feelings of speechlessness, which in turn motivated a search for more *formal* religious knowledge. This type of knowledge was considered an important condition for acquiring a language that would enable them to *talk* about Islam and be understood by Others, thereby also allowing the women to represent their own difference better. I shall limit myself here to experiences the women had at school because they instructively foreground the different ways in which the German and French school systems construct and deal with Otherness.

In Germany I was often told that children of Muslim background were frequently called on at school to serve as "expert on Islam" by giving presentations or serving as spokesperson during question-and-answer sessions. In these situations, many children encountered the difficulty of putting their familiarity with Islam into words, which elicited a painful awareness of how little communicable knowledge on Islam they possessed. Consequently, these young Muslim students were driven to search for palpable knowledge, especially by reading books. Such was the case with Gülden, one of my former classmates at university whom I fortuitously met again during my fieldwork at the BFmF. A woman of Turkish background in her early thirties and a PhD candidate in the French language and civilization, her devout parents had sent her to mosque classes from an early age.[5] Yet she still felt that her knowledge was insufficient to the task expected of her at school.

> At school you are declared the "expert," and you need to know quite a lot of
> things. This is how my interest grew, in order to explain things to others, not

only for my own practice. So I developed a sort of professional interest, quote unquote, in this topic. And I started to defend Islam—at times I could become very aggressive.

Gülden's experience not only quite subtly highlights the "Humboldtian" approach taken by German public schools—which, following certain humanist ideals, invites each pupil to express his or her individuality—but also exposes a political culture that fixes the Otherness of "foreign" children.[6] Thiel Suniers (2004: 222) observes that in German schools the idea of a cultural difference between Germans and foreigners marks relations between pupils as well as among the teaching staff, which systematically reinforces cultural boundaries. To have one's individuality limited to one's belonging to a certain religious group (Turk or Arab being considered synonymous with Muslim) is doubtlessly essentializing. If such an approach is experienced by many students as a stigmatization that does not conform to their own self-image, my interlocutors seemed to respond to this interpellation rather positively: being Muslim was already an important element of their self-identity and it potentially valorized their difference. At times they even confided that these moments when they were considered "experts" helped them to gain "self-confidence" and "self-esteem." Nevertheless, they initially felt utterly unprepared for the task of representing Islam in the classroom.

The women I met in France did not share these experiences. In the French republican school system, "the crucible in which citizens are formed" (Joan W. Scott 2007) through the inculcation of a universalist perspective that seeks to transcend the "particularities" of ethnic, religious, and cultural identities, the experiences of minority groups are generally marginalized (Keaton 2006; Mannitz and Schiffauer 2004).[7] For the women, who were socialized in the French system, this attitude meant that their "expertise" was not welcome. When they engaged in discussions about Islam with teachers in philosophy, history, and French literature classes—all of which persistently focused on negatively perceived gender questions, such as Islam's supposed oppression of women—they often experienced those encounters as hostile confrontations. These situations also provoked feelings of powerlessness and speechlessness in the women, due to their inability to counter these discursive attacks with convincing arguments. This was the experience of Emna, a spirited woman of Moroccan origin in her early twenties who enrolled as a student at CERSI while also preparing to receive her high school diploma at a school for adults. Raised as an only child by her widowed mother, Emna grew up in a *banlieue* east of Paris. Her mother was religious and tried to teach her the basic rules of Islam, but without explaining "the deeper meaning of things." Emna's memories from her school days were not pleasant, marked as they were by unsympathetic attitudes toward Muslim sensibilities, and she was eager to leave school and start working, even without graduating from high school. She recalled the following:

> I always had these debates with my French teacher. He always tried to provoke me—like the debate about God: does he exist? Or on Islam, about the position of women—it was always like that. And back then I didn't have the argument to make them change their mind. . . . This is what incited me to learn [about Islam], and I read a lot afterward.

But even if some women had the capacity to formulate a defensive discourse, they still felt that their opinions were delegitimized, especially if they were recognizable as "religious Muslims" (because of their headscarf).[8] Aziza was a young, attractive journalism student of Tunisian origin who had just turned nineteen. Her parents were active members of the revival movement in France, running an establishment for the religious education of young children in a *banlieue* north of Paris. Thus, unlike many others, she had been exposed early on to a more scholarly approach to Islam. Consequently, she felt confident and entitled to argue with her teachers on the matter. However, she too conveyed a similar sentiment:

> When he [the history teacher] talked about Islam, he often confounded religion and tradition. He talked about female genital mutilation, he talked about all that. And me, I always wanted to tell him that he had to distinguish between the two. But he didn't like that. . . . Whatever I said, it was the *intégriste* [fundamentalist] speaking, because I had this thing on my head. They thought that I was immediately subjective.

These different experiences within the German and French school systems—which corresponded quite neatly to the respective countries' national political and discursive cultures of dealing with racial, ethnic, and religious difference—all triggered a sense of urgency to learn to *talk about* Islam, to communicate Islam in order to explain themselves to others in ways that would be recognized as the condition for "having a religion" (Keane 2007: 213).[9] Moreover, the ability to communicate Islam discursively was perceived as the very first condition for combating the negative image of Islam, even if this ability did not guarantee, as Aziza's example shows, that the arguments would actually be heard.[10]

Once their interest was piqued, many women began reading alone. At this early stage, they read everything they could easily acquire, from the foundational texts—such as translations of the Qur'an and biographies of the Prophet Muhammad (*sira*), texts that were often easily accessible at home or in the mosque—as well as literature available in mainstream bookstores that introduced a larger public to issues regarding Islam. In addition, women of Turkish origin usually found in their homes Turkish-language *almihal* literature, a genre that developed in the Turkish context and constitutes a sort of Muslim catechism.[11] This genre can be considered a precursor to contemporary "Islamic books," which are written in easily accessible language and provide practical information about pious conduct (Gonzales-Quijano 1991). This proliferating pedagogical literature, often translated from Arabic into various European languages and available in the numerous Islamic libraries that increasingly are visible in French and German urban centers, has gained popularity among young Muslims in search of religious knowledge. Furthermore, many women of Turkish background complemented their educational literature with Islamic novels, another increasingly popular genre within Turkish revival circles. Though not considered a vehicle of knowledge per se, this literature was appreciated for its capacity to arouse Islamic sensibilities by providing emotionally touching stories about Muslim heroines.[12]

Women remembered this first stage of rediscovering Islam—whether it took place in a family setting, in a circle of friends, or as a strictly solitary endeavor—as a highly independent and personal self-education. In retrospect, they appreciated it for helping them to develop an "Islamic personality" at their "own pace," without any external pressure. For many authors writing about Islam in Europe, this private quest for knowledge has been taken as welcome evidence of the hypothesis that "individualization" has become an element of Islam in Europe.[13] Such a trend may indeed be observable among many Muslims born in Europe, but for my respondents, an exclusively individualized form of knowledge acquisition could not substitute for the importance of communal structures.

All of the women I spoke with insisted on the insufficiency of learning merely for oneself, especially once they no longer wanted simply to search for cognitive knowledge but also wanted to put this knowledge rigorously into practice. Often it was the desire to resolve very practical questions that led them to seek out institutional structures. In our early conversations, I often heard statements like "I started the work by myself but at some point I felt the need to ask questions," or "I needed to understand why we had to do this, and why this was not allowed." In this context, the discovery of novel forms of Islamic learning provided through conferences, classes, or entire course systems by recently established Islamic centers was experienced as the next and most significant step in the women's religious journey.

Studying Islam's primary sources with the help of qualified people formed part of a quest to live an "authentic" Islam rooted in solid knowledge and deep understanding. The women's critique of their parents' "traditional" religiosity was generally formulated on the grounds that it was not only a nonreflexive, pre-discursive emulation but, more gravely still, an inauthentic, even false knowledge that unacceptably mixed cultural customs and religious norms and practices. Access to the primary sources—the Qur'an, the Sunna (the tradition of the Prophet and his companions), and *sira*—was always judged to be of major importance, because only these sources could provide direct, uncorrupted knowledge. At the same time, these sources required interpretation to reveal their true meaning and establish correct and authentic knowledge. Conscious of the difficulty for the lay believer and nonspecialist of arriving at a proper interpretation, the women advocated studying with recognized teachers in the community who could correctly transmit that "authenticated" (Deeb 2006) knowledge. In this sense, they were already responsive to the revival movement's overall concern for the maintenance of institutional orthodoxy.[14]

Furthermore, their participation in these Islamic institutes of learning made them approach the available outside sources for learning about Islam— the print and digital media—more carefully. In these institutions, women learned who the trustworthy scholars and preachers were. Interestingly, the women expressed a rather vague definition of this group of scholars, roughly identified as representatives of an "Islam of the Middle Way." This group was not so much demarcated by a clear intellectual lineage as it was distinguished by who was excluded from it, namely those who were too "soft"—meaning that the stances they took were too "liberal"—or conversely too "extremist."[15] Similarly, it was also in these centers that important information circulated regarding whose sermons were available on CD or DVD or downloadable, and what books were the must-reads.[16] While the (especially emotional) benefits of the new media technologies were widely acknowledged, it was the act of reading that was encouraged as the quintessential experience of Islamic learning and knowledge acquisition.[17] This preference was emphasized repeatedly in classes and conferences; the first revelation received by the Prophet Muhammad, which started with the word *iqra'* (most often translated in these contexts as "Read!" rather than "Recite!") was upheld here as the paradigmatic example. At all the centers I visited, reading was highly encouraged, and they each had a small library or bookstore section, regularly organized book sales, and at times even held reading contests.

The insistence on the necessity of studying Arabic similarly derived from a concern for authenticity. Many women took Arabic lessons at the Islamic centers, at university, or in language schools abroad in the Arabic-speaking world. For most of my interlocutors with roots in Arabic-speaking countries (the Maghreb or the Middle East), the study of literary Arabic was a crucial part of the learning process. Knowledge of classical Arabic appeared as the key to "pure knowledge," that is, to the ability to understand the Qur'an in the original text. Although translations were generally used, there was an underlying awareness of the potential of translation to distort the text. "To translate is to transform" was a remark I often heard in this context. In France, women of Maghrebi background, who generally were fluent in local Arabic dialects (unless they were Berberophone), persistently expressed their regret at not having learned classical Arabic in their youth. And while many women of Turkish background similarly invoked the importance of studying Arabic and were at least able to read the Qur'an in Arabic (even if they did not understand it), they nonetheless equally valorized the Turkish language, which they could generally read and speak quite fluently, as possessing an Islamic connotation, and therefore considered it too a legitimate and authentic language of Islamic learning. Most important, however, was that the Turkish language elicited in them, as Arabic did for many others, the *feeling* of Islam. I often heard statements like "I read a lot in Turkish. I don't like reading in German; it does not give me the same feeling." This perception also indexes the important relationship the women established between Islamic knowledge and emotional dispositions, a relationship at the heart of the learning process that was encouraged in the Islamic centers.

"Objectification" of Islam

The critique that young pious Muslims in Europe leveled against their parents' "traditional" Islam, as well as the importance they consequently attributed to acquiring a formal religious education, clearly reflected modern conceptions about education as necessarily being "formal" and objectified through language (Keane 2009). Literature on European Islam often concludes that this quest for knowledge has established a new relation to religion, one that is more reflexive, intellectual, and rational. The arguments developed are largely congruent with religious modernization paradigms that revolve around the idea of the "objectification" of Islam, articulated in the European context by Olivier Roy (2004), but building on a hypothesis originally formulated by Dale Eickelman and James Piscatori (1996). According to these two authors, the new possibilities of access to religious knowledge through mass education and new media technologies have enabled the development of an objectified Islam that is defined by heightened self-consciousness, reflexivity, and systematization of the religious tradition.

The conjecture that defines objectification processes as specifically modern phenomena has been criticized by several authors (Asad 1986, 1993; Deeb 2006; Mahmood 2005; Salvatore 1998). Saba Mahmood (2005) is one of those voices that question the implicit assumption contained within this hypothesis that a formerly unreflective "traditional" mode of religious practice is being replaced by a contemporary reflective and thus "modern" mode of practice. The critical debate on the objectification of Islam thesis reflects unease with accepting the linear modernization paradigm (along with its underlying teleologies and epistemologies) that prevails in certain currents of the study of religion.

Although I agree with this critique, I also believe that the term *objectification* has the potential to conceptualize the specific understanding of "knowledge" that my interlocutors so clearly display. Webb Keane's (2007) reflections on objectification offer, in my opinion, a way to make this concept fruitful without endorsing it as a normative model.[18] He too criticizes objectification, as commonly employed, for being not merely a "neutral" heuristic concept but rather, as he puts it, one of the central claims that distinguishes what he calls the "moral narrative of modernity," an epistemological claim with moral implications (2007: 10). As such, objectification is part of a larger process in which the subject, clearly distinguished from the object, asserts its freedom, agency, and autonomy. Yet Keane still wants to hold on to the term for its usefulness in thinking through processes in which something, be it language or something material, becomes an object of experience and thus an "instance of a more general principle of reflexivity within the ongoing creation and transformation of social phenomena" (2007: 18). The term *semiotic ideology* provides him with a conceptual tool for thinking of objectification as not derived from "the teleological destination of modernity" (2007: 21).[19] Semiotic ideology is what one believes about language and objects, material or otherwise, and how one acts on the basis of those beliefs; it therefore always also points to awareness and reflexivity, and thus to some form of objectification. Significantly, Keane argues that the particular structure that objectification processes take, whether "modern" or not, depends on the resources provided by people's respective traditions, of which semiotic ideologies are a crucial component (see 2007: 256).

The insights that Keane has developed around semiotic ideology as a way to think about objectification without taking on its moral and teleological baggage seem extremely useful for analyzing the specific modes of discussion and reasoning that I encountered in the Islamic circles. Such an approach is useful for exploring how value is attributed—or not—to certain modes of speaking and conducting oneself in relation to a religious tradition. It helps account for the critiques that my interlocutors voiced about their parents' way of being Muslim. It provides a useful framework for thinking through the new kinds of learning experiences and pedagogical approaches that are employed in revival structures as a response to new understandings of what "learning Islam" entails. Finally, because the concept is embedded in and connected to a specific semiotic ideology, it highlights the fact that Muslims' "ready availability for talk" (Keane 2007: 257) about the correct meaning of Islam is not an isolated feature of European modernity but instead is consequential to Islam's rich scriptural (and oral) traditions and to the way they have developed under particular modern conditions.

The Relationship between Knowledge and Faith

Everyone I talked to posited that the formal, reflexively acquired type of religious knowledge was the condition *sine qua non* for effecting a general transformation of the self that was indispensable for adopting a "real" Islamic lifestyle. Even if the intended self-transformation often turned out to be more difficult than initially imagined, the idea of self-transformation as an essential process was ubiquitous in the women's discourse, as well as in the teachings at the Islamic centers. This "work" on the self, most often captured in the Arabic locution *jihad al-nafs* (struggle against the lower self), became an object of constant reflection and discussion, whether in regard to the various devotional practices and the discipline they required or in regard to general life conduct.

Here again, ideals of the modern subject—such as choice, knowing, self-awareness, and the capacity for self-transformation—created a discursive environment in which Islamic traditions of self-cultivation became inhabitable. The emphasis on self-cultivation, often discussed by Islamic scholars of the past—most notably by scholars embedded in the Sufi traditions—seems to have become increasingly popular through the burgeoning activities of Islamic revival movements (both orthodox and Sufi varieties) worldwide. Thus, while these movements are not simply echoing modern (liberal) assumptions of self-transformation, these assumptions nonetheless make available an important semiotic and psychological background that renders self-cultivation plausible. Through and against this background pious practitioners elaborate their own language for that ethical work that accounts for their own sense of self and their relation to community and religious authority.

Such a comprehension of the tight relationship between knowledge and the transformation of the self that could issue in the strenghtening of faith was explicated by my interlocutors in multiple ways. First, the pursuit of knowledge was driven by the necessity to understand, to be convinced. Finding plausibility and coherence in the Islamic dogmas so that they were convincing to oneself was a primary condition for strengthening one's faith (*iman*). Primordial here was the role of the Other, who had the capacity to make one question the internal coherence of one's belief. Time and again I heard statements positing that the ability to respond convincingly to questions and criticisms from non-Muslims was an important condition for sustaining this internal coherence. And it was the gender issue that served as the ultimate touchstone. Confronted with an image of Islam that is particularly negative in this regard, it became essential for women to prove to themselves that this representation was wrong. Ümit, for instance, was strongly influenced on her personal and professional trajectory by such an experience. A woman of Turkish origin in her early thirties, a widow and single mother, Ümit worked full-time at the BFmF, developing interfaith programs as well as teacher seminars on Islam. When I asked what had triggered her participation in Islamic classes, she responded as follows:

> You are also continuously questioned by the environment about all sorts of things. You have to agree with what you say yourself. Explanations for others, OK, but also an explanation for oneself. You also have questions as a Muslim— why this, why that? And if you don't have any explanation. . . . Are women really disadvantaged? Are my rights recognized? This knowledge you need to have for yourself. The more you know, the more it seems logical to you, the more your faith is strengthened. You believe more intensely.

Another frequently highlighted dimension of this link between knowledge and faith was the idea that faith can never be fully acquired but must, on the contrary, be continuously cultivated and worked on.[20] This idea was also extensively discussed in the conferences, lectures, and classes provided at the Islamic centers. Naima, for instance, never grew tired of insisting on this dimension. A young, charming, athletic woman of Moroccan origin in her late twenties, she had, by the time we met, completed her training in nursery care, taken two years off to study Islamic sciences at Château Chinon,[21] and just started her specialization training as a pediatric nurse. I accompanied her to many of her religious activities. We developed an amicable relationship and it was with her that I had some of the longest conversations. She was most outspoken about her inner struggles in regard to her religious journey. One Saturday afternoon, after attending a class in one of the buildings of the Grande Mosquée de Paris (Grand Mosque of Paris),[22] we sat together in the tea salon at the mosque compound enjoying green tea with fresh mint and engaging in one of those long and insightful conversations. On this particular day, when I inquired about her motivation to continuously take Islamic courses, she replied,

> For me, [religious] knowledge [*la science*] is indispensible. All kinds of knowledge, you know, you taste a little bit and you want to know more; and the more you know, the less you have the impression that you know anything. So, when it comes to *din*, spirituality, it's the same thing. It's as if you plant a seed in your heart and it starts to grow, and then you need to nourish it even more. . . . Because your faith, at one moment, if it is not nourished by knowledge . . . this has occurred in my life; there have been ups and downs in my faith. The Prophet, *salla Allahu ʿalayhi wa sallam* [May Allah honor him and grant him peace], said at times your faith will increase, and at times your faith will decrease. What has always helped me to keep my faith growing, so that it never diminished too much, was knowledge.

Note first that Naima refers to Islamic knowledge with the term *la science* (rather than *savoir*), thereby building on Islamic epistemological traditions that have not incorporated modern positivist assumptions, which oppose (rational) knowledge and (irrational religious) belief to each other.[23] I also want to highlight another aspect of Naima's statement. Although she emphasized the primordial importance for the pious believer of dwelling on religious sciences in order to build up a strong faith, she also recognized the fragility and nonlinearity in that process. Her awareness of the potential instability of faith reflected well all my interlocutors' conception of piety. A faith that weakened was understood as "regression," a faith that strengthened, as "progress." Especially women who were invested in a professional career or family life complained about the difficulty of maintaining the necessary discipline and time investment to regularly attend Islamic learning activities. Overwhelmed by the quotidian stress of a hectic life in which the cultivation of Islamic sensibilities did not have much space, the effort to invest oneself in religious sciences was not equally intense at all times and often got weaker over time, which in turn was felt to have a negative impact on an individual's faith.

Sevim, whom I quoted extensively at the beginning of the chapter, was such a case. During her student years, she went through an intensive phase of pious self-cultivation. She attended religion classes and practiced in a scrupulous manner. She also began to speak publicly at Islamic conferences throughout Germany. Indeed, I had met her in the early 1990s when I was an undergraduate at the University of Cologne, where she was active in the Islamic student association. I even attended one of her talks. During my fieldwork, I met her again at the BFmF. In the meantime, she had completed her studies, gotten married, and started working as a translator and language teacher. She had been significantly impacted by the changed rhythm of life and intensive work hours, which is why, when I met her again, she was much less involved in Islamic communal activities. The hours when she taught at the BFmF were the few hours per week that she spent in an Islamic environment. We had enjoyed many chats in the BFmF cafeteria, and one afternoon she invited me to her translation agency in a small town outside Cologne. Over tea and cake she discussed quite frankly her own struggles to maintain her former degree of piety, stating with regret:

> Right now I am stagnating, unfortunately. When you work a lot, you don't have the time to study. Often I find I prefer reading a regular novel rather than the *sira*. I have so many books on the *sira* but I don't read them. Because, my God, I tell myself, you have to concentrate. Regular novels, I can read them like this, without effort. No, you have to be continuously in movement; otherwise, your Islam is gone.

Difficulties similar to those experienced by Nevim were often acknowledged and thematized within the circles. Salwa, the social worker at the BFmF who taught the class "*Tafsir* and *Fiqh*: The Signification of the Islamic Sources for the Daily Life of Muslim Women" (see Chapter 1), had repeatedly reflected on these issues. A woman with friendly but resolute manners who was much respected in the center for her religious and professional expertise, she therefore offered a new class specifically designed for the staff. After returning to Cologne for another round of fieldwork, one year after my previous visit, I noticed this additional class on the schedule and asked Salwa about it. She answered,

> We realized that our own teachers, who should live and breathe Muslim piety, are often overwhelmed by their daily lives and, as a consequence, become less and less Muslim, inside. They start neglecting the prayer times. Islam then becomes just an outside cover. So we thought we had to do something to combat this trend. We have to give reminders not only to the women who come to us, but our own staff needs reminders too—we all do. Although it is not an obligation for our staff to attend every session, they should try to attend as often as possible. These classes are similar to my "*Tafsir* and *Fiqh*" class. I try to remind them of things they already know, so that their Islamic awareness and faith stay intact, and do not decrease.

Because the potential instability of faith was so readily acknowledged, the pedagogical strategies that teachers like Salwa enacted were geared toward mitigating the possible consequences of that fragility. One finds here too the intrinsic link between knowledge and faith that Salwa further explained to me on another afternoon as we sat together in her office after her class:

> It is like in any other relationship. To lead a good relationship, whether as a spouse or as a friend or in parent-child relationships—all relationships require hard work. For the God-human relationship it is the same thing. This is work on the God-human relationship: through the acquisition of knowledge, you get closer to God. It is the interaction of the cognitive and the spiritual aspects of faith. On the one hand, it is the cognitive acquisition of simple knowledge, facts, *hadith* [the authoritative records of the Prophet's sayings and deeds], Qur'an verses, and the meaning of their contents. On the other hand, it has an effect on the relationship to God. The more knowledge I have, of course—provided that I am convinced of these things—the more I am fulfilled by faith, the more proud I am of my faith, and the deeper are those roots, the more my faith becomes unshakeable. Spiritual growth is absolutely linked to cognitive growth, which one achieves through access to the sources.

Yet the women did not consider "spiritual growth" to be the quasi-natural outcome of any kind of Islamic knowledge transmission. It was precisely according to the ability to incite "spiritual growth" in the learning encounter that teachers of the Islamic classes were judged. I often heard, for instance, after classes at the BFmF or CERSI, students gathered together discussing their teachers' respective styles, which they lauded for their capacity to touch the students emotionally and to make their faith "grow." Following the same reasoning, my interlocutors, whether teachers or students, constantly recommended listening to rhetorically talented preachers (at conferences and on DVDs, CDs, and the Internet) who did not merely convey knowledge but simultaneously stirred pious emotions. Naima, for instance, frequently commented on the significance of listening to those teachers, preachers, and scholars who were able to "touch the heart." During her movements throughout the city, she would listen, like many of her peers, on her MP3 player not only to Qur'anic recitations but also to sermons by those preachers she deemed most eloquent. During the afternoon that we spent at the tea salon at the Grand Mosque of Paris, for example, she invoked her enthusiasm for listening to the Egyptian TV preacher Amr Khaled:

> What helped me a lot were the conferences of Amr Khaled; you must know him. I discovered him at the Bourget three years ago,[24] and it was like a revelation. Amazing, I was speechless in front of his presentation. . . . *Masha'Allah* [God has willed it], and he had this way of talking with a particular eloquence. . . . There are people like this who are very talented; it comes from God, *al-hamdulillah* [praise to God], it's a gift. And then I listened to his cassette on *khushu'* [humility] and on *qiyam al-layl* [prayer at night], and this helped me enormously to develop my love for God.

Again and again I was told how important it was not to limit oneself to rational learning, because Islamic knowledge had to be acquired through a spiritual approach. Naima continued her reflections on this perspective, between sips of tea and bites of baklava:

> *La science* without spirituality, this is mechanical knowledge: I learn this *sura* by heart, I learn the *fiqh* by heart. There are those who limit themselves to this kind of mechanical knowledge: the *fiqh*, okay, there are four schools, if you don't pray you are an unbeliever. If you don't have spirituality, what can you do with this science in your daily life? My faith is nourished by knowledge *and* spirituality.

Here she distinguished modes of knowledge that have an affective ("spiritual") impact from those that do not (which she called "mechanical"). This emphasis on a spiritual, affective approach to Islamic knowledge was ubiquitous in conversations and class discussions. During one of Salwa's classes, for instance, in which the importance of a spiritual approach to knowledge was highlighted, one woman related how she had initially chosen to pursue Islamic studies at the local university, motivated by her desire to deepen her knowledge of Islam. However, she changed disciplines after the first term, when she found that the academic approach was too "cold" and "rational." Such a secular acquisition of knowledge *about* Islam was not suitable for eliciting the desired sentiments. The learning experience was, on the contrary, expected to create emotions that would serve as the foundation on which faith was to be constructed.

These reflections are in line with established Islamic pedagogical traditions. In these traditions, knowledge received the status of a moral virtue and was understood to be in a causal relationship with faith. Faith emerges and can grow through knowledge. Numerous classical thinkers have elaborated on this notion (Rosenthal 1970; Wan Daud 1989). This is why classical scholarship has turned *'ilm* (knowledge) into a central Islamic "metaphor" (Lapidus 1984). To illustrate this particular understanding of the strong relation between faith and knowledge, many women cited during our conversations the Qur'anic verse "Among his servants, only the knowledgeable fears Allah" (35:28). They thereby pointed to the idea that knowledge not only should transmit information, but also should help the believer become immersed in an ambience of divine presence. In return, this immersion should arouse specific emotional states, such as feelings of love and fear toward God, humility, and confidence in God (*tawakkul*).

This Islamic pedagogical tradition—which follows closely in the footsteps of the Aristotelian model of ethical pedagogy—invigorates the insight that learning is always related to the domain of the affective and must be understood within a politics of feeling.[25] Scholars of critical pedagogy have recently recovered these insights, claiming that knowledge is not simply "something to be understood; it is always, understood or not, felt and responded to somatically, that is, in its corporeal materiality" (Giroux and McLaren 1991:170).[26] Learning as ethical cultivation thus refers to the process of being properly affected, of being "open to certain affections and closed to certain others," to "being discriminatingly receptive and resistant" (Kosman 1980: 106).[27] *'Ilm* (knowledge) seeks to fashion certain inner dispositions, visceral and affective, that in the long run will sediment an Islamic habitus.

Affective Knowledge and Communities of Learning

One Sunday, in the "Islamic Morals" class at CERSI, Olfa devoted the session to the question of brotherhood in Islam, which as she mentioned during her introductory words was intrinsically linked to the notion of *taqwa*

(God-consciousness). As she put it, "the path to God is traveled in a group." Throughout her lecture, she offered advice on how to deepen the bonds of brotherhood (or sisterhood) among believers and listed which were the necessary virtues in that regard. To bolster her argument, she quoted extensively from the Qur'an and the *hadith* literature. After dictating to the students a few *du'a* (invocations) that demanded divine help in establishing these bonds, which she said they should learn for the next week, Olfa insisted that the students meet with their peers as often as possible, to remember God together, to learn together, beyond the framework of the institute. In contrast to the notion that piety could be cultivated in an individual, private space, she claimed that it was literally impossible to get closer to God all by oneself, and that everyone needed constant reminders from other believers. For this reason, one should always feel deep love for one's brothers and sisters, because it is also thanks to them that one may earn a place in paradise. She concluded, "Always remind yourself that you love your brothers and sisters in God [*aimer en Dieu*]. And our class is also important for this reason—that you are in a community."

Olfa's teaching that day clearly demonstrates that the model of learning put forward in the Islamic centers connects the emotional experience of learning to its pronounced *relational* character. Learning occurred through a relationship between the teacher and her students, but also through the relationships among students. Earlier I mentioned that all my interlocutors considered the study of Islam within Islamic communal structures to be pivotal in their own pious trajectories. This experience was crucial not merely because they felt they could acquire a deeper and more "authentic" knowledge only in such settings, but also for the emotional benefit of learning *together*. Because they were confronted with an outside world that did not share the same religious and spiritual sensibility, learning together became a resource for mutual motivation. Everyone highlighted the importance of spending time studying with their classmates. "I need to be in touch with the sisters" was a constant refrain. This emphasis on togetherness was insisted on not only in the class just described but also in several other classes and conferences. For the women I talked to, curtailing this experience of learning together would almost certainly provoke stagnation in their faith.

In her work on Qur'anic recitation in Indonesia, Anna Gade (2004) highlights the necessity for studies on Islamic schooling to examine what a specific educational system "entails situationally in terms of personal or social experience." (Gade 2004: 118). She thereby wants to pay attention to "affective associations, ambivalences, and patterned emotional textures" that envelop the experiences of Islamic learning in a specific context. Building on work by social learning theorist Jean Lave (1991), Gade develops an understanding of religious learning as a developmental "learning identity." Lave highlights learning as a practice that forges subjectivity in direct relation to that practice. Several learners engaging together in that practice come to be accepted into "communities of learning" (Gade 2004: 123). Indeed, the situational activity of learning together with other (young) Muslims in an Islamic center created close, emotional ties between practitioners, extending the simple socialization of the classroom. Being attentive to the experiences established through these "communities of learning" allows us to comprehend better the difference between "traditional" modes of Islamic teaching and the type of learning provided in these centers. At the core of this perception is a distinct teacher-student relationship. Listen, for instance, to Salwa, the teacher of the "*Tafsir* and *Fiqh*" class at the BFmF as she describes her own position in this relationship:

> When I was on maternity leave . . . the *tafsir* class was cancelled, and a lot of students came to me and said, our *iman* is growing weaker. And I myself noticed that the *tafsir* class was not like, I am the teacher and these are my students, but it was for all of us . . . a group in which we remembered God. We are all the same, and for me it is a genuine filling station. . . . I also need that *tafsir* class. Therefore, it is important, these groups are important, for mutual support.

In addition to highlighting the importance of studying together in a group for sustaining individual faith, Salwa also emphasized her own position in the class as merely one member among equals. She did not perceive her situation as being in a hierarchical teacher-student relationship. This viewpoint reflected an observation I made in several other centers. It was not unusual to see amicable personal connections develop between students and their teachers. The close teacher-student relationship has often been observed as a central feature of traditional Islamic education. For example, Jonathan Berkey (1992), in his study on Islamic education in medieval Cairo, discusses this relationship using the Arabic term *suhba*. Although the word also implies "companionship," he prefers "discipleship," because the traditional teacher-student relationship, albeit extremely close and personal, was a highly authoritative one that created an "insuperable psychological gulf" (Berkey 1992: 35) between teacher and student. A student should learn with one *shaykh,* and the relationship should ideally last a lifetime. This relationship model required a specific etiquette in which the student constantly performed respect and obedience to the teacher.[28]

The personal relationships between students and teachers that I observed in the circles I studied, however, could be more properly described as "companionship." They were highly democratized—which was also due to the type of training the teachers had received. These teachers, who were often quite young and not so distant in age from the students they taught, had themselves benefited from the new educational facilities in Europe. Olfa and Salwa were two clear examples of this new type of teacher. The ambience in their classrooms was generally relaxed, leaving time for laughter and relaxation. The teacher could easily be interrupted, interrogated, and even contested, which often gave way to lively, even passionate discussion. That the relationships between students and teachers in these centers were conceived as nonhierarchical was further indicated by the fact that teachers and students spoke respectfully of each other as "sister" (and if applicable, "brother").

It was precisely the nature of the relationships established in these contexts of learning that was highly appreciated and that so sharply contrasted with the atmosphere that many students had experienced during childhood at the Qur'an school. The latter instruction was generally dispensed by an older imam, a *shaykh* or *hodja*, who often had arrived in France or Germany at a relatively advanced age (and generally, therefore, was unaware of or even hostile toward the local culture), and the emotional relationship between this instructor and his students, if any, was one of fear and timidity. This new learning atmosphere in an Islamic context, where teachers were "like them" (that is, raised and socialized in European society), was highly appreciated by the participants, and new arriving students at CERSI and BFMF welcomed this novelty particularly enthusiastically.

My interlocutors persistently stressed the importance of teachers being capable of relating to the specific problems of European Muslims and of adapting their teaching styles and content accordingly. They insisted that they wanted to feel welcome and comfortable in the Islamic centers and to develop warm relationships with fellow students and teachers. One could witness exactly such an ambience, for instance, in the hour preceding the "*Tafsir* and *Fiqh*" class at the BFmF, when participants would trickle into the cafeteria, affectionately greet their "sisters" with hugs and kisses, and begin chatting with one another (while enjoying the fresh cake for sale there), often with Salwa among them. Similarly, at the CERSI, during breaks between classes and especially at lunch break, when a buffet would be set up in the front hall, a similar ambiance reigned, allowing students and teachers to mill about, chatting and eating together. This atmosphere—personal and egalitarian—fostered relationsships between teachers and learners that established an emotional "community of learning." Additional events held in these centers—such as celebrations, *qiyam al-layl*, cultural programs, and organized vacations—further cemented these communities. Students often developed deep and long-lasting friendships with both teachers and fellow students—the women with female teachers, with whom they often spent time outside of the center.

This is not to say that learning with older generations of scholars, whose status did not allow for the same close and egalitarian relationships, was rejected. Given the deep respect that these pious young Muslims held for Islamic scholars, and their recognition of them as the bearers of religious authority and the ultimate source of authentic knowledge, they deeply appreciated occasions to listen to them. Nonetheless, their esteem for these scholars, referred to as *'ulama* or *shuyukh,* did not replace their desire to find themselves among peers with whom they could interact closely, nor did it dispense with their need for role models who were intimately familiar with the students' daily struggles as French or German Muslims. This need for homegrown role models also explained the admiration that the women generally expressed for European-born preachers, such as Tariq Ramadan or, in France particularly, Hassan Iquioussen, both of whom were capable of "speaking our own language." It is also for this reason that women in Germany often expressed regret about the lack of native-born German-speaking preachers.

To respond to these expectations, teaching methods were adapted. Teachers like Olfa and Salwa, who sought to transmit knowledge that was relevant for everyday life, made use of materials that were proximate to the specific context of Western Muslims, and thus employed an extremely wide range of resources and literary genres. Certainly, they used the Qur'an, the Sunna, the sira, classical literature (from the founders of the four schools of law to Ibn Taymiyya), and in spite of some reservations about Sufism that are observable among some revival circles, early and classical Sufi writings (especially by medieval scholar and mystic Abu Hamid al-Ghazali).[29] They also drew on literature and media products produced by contemporary Muslim preachers and scholars who were globally popular (such as Yusuf Qaradawi, Amr Khaled, Tariq Ramadan, Tareq Al-Suwaidan, and Hamza Yusuf). And they did not hesitate to refer to popular self-help literature and recent TV talk shows in order to derive—either positively or negatively—lessons from them.

Because these Islamic centers were tasked with establishing "communities of learning" in a diasporic context, where living as a (often visibly) pious Muslim provoked skeptical or even inimical reactions from the world outside of the orthodox Muslim community, they were not merely significant to shaping an Islamic habitus, but they were also crucial to providing a community *tout court*. For my interlocutors, the centers often became a second home, a space of comfort and belonging, which some of them had not found even in the households where they grew up. Thus these centers were pivotal for the formation of a European and diasporic type of revival Islam, and for forging networks and elaborating new modes of pious sociability.[30]

Disseminating Knowledge and *Da'wa*

The Islamic centers that are now thriving all over Europe provide young Muslims with unprecedented opportunities to instruct themselves in the religious domain. Young men and women who have gone through these institutional structures are now also able to participate in the field of Islamic knowledge dissemination. Indeed, throughout my fieldwork, I encountered numerous women who were engaged as teachers in Islamic institutes, as conference speakers, or as organizers of informal study circles. This work of knowledge dissemination is intrinsically linked to the larger field of *da'wa* activities, which are so central for Islamic revival movements worldwide. Arabic for "call" or "invitation," *da'wa* is a type of moral guidance that seeks to encourage Muslims to follow Islamic prescriptions.[31] Scholars who have traced the shifts in the discourses and practices of *da'wa* in modern times have stressed that the "democratization" of *da'wa*, favored a general tendency toward "the individualization of moral responsibility" (Mahmood 2005: 64).[32]

This more recent reconfiguration of *da'wa* was evident in the understanding of *da'wa* and its implementation in the Islamic circles I studied. All of the women, whether or not they were directly engaged in organized activities of religious knowledge transmission, expressed a clear sense of their personal duty to conduct *da'wa*.[33] Salwa, the "*Tafsir* and *Fiqh*" teacher in Cologne, for instance, explained her own teaching activities:

> From an Islamic point of view, it is '*khayrukum man ta'allama al-qur'an wa 'al-lamahu* which means "the best among you are those who learn the Qur'an and teach it." This is of course, for me, a theological motivation. Furthermore, it is a responsibility for which you will not only be rewarded but held accountable if you don't hand down this knowledge. In this respect, I see it as my duty.

Daʿwa was not, however, experienced merely as a moral obligation; rather, many women described it as a deeply felt personal desire. Naima repeatedly expressed this sentiment in our conversations, and I followed her in her various efforts to set up a study group of her own. One day, after not seeing her for a couple of months, she called and informed me enthusiastically that she had succeeded in gathering together a small, informal group of "sisters" to whom she taught *tajwid* (Qurʾanic recitation) on a weekly basis at a small mosque in a *banlieue* east of Paris. She invited me to join them and explained, "I really felt this need. I told myself I will be thirty soon, and I need to give what I have. I proposed that we work through the Qurʾan together, just basic things, once a week. And now I feel good; I really felt a lack in this sense."

Because of the diasporic context, this kind of *daʿwa* work acquired a deep urgency. The transmission of Islamic knowledge to Muslims of the next generation appeared to be the condition for the community's survival in the diaspora. This transmission was critical because the pressure to assimilate, particularly for women, was strongly felt and everyone was aware of the difficulty of resisting the "seductive" Western way of life. One of the most compelling themes I encountered during my discussions with women was the omnipresent fear of loss.[34] I listened to numerous stories about friends and family members who had abandoned all commitment to Islam in order to endorse a fully secular lifestyle (going along with practices that were considered sinful from an Islamic perspective). For the devout women, witnessing these developments was a painful experience. One of my interlocutors in Cologne, Sena, a young woman of Turkish background whom I met at the Islamic Student Union at the local university, related such fears to me. At the time I got to know her she was completing her teacher training and offering classes in Islamic instruction to adolescent girls at a Milli Görüş community center. She emphatically maintained, "They have to learn it [Islam], we have to meet in groups and do something. How else can they get to know Islam? Otherwise they will become Germanized [*verdeutscht*] and we will lose our community."

Beyond this fear of loss, however, was another significant dimension that was reflected in the discourses of *daʿwa*. *Daʿwa* was not simply about the ultimate salvation of the members of the Muslim community, but also very much about the well-being of the community (*umma*) as a whole. Proper knowledge of Islam was deemed a precondition for the welfare of the Islamic *umma*. Literally everyone identified "ignorance" of "genuine" or "authentic" Islam as the reason behind the crisis they perceived to be affecting Muslims on both a local and global scale. Issues as varied as terrorism, youth delinquency and drugs in the impoverished neighborhoods, and the weak status of women in Muslim-majority societies and in the migration context (as epitomized in the "forced marriages" and "honor killings" that were fodder to the media) were all invoked as symptomatic of the *umma*'s crisis.

This insistence that ignorance of authentic Islam was the cause of crisis for the *umma* recalls certain recurrent tropes in the dominant contemporary Islamic discourse.[35] Started by the Islamic reform movements that began at the end of the nineteenth century and continued through the beginning of the twentieth century, and disseminated by successive Islamic movements, *'ilm* and the corollary notion of *tarbiyya* (education) became key strategies for social and moral reconstruction—captured most powerfully in the terms *tajdid* (renewal) and *islah* (reform)—of both the individual and the Muslim community, the latter of which was perceived to be in a state of decline (Shakry 1998). The weak state of the *umma* was denounced by Reformists and Islamists alike and explained as resulting from the "ignorance" of the Muslim population. This condition was captured by the Qur'anic term *jahiliyya* (age of ignorance), which refers back to the pre-Islamic period. This term was frequently invoked in the environment where I did my fieldwork. According to this perspective, only the dissemination of a "pure" Islam, stripped of all traditional deviations, could reestablish the glorious state of past Muslim civilizations.[36] Thinkers from Ibn Taymiyya to Muhammad Ibn Abd al-Wahhab established a historical precedent by adamantly warning against the dangers that ignorance poses to Islam. But it is especially since the reform movements of the late nineteenth and early twentieth centuries that ignorance has been perceived as inseparable from the supposed "backwardness" of Muslim societies, and the cause of Western domination (Gasper 2001: 78–79). Only the dissemination of an "authentic" Islam—that is, an Islam freed from the sclerotic accretion of tradition—can permit the Muslim community to regain its former strength. The project to reform society is thus inherently connected to a project of authenticity.[37]

In this sense, I was told that the critique of "cultural" Islam and the knowledge of "true" Islam were the conditions *sine qua non* for improving the status of Muslim women. Overly patriarchal or misogynic interpretations and practices in Muslim communities that prevent women from developing themselves and taking their full place in society were regularly discredited. Frequent media accounts of violence against women in Muslim majority societies and in diasporic contexts were registered with horror and sadness, and with the response that it was only by obtaining *authentic* religious knowledge that Muslim women could become truly empowered. This topic appeared as a leitmotif throughout our conversations, as well as in the classes, conferences, and meetings I attended.[38] In this sense, *da'wa* work that addressed women was viewed specifically in terms of empowerment. In our conversation about her teaching, Salwa noted that "the objective of this acquisition of knowledge is . . . I have a completely new Muslim self-confidence, as a Muslim woman. Therefore I have hope that I can broaden the horizon of other women and girls through the classes I give. . . . It [Islamic knowledge] was my form of emancipation as a Muslim woman."

The dissemination of religious knowledge therefore was not only aimed at the individual believer's salvation but also became a means of improving the social condition of Muslim populations in the diaspora. Consequently, the women I interviewed did not conceive of Islamic knowledge merely in terms of the individual subject aspiring to piety. On the contrary, knowledge acquisition was absorbed into a broader social logic in which it was articulated with a sense of responsibility for the welfare of the Muslim *umma*. *Da'wa* was an individual duty that one owed to the community.

Ethical Know-How and the Islamic Way of Life

Even though the dimension of the broader collective was never neglected in the stories my interlocutors told me about their lives, their acquisition of religious knowledge was initially always linked to the idea of transforming their personal life according to Islamic norms. It was from this perspective that Olfa defined the core objective for her class "Islamic Morals" when I asked about her approach to teaching. She said, "Knowledge must be a useful science ['ilm nafi']; if it is not useful, than it's good for nothing. It is in this sense that I talk about morality, so that I can use it in everyday life." Conferences and religious classes were often geared toward providing knowledge that could be applied to day-to-day life. When classical manuals of Islamic science were reviewed in these classes, they served especially to foster understanding of the implications of these rules for daily conduct. The need for concrete guidance in everyday life was also fulfilled through the wide market of contemporary Islamic pedagogical literature. These booklets cover a range of topics, from the formation of an ethical and moral character to conduct toward parents and among married couples and the importance for women of adopting a particular dress code. The concern for correctly applying Islamic precepts in daily life was furthermore reflected in the popularity of muftis among European Muslims; these experts on Muslim law were consulted (whether in person, by telephone, or via the Internet) to issue fatwas on these various matters" (Caeiro 2010, 2011).[39]

In this conception of religious knowledge, the pious self-cultivation initiated with its acquisition was supposed to lead to the adoption of a new mode of *Lebensführung,* which means, to use the Weberian formulation, consistent and methodical life conduct—in this context, conduct defined by Islamic codes and virtues. This understanding was in keeping with the classical Islamic understanding of knowledge, according to which knowledge is the basis of action and must lead to action (Lapidus 1984: 39). Numerous classical treatises further establish a link between knowledge and *adab,* which Georges Anawati defines as a "code of etiquette that combines the obligations of a well educated man who is at the same time concerned to behave well in the presence of God" (Anawati 1976: 240). For Ebrahim Moosa (2005), *adab* transcends the mere domain of "etiquette"; he explains it as "that pedagogy that results in the cultivation of a virtue and motivates all human practices. It is both the education itself and the practical formation of norms for right and exemplary conduct; and, more, it is the internalization of norms in order to ingrain into the psyche a certain virtue (*fadila*)" (209). What both authors emphasize is that knowledge and *adab* are conceived as in a close relationship in which one materializes in the other: knowledge is acquired with the objective of leading a virtuous life (see also Lapidus 1984: 34). *Adab,* in this sense, is a "disposition towards knowledge" (Moosa 2005: 210).

Abu Hamid al-Ghazali, who was held in high esteem and frequently referred to in the circles I attended, has extensively elaborated on this link between knowledge and virtuous conduct.[40] *Ihya 'ulum ad-din,* his monumental oeuvre, aims to give the individual believer essential information for living a life distinguished by ethical rectitude in order to attain salvation (Moosa 2005). According to al-Ghazali, the soul, as the essence of every human being, is the divine spiritual substance, but it can be corrupted by the desires of the body.[41] This is why the believer has to try to purify his soul throughout his life (Lapidus 1984: 46–48). This purification implies the acquisition of knowledge. For al-Ghazali, knowledge is a means *and* an end. It has to generate qualities of the soul that translate into just actions, which in turn strengthen dispositions toward goodness. Familiarity with the principles of faith, with the deeds of the Prophet, and with the required, forbidden, and advised acts as well as with the faculty to prevent negative instincts, all stem from this knowledge. According to al-Ghazali, in whose work Aristotelian practical ethics resonates, 'ilm is much more applied than learned. Every action, he says, engraves a thought, an idea into the soul (Lapidus 1984). This "knowledge of the heart" is more than information to be learned, because it induces the desire to put it into practice.[42]

As al-Ghazali emphasizes, the knowledge of recommended, forbidden, and obligatory acts is indispensable to living a virtuous lifestyle according to Islamic norms. Indeed, it was this practical and concrete ethical know-how that was most crucial for all of my interlocutors who had recently embarked on their conscious turn to Islam. I discussed earlier the significance for these women of "understanding" Islam at the beginning of their religious journey, especially in relation to their minority status. Indeed, understanding precisely the meaning of religious practices and norms, which contained many (often highly gendered) restrictions, was even more urgent within a Western context governed by a logic of modern secular existence that celebrates freedom and autonomy and in which obedience to religious norms, and in particular to Islamic norms, is viewed as tantamount to sacrificing freedom. This understanding was thus an essential condition for interiorizing and practicing these virtues. When Naima recounted her early quest for knowledge that accompanied a growing interest in practicing Islam, she mentioned precisely this dimension:

> I wanted to understand these things—Why the headscarf? Why should I not talk with men?—concrete aspects of daily life—Why should I obey my parents when I didn't feel like obeying? I really needed to ask questions. [In the beginning] I always had the telephone number of the Paris mosque with me, to ask questions.

Here again we witness the significance of individual "understanding," of intimately comprehending the requirements, interdictions, and etiquette that characterize the Islamic mode of life as interpreted by the revival circles. It was crucial to appropriate these rules and restrictions in a conscientious and free manner rather than have them imposed by others (notably parents). Hanan, a witty young woman of Moroccan origin in her late twenties, was a teacher of French as a foreign language. She had consistently and vehemently emphasized a deep resistance to any religious conduct that was not preceded by independent learning and understanding:

> When I went to jam'a [mosque], it calmed me down. I was not particularly agitated, but there are plenty of things that I did not do but that I would have done if I had not gone to the mosque. It helps you to stay calm, to give you a sense

of calm. In the beginning, when your parents tell you, you can't go out because you're a girl, you say fine, but you're not the type of person who listens to their parents. So you don't abstain from doing things because your parents told you so, but because you yourself prohibit this. Perhaps it is good to do this and that, and so I will follow this.

Hanan's statement clearly indicates that certain notions of freedom affected how the enactment of an Islamic lifestyle was experienced. If religious norms were freely accepted, then it could be presumed that inwardness, conviction, and sincerity were present—a supposition evocative of what Keane (2007) refers to as the moral narrative of the modern subject. This narrative left clear traces on my interlocutors' conceptions. Although they did not aspire to be freed from religious conventions, they claimed that submission to these conventions must be mediated by a personal conviction grounded in knowledge. It was through this preliminary understanding that the act of submission to a transcendent will, to religious norms and the authority that administered them, could be experienced as consonant with the surrounding secular society's dominant standards of freedom and choice, even if many of the underlying assumptions were quite distinct.

Webb Keane (2007), drawing on Talal Asad (1993) and Charles Taylor (1989), reminds us that sincerity has played an important role in European discourses on the construction of modern selfhood, which is strictly tied to notions of freedom. Seen as the locus of individual interiority, sincerity became the "chief site of that which might elude political coercion" (Keane 2007: 214). According to Keane, sincerity in modern, especially Protestant, forms of religiosity became associated mostly with speech acts, with propositions of faith to which one sincerely subscribed. These speech acts, following Keane, are thus "compelled by nothing that might lie outside the speaker" (2007: 214).

Participants in Islamic circles, however, associated the demand for "sincerity" first and foremost with embodied practice, that is, with embodied disciplines and ritual activities, all of which nonetheless also involve speech acts. In their logic, sincerity not only constituted one of the conditions for rendering voluntary any submission to religious norms and compliance with specific practices, but also became pivotal for success in undertaking the process of self-transformation. Given that sincerity, with its underlying assumption of freedom, had become a moral norm in modern religious life, this and similar notions also became important discursive strategies for severing the connection between Islamic religious practices and oppression that had been established in many contemporary European debates on Islam.[43]

Another point in this particular understanding of applicable knowledge is the relation of such knowledge to ethical life conduct. In the sense that the knowledge acquired was concerned not only with questions about doctrine (ʻaqida) and worship (ʻibadat) but also with the domain of social relations (muʻamalat), Islamic knowledge was understood as impacting and transforming *all* aspects of the believer's daily life, however "profane" they might appear. In this logic, every righteous action might be turned into an act of worship, as Salwa tirelessly emphasized in her classes: "You can turn your whole life into worship; even preparing food or other housework can become worship with the right intention." Such an activist conception of piety—which revival Muslims claim is an Islamic "specificity" that must be maintained even in the diaspora (Ramadan 1995: 426–427)—refused to adhere to the ideal of secularized societies, where religion is supposed to be practiced in certain well-delimited spheres.[44]

Such an attitude demanded strict vigilance, requiring the continuous monitoring and governance of one's own conduct. Acts of daily life were examined in a self-critical and reflexive way in order to determine whether they conformed to Islamic ethics and norms or required rectification. In the courses and classes I attended, participants often discussed different techniques that helped to bring seemingly insignificant aspects of their life into compliance with the norms of Islamic piety. Many times I witnessed lessons shift from their original topic to a discussion of the difficulties that the young women (and men) faced in conforming themselves to Islamic norms and ethical requirements in their everyday life (especially in the context of contact with the non-Muslim Other). In informal meetings between friends too, these topics were often debated, and even women I considered to be advanced on their religious path openly admitted how they had failed (again) to uphold these standards. These types of discussions should alert us to the fact that self-cultivation, rather than pointing to a completed self-transformation, remains an eternal project and is never fully completed.

The Islamic centers thus became the central places for instigating a program of self-transformation and self-cultivation that would enable participants to develop a different kind of relationship to themselves. In this sense, the work of these institutes, and of the revival movement in general, provides a context for the enactment of a distinct disciplinary regime through which participants in these movements progressively come to govern themselves. The mode of self-governance that the revival movement promotes, while crucially building on Islamic traditions of ethical self-cultivation, can only be fully grasped when taking into account various discursive projects (including, among others, those invoking modern narratives of the self as well as those building on different historically contingent understandings of "authentic" Islam). Again, one should not presume that these "regimes" succeed in becoming all-encompassing in an individual's life, nor that they circumscribe stable or static formations.

In the following chapters I chronicle in detail the many difficulties that the women I interviewed faced in this process of self-transformation—their doubts, ambiguities, and tensions—which point not only to the impossibility of being fully governed by a regime, but also to the unlikeliness, in today's world, of being governed by merely *one* regime. Indeed, my interlocutors are exposed to several discursive projects, each with its own corresponding semiotic ideology, which delineate distinct ways of defining the relation of self to self and of governing the self. The diverse modes of being they promote and the various affects and desires they produce all interfere with, complicate, challenge, and at times reinvigorate my interlocutors' quest for pious self-cultivation.

3 "YOUR *NAFS* PULLS YOU DOWN, YOUR SPIRIT UP"

Struggling for Virtue

Know that the man who is dominated by sloth will consider unpleasant any spiritual struggle and discipline, or any purifying of the soul and refinement of the character. Because of his deficiency and remissness, and the foulness of his inward nature, his soul will not permit him to undertake such a thing; therefore he will claim that the traits of a man's character cannot conceivably be altered, and that human nature is immutable.

—Al-Ghazali 1997, p. 24

Worship God with pleasure. And if you cannot, then with perseverance, for perseverance in something which you dislike contains much good.

—Hadith

LAMIA WAS a twenty-something French-Algerian woman, with a calm and composed attitude that concealed a sensitive personality. She had just received the equivalent of a BA in English but had enrolled in another program and, by the time we met, was in her first year as an undergraduate student of Arabic and in her third year at the CERSI. When I interviewed her, she told me about her religious trajectory—her *cheminement spirituel* (spiritual path), as she called it—which she had embarked on during her teen years, following the premature death of her cousin. Like many others, she insisted on the importance of starting her religious journey by herself, detached from the many harsh voices rampant in the Muslim community. And what became apparent in her remarks was the critique of an approach to piety that was too demanding and rigid, and that did not recognize the multiple obstacles that arose in the journey of each individual:

I developed this relationship with Allah, and this relationship was such that I knew that what he asked us to do was in our interest. So I told myself, every day I have to do a little more. But it's true, this is not easy; there were a lot of moments with real challenges. But whenever you succeed, it's true, you feel the satisfaction.

However, I did not approach Islam from a perspective of licit, illicit. I really didn't like that in the Muslim community; I thought it was very aggressive. When you arrive and you are new, it is very aggressive. I remember in the beginning, when I started wearing the hijab, I wore it in the African style [attached at the back] and some sisters would not reply to my *salam* [*Salam alaykum,* Peace be upon you]. So I wanted to learn to know God by myself, because for me Islam is learning to know God; and in order to discover the beauty and the sweetness of Islam, you have to go really toward God. Often people turn toward the community and they will depart disappointed. When I listened to certain people, I said this is impossible: Allah is just, He is soft and forgiving; but there was no pedagogy. It was very categorical; the content is perhaps correct, but the form is not. So, in the beginning I didn't want to go to the community, I just wanted to get closer to God. But at the same time you want to search for knowledge [*la science*], so necessarily you end up going to the community. I was lucky when I found the conferences by Tariq Ramadan, and then CERSI.

But really, when you go to certain circles, the discourse there is so shocking: very quick to judge others. . . . But the first thing you should know is that you must be humble. Look first at your own mistakes, at our own struggles and challenges in our journey [*cheminement*].

Like Lamia, Gülden, the German-Turkish student introduced in the previous chapter, spoke in a straightforward manner and did not hesitate to stand by her own opinions, even if they did not necessarily please everyone else. One day, during one of our countless conversations at the BFmF, Gülden spoke frankly about the complications she continued to encounter in her religious practice, in spite of having been a practicing Muslim for many years. Although her struggles may have been far less troublesome than those of many of her peers, she still felt the desire to improve her deficiencies in this regard. Yet, in spite of her efforts, she refused an understanding of piety that did not account for such difficulties:

I am not among those who continuously listen to the Qur'an on their Walkman or at home; and also with other things, such as prayer and so on, I am not an overachiever. Unfortunately I am also very lazy. My everyday life is so busy that I am always glad to get my five prayers done. It's true, I really need to improve my prayer, to be more punctual, to wake up especially for *fajr* (morning prayer), and I would like to take more time to read the Qur'an and to continue learning more. But you know, and perhaps this sounds a bit heretical, I think that Allah also loves us with our mistakes, because it is through these mistakes that we get our feet back on the ground.

If I feel that because I pray my five prayers plus *nafila* [supererogatory] prayers, I fast every Monday and Thursday, and I do this and that and I am living a completely God-pleasing life, I don't need to worry anymore, then, for me, I am overestimating myself. In this sense, mistakes have their benefit too. They remind us that we are not perfect, they keep us down to earth. Allah is merciful, but this does not mean we should use that as a free ticket to always make the same mistakes. No, that's not it, but it gives you confidence and trust in Allah that he will forgive, insha'Allah [God willing]. And also, you know, your relationship with God is one thing, while the relationship with your fellow human beings is another. And in this regard we need to learn humility, and to actually practice that.

Both of these women had a quite disparate trajectory. Lamia, when I met her, practiced meticulously and was strongly invested in studying Islam. Her Arabic studies were closely connected to that objective. Gülden, by contrast, felt so overrun by her daily life, between her job at the BFmf and attendance at university, that she found it hard to adopt a mode of practice similar to the one enacted by Lamia. In spite of these differences, however, both criticized in very similar ways two attitudes that they saw as prevalent among certain Muslim practitioners. On the one hand, Lamia and Gülden objected to the self-righteousness of certain practitioners who claimed to embody piety and virtue and denounced others for their imperfections—an unforgiving stance that the two women felt betrayed the religion's merciful nature. For Lamia, this attitude went hand in hand with a clear lack of "pedagogy." On the other hand, both women defended a vision of the religious journey as advancing at a very slow pace, thus accounting for the long-term struggles and failures involved in the process.

These insights frame the twofold goal of this chapter. First, it examines the difficulties, impediments, and far-from-linear developments that my interlocutors encountered in their efforts to realize the virtuous self as it is defined by orthodox Islamic traditions. Second, this chapter exposes the pedagogy elaborated in the centers that these women attended—a pedagogy that precisely sought to distinguish itself from the more severe approaches criticized by women like Lamia and Gülden. And because they did not take pious self-reform for granted—and certainly not the enactment of practices understood to be key to that process—these women spent a great deal of time talking about it, inside and outside of the centers. Reasoning, reflecting, questioning, and justifying their own approach to certain practices and modes of conduct as well as listening to the advice from their teachers was as much a part of the process of learning Islamic conduct and practice as was the repetitive enactment of those practices. In my investigation of these accounts of self-cultivation, I focus specifically on ritual prayer (*salat*) and on female modesty, because I found them to be at the heart of my interlocutors' struggles. I analyze these issues as bodily *and* discursive practices because, as we saw in the previous chapter, speaking about Islam and Islamic practices is an important element of the process of self-cultivation. Indeed, discussing, explaining, and justifying a practice constitute an important part of the practice, as Webb Keane (2007: 257) has correctly noted: "speech about practice is itself a practice."

The Discipline of Prayer

The fundamental character of worship (*'ibada*), and in particular *salat*, was one of the most discussed topics in the classes and gatherings I attended. Unanimously considered an act of faith and piety, prayer was at times assessed as one of the conditions of membership in the Muslim community. It was in this sense that *ahadith* like "The prayer is the pillar of religion. Who abandons it, destroys religion" and "Faith grows and falls with prayer" were frequently mentioned and examined. Indeed, early in my fieldwork in the French revival circles, I took for granted the performance of prayer among the participants while also being impressed by the seeming ease with which the women I encountered enacted the five daily prayers. They always appeared to have the prayer times in mind, regularly checking their watches and promptly interrupting our conversations when prayer time was due. My first conversations with these women seemed to confirm the idea that prayer comes "naturally" with the process of becoming a practicing Muslim. As I mentioned in the previous chapter, in these early exchanges the women gave rather linear accounts of their own trajectories; once they had achieved the necessary conviction, prayer had been implemented in a swift manner, followed more or less quickly by the donning of the hijab. It was only after spending a considerable amount of time with these women, listening again and again to their self-critical examinations of the many difficulties they faced in the proper exercise of *salat*, that I reconsidered my impression that prayer came easily to them. This type of testimony came not only from women who had recently initiated their "return to Islam," but also from women, like Gülden, whom I had considered to be "senior" practitioners. By the time I started my fieldwork in Germany, I had already acquired an awareness that prayer was not just an act one decided to do, but instead necessitated a permanent effort.

This insight initiated a close investigation into the different prayer trajectories of my informants. Some had been familiarized with *salat* since childhood.

If the parents prayed regularly and wished to transmit this practice to their children, they often started teaching it to them in a playful fashion. They would direct them progressively toward more regular and punctual prayer. This was especially the case for women whose parents themselves had been affected by the Islamic revival. Many parents, however, prayed without actively initiating their children into this practice. In their case, as in the case of respondents with nonpracticing parents, they generally started to perform *salat* after their "conscious" turn to Islam. Their first occasion of praying in a deliberate and conscientious way was often remembered by my interlocutors as a pivotal moment and described as a spiritual experience that enabled an unprecedented feeling of closeness to God. But the zealous spirit of the first days was often of short duration. The routine of prayer turned out to be quite hard to acquire. Again and again I was confronted with testimonies that emphasized the difficulty encountered in regularly and punctually accomplishing the obligatory prayers in the midst of their daily lives.

Not only at school, university, or work but even at home, praying could be felt to be a burden and a "disturbing" interruption. This was particularly true of *fajr,* which took place, depending on the time of the year, between 3:30 and 6:30 in the morning and was often experienced as the most challenging. In spite of the hardship, *fajr* was constantly lauded as an outstanding prayer, because in the morning the spirit was still "fresh" and "free," untouched by the impressions of the day, which facilitated *fajr*'s meditative quality. And because of the difficulties it involved, *fajr* was also often invoked as an important element of *jihad al-nafs* (struggle against the lower self), because it required combating one's physical and mental weakness. If one was capable of such an effort, the punctual accomplishment of the subsequent prayers became easier. Indeed, women who claimed to perform *fajr* consistently on time were generally the most rigorous in the punctual accomplishment of *salat* throughout the day.

Punctuality was perceived as intrinsically linked to the duty of prayer, yet many practitioners went beyond the simple aspect of duty. According to them, punctuality in prayer stood in close relation to the correct attitude one had to adopt during the ritual. Missing the prayer times during the day and combining several prayers in the evening made it difficult if not impossible to concentrate. Lamia conveyed exactly that sentiment:

> When I started praying, . . . I didn't know where to pray during the day [on campus], so like everyone else I made up my prayers in the evening. But you realize that when you make up prayers, it's not the same thing. When you make

up five prayers, that's very heavy; above all you are tired, it's the end of the day. This has more of a negative impact than a positive one—oh gosh, I still have to do so many prayers—that's heavy.

Yet punctuality was also not a guarantee of a correct state of mind. One of the fears regularly expressed was that once a certain kind of routine was finally established, prayer could then easily become mechanical, "like gymnastics" or "like eating, without thinking."

Although everyone acknowledged the significance of praying in a state of concentration, they also admitted how difficult it was to achieve this state. I was told numerous times that the mind-set of prayer must be the object of continual effort; it was never fully acquired, but required, similar to faith itself, constant cultivation. Many classes in the centers and informal meetings between "sisters" were devoted to this topic and the participants spoke openly about their difficulties in reaching this state of concentration. Teachers tried to provide their students with a method to help them on this path. Olfa, who taught "Islamic Morality" at CERSI, for instance, was always inclined to stress the significance of the intention (*niyya*) to achieve this goal. As she usually put it, "It is not the result alone that counts; we will always try to follow this approach, because what counts in the end is your intention." In her *tafsir* class at the BFMF, Salwa pursued a similar logic, highlighting the transitory nature of the state of *khushu'* (humility and submission) and the difficulty of reproducing it every day:

You never pray with the same enthusiasm each day, and you have, of course, other things in mind. You continuously think of profane things during prayer, and this is normal. But you have at least to try to leave daily life behind you. This state, this is not something static that you accomplish just like that. You have to achieve it every time anew.

Students appreciated their teachers' more realistic and comforting approach. Hanan, whom I met while she was studying at CERSI, had taken classes in several mosque associations in the past. Compared to the pedagogy employed at CERSI, she found the teaching styles at the mosques out of touch with reality:

The teacher will tell you, prayer connects you directly with God; it is a vertical relation with God and you are in front of God. This is true, but you also have to say that this is a superior spiritual state toward which you strive; then you can give yourself more reasonable objectives. If you know that this is an ideal state, then you can see your path more clearly.

In an effort to make available certain techniques that could help practitioners improve their inner attitude during prayer, teachers would often draw again on the work of al-Ghazali. Identifying "humility" and "presence of the heart" as the conditions that make a prayer valid (al-Ghazali 2000: 334), al-Ghazali provided concrete advice, such as to pray in a calm room in order not to be disturbed.[1] Recent manuals available in Islamic bookshops throughout Europe and widely consumed in the revival circles I attended have adapted these considerations for the contemporary context. They recommend eliminating every source of distraction—for instance, switching off the TV and radio, disconnecting the telephone, and so on (Ismaïli 2003). Similar council was given in classes. All discussions and texts devoted to the state of mind to be adopted by the practitioner during prayer suggested that these inner states are not only not innate—therefore requiring intense labor (Mahmood 2005)—but could at no stage be understood as definitively achieved.

This extremely conscientious and self-critical approach to prayer was what distinguished these practitioners, in their own eyes, from the generation of their parents, whom they often criticized for taking the "traditional" approach and practicing Islamic rituals in a "mechanical" manner and without the necessary mind-set. One young woman's comment during a discussion in one of Salwa's *tafsir* classes was typical in this regard. She related in a slightly irritated way how she had to admonish her mother regularly for letting her eyes stray toward the illuminated television screen while praying in the living room. In this sense, prayer had become another site for contesting "traditional" Islam, with inwardness, consciousness, and genuineness serving as indications of the authenticity of one's approach.

These assumptions about what distinguishes an "authentic" from a "traditional" approach to worship bring us back to a conversation on sincerity initiated in the previous chapter. In his analysis of the contrasting views on ritual and ritual speech of Dutch Calvinist missionaries and the Sumbanese, Webb Keane shows that Calvinists criticized Sumbanese rituals for their supposedly overly fixed and formalized speech in contrast to the presumably sincere individual speaker performing a Protestant prayer. For the Calvinists, prayers that had their source in the inner individual space were sincere compared to a speech that displaced the agency to outside the speaker: "Protestant anxiety about the apparent insincerity of pagans seems to imply a linked concern with the apparent domination of the . . . individual by the rules of society" (Keane 2007: 185). This critique has been shared by Orientalists writing about Muslim societies who have criticized *salat* as being overly ritualistic, devoid of sincerity, a mechanical repetition of formulas, and generally evocative of "Islamic formalism" (Grunebaum [1951] 1976).[2]

The women I worked with seemed to sit at the intersection of two discourses with entirely different histories. Without questioning the sanctity of Islamic ritual prayer, they conditioned its validity on the standard of sincerity—a conscious and devoted inner state that gave sense to outward acts. In other words, the deliberate effort to reach the desired inner state was at the heart of what was defined as legitimate practice. Such an approach followed earlier Islamic traditions of religious instruction, as epitomized in the work of al-Ghazali. Yet the critique of "traditional" modes of religious practice as ritualistic and nonspiritual resonates with specific modern concerns related to sincerity. It is these concerns, it seems, rather than al-Ghazali's insistence on the conditions of prayer, that explain why so much anxiety was projected on the parents' generation as the embodied representatives of "traditional" Islam.

The Affective Economy of Salat

Once a month, the BFmF held its Sunday seminar, a whole-day event to which an outside speaker was invited to address a particular topic. For a minimal fee, female participants not only could attend the seminar, but also were offered lunch and, if needed, provided with child care in another part of the building. One windy, grey day in April, the speaker, a young woman of Turkish origin and a trained pedagogue, lectured in the center's seminar room on the religious education of Muslim youth in Germany. She started her talk with a particularly vivid critique of her parents' generation for their failure to transmit love for God to their children. This was one of the reasons why, according to her, many Muslim youngsters had abandoned the Muslim way of life. She scolded:

> Our parents have always told us, you must not do this, you must not do that. Don't do what the unbelievers do, otherwise you will be punished, especially girls. Islamic education is not about being so prohibitive and exclusive; it must be loving and spiritual in an all-encompassing way. But we failed to emphasize love for Allah. Islam is not only about *fiqh*; it is about spirituality. You have to find the middle ground. This is why we say, "Only in the remembrance of Allah do hearts find ease." Many imams also do not know how to transmit spirituality; they do not know how to talk to Muslim youth in Germany. We do not have preachers in Germany who transmit Islam in attractive ways, with spirituality.

This is also why Islam has a bad image and why young Muslims turn their back on religion. . . .

And look how the prayer is taught. Of course Muslim parents do have an obligation to teach Islamic duties, and yes, they need to insist on this; we do not agree with the Western principle that everything is totally voluntary. But prayer needs to be transmitted as something beautiful, so that the child can learn to love it. Prayer is a gift from Allah; it allows you the closest rapprochement possible to God. You have to do it with the feeling of love.

I listened over and over to similar critiques addressed to parents, "traditional" imams, and to "hard-line" scholars of various tendencies for not sufficiently insisting on feeling love for God. Many parents, as well as traditionalists and hardliners, were deemed to be inhabited by a different set of feelings toward God—most notably fear: the fear of a punishing God and the fear of hell. It was this category of emotions that had often been conveyed in their own education—particularly in regard to daughters, the critique went, in order to justify a whole set of prohibitions. The acknowledgment of love's pivotal role, then, had become another indication of an "authentic" approach to Islam, as opposed to a traditional (or radical) one. For my interlocutors, it was only the "authentic" Islam that could guarantee the sustainability of Islam in the diaspora, because it spoke more to young Muslims' need for spirituality.[3]

In one way or another, this topic was tackled in numerous conversations. Some women told me that they had initially rejected all references to the idea of a vengeful God, preferring to build their faith solely on love. Others explained that they had learned the significance of love as they had progressively acquired a deeper understanding of the religion, which had allowed them to cultivate this sentiment. Sena, the German-Turkish woman who was completing her teacher training in Cologne, stressed the latter:

I just recently learned to understand the feeling of love [for God]. Before, I was not really aware of it. . . . *Al-hamdulillah,* I am much more involved in it [Islamic studies] right now. You have to build on it. I am right now in the phase of building on it. I have read several times that this is very precious. . . . For example, God is ninety-nine times more clement than a mother toward her infant.

As this excerpt indicates, my interlocutors explained this love relationship between believers and God by referring to two of the key divine attributes: the merciful (*al-rahim*) and the compassionate (*al-rahman*). These attributes, they claimed, evidenced God's graciousness toward his creatures, an attitude to which justice could not be done with reference to fear alone. This dimension was considered so fundamental that entire course sessions and conferences were dedicated to it. And despite the earlier-mentioned mistrust of the "exaggerations" of Sufism, it was once again classical Sufi literature (the female mystic Rabi'a al-'Adawiyya was most frequently mentioned) that enjoyed widespread popularity because of its capacity to build up and sustain this "love relationship."[4] At the same time, this insistence on love did not completely displace fear of God. Fear continued to play an important role in the relationship that my interlocutors cultivated with God. Love and fear, so I was told, complemented each other.[5] Thus the valorization of love did not point to a mode of spiritualization that exonerated the believer from the assiduous accomplishment of religious duties or the meticulous respect for religious norms. It pointed to a spiritual relationship that produced specific acts (such as prayer) that necessitated continuous effort so that love could fortify and be proved to the object of love.

Love was clearly more explicitly problematized and highlighted than fear, precisely because participants considered it to have been marginalized by an exclusive emphasis on fear. At one of the Saturday morning "sister brunches," for instance, Olfa elaborated on the supremacy of love over fear as a motivation for pious acts. Referring once again to al-Ghazali, she explained that "believers motivated to act piously out of love for God will be promised a higher level in Paradise than believers who act piously out of fear of divine retribution or in expectation of rewards."[6] This assertion provoked a vivid discussion. Some women expressed wholehearted approval, claiming, as one put it, that she had always "preferred this idea to notions of fear and reward," which she deemed a bit "too calculative." Other women expressed their puzzlement. One, for instance, stated, "Now I am a bit confused. I have always been taught that doing *hasanat* [good deeds] will bring us *'ajr* [rewards]; even you, Olfa, regularly talk about that. Others here at the center do as well. How should I understand that now?" In her response, Olfa validated all of the various reasons for encouraging pious conduct, but clarified:

> They correspond to different stages and capacities of the believers. You know, Islam has always been a religion that takes into account the differences among human beings, their strengths and weaknesses, and the different stages on their paths. For many believers, especially at an early stage, it is the idea of fear of punishment and expectation of reward in the Hereafter that motivates them to abstain from forbidden acts and implement the required rules. They need that

incentive to act properly, to do their religious duties. This is also what more basic understandings of religion generally convey.

But for those whose *iman* [faith] and *taqwa* [God-consciousness] have been developed so intensively and intimately, who love *Allah subhanu wa ta'ala* so deeply, they do not need these additional incentives anymore, because this love fulfills their entire being and motivates them on its own account. So, while all the various motivations are legitimate, every believer should strive his whole life to attain this highest degree, which is also the most satisfying on an individual and spiritual level. But it is hard to reach this degree and only a few actually attain it.

One central aspect of this emphasis on love, to which Olfa alluded at the end, was the proposition of a certain kind of Islamic subject who experienced herself as unique and singular. Again and again I heard testimonies about the very intimate kind of relationship between the Divine and the individual believer that Olfa described, as did so many other women, with the Qur'anic reference, "We are closer to him than his jugular vein" (50:16). Over and over, people would emphasize the particular value of the individual in the God-ego relationship.

In his seminal work on the Protestant ethic, Max Weber describes focusing on God as a vector for individualization. By addressing oneself to God alone and by commanding obedience to God alone and not to human beings, Protestantism has transferred authority, which traditionally was in the hands of intermediaries (the clergy), to the individual. By abolishing all mediation between God and human beings, this specific form of Christianity counts on the capacity of each individual to organize and consciously control her own conduct. This, according to Weber, allows for the constitution of autonomous and responsible subjects. Weber saw in this faith tenet the historical foundation for the development of modern individualism (Weber [1930] 1996). If one follows Web Keane's claim that Protestantism has given rise to a new "world-historical configuration that exceeds particular doctrinal identifications," a configuration that is associated with the overarching narrative of modernity and a novel conception of personhood, then one can certainly argue that the discourses encountered during my fieldwork reflect the sedimentation of this "world-historical configuration" within contemporary understandings of Islamic practice.[7] In this case, these reconfigurations were made inhabitable by grounding them in a robust reading of the tradition, one that focuses on those elements which allow to give value to individual agency and to inwardness. It was for this reason, one might suggest, that classical Sufi scholarship proved so pivotal when formulating this particular God-ego relationship.

Now, to return to the question of ritual prayer and its relation to love: I was told that love was supposed to be actualized during prayer, but it was also love that enabled this relationship in the first instance. This approach seemed to respond to the demand for a certain kind of emotional experience, which could not be granted by an exclusive emphasis on punishment or recompense in the Hereafter. And if *salat* was performed out of love for God, it was not experienced as a constraining duty anymore but as the consequence of one's own desire, and therefore as in tune with one's own free will.

We saw in the previous chapter that this notion had acquired an important place in my interlocutors' self-understanding. Furthermore, it corresponded with another understanding of prayer, laid out by my interlocutors, as having immediate emotional, spiritual, and even physical benefits, and often framed as "doing yourself good." Frequently I heard women discussing the various benefits of *salat* (as well as of *wudu'*—the ablutions, or ritual purifications, that precede salat—and fasting) for personal well-being. When Salwa, for instance, evoked the therapeutic benefits (spiritual and medical) of *salat* in one of her classes, it gave rise to a fascinating discussion. Several women present who had apparently read similar arguments provided additional information that confirmed Salwa's point. One woman, for instance, pointed to the fact that the Islamic ritual prayer involved all of the most important yoga positions. Someone else referred to the specific psychological and physiological benefits of wetting hands, arms, feet, and especially the scalp with water during wudu'.

Another consequence of this new prayer pedagogy is that prayer can become a "pleasure" capable of "competing" with other ("profane") pleasures, as the title of an article by Ayşe Saktanber (2002) suggests so accurately: "We pray like you have fun." Whenever I spent time with some of my interlocutors during informal gatherings at their homes, I observed that ritual prayer constituted an integral part of their sociability. When prayer time came, they would interrupt their activities and conversations, do their ablutions, then perform their prayer collectively. The designation of someone to play the role of *imam* (prayer leader) and perform the *idhan* (the call to prayer) was frequently accompanied by jokes and lighthearted chatter. If, for instance, the designated woman was reluctant, efforts to convince her could include teasing appeals such as "Come on, you know how to do it" or "*Yallah* [Come on], don't be shy." After the prayer, conversation might include discussing the mistakes the designated prayer leader committed, such as misquoting the Qur'an during the recitation. Far from delineating a disruption, *salat* was an intrinsic part of the convivial atmosphere that was characteristic of these gatherings.

By pointing to the new economy of emotions and the novel languages through which the ritual duties are experienced and expressed, I do not mean to imply that revival circles have increasingly enacted a type of New Age religiosity, as certain authors have argued (see, for example, Roy 2004). Without a doubt, the emphasis on pleasure and "wellness" is one of the numerous ways in which Islamic religious experience has been rearticulated. Discourses on the modern self that have enabled the rearticulation of religious experience more broadly (and given rise to so-called New Age religions, among other things) definitely constitute one of the conditions of possibility for the reconfiguration of Islamic orthodoxy in Europe (and beyond), which points to new sensibilities and subjectivities that read the Islamic tradition in novel ways. This approach does not, however, imply an indulgent or individualist understanding of religious practice. Rather, a rigorous discipline is communicated, reasoned, and made possible through the help of a different language, a language that has fashioned the members of the revival circles, including creating specific desires in them. The individual aspiration for "well-being" and for "doing yourself good" is increasingly stimulated in late capitalist societies. Moreover, the emphasis on pleasure and "wellness" carries the potential to provide better discursive representation of Muslim practices to a broad public that has been informed by Orientalist images of a ritualist and formalist Islam characterized by a fearful God—notions still perpetuated in post-9/11 debates on (radical) Islam. Such ideas are not particularly disposed to granting a gratifying spirituality to Islam.

Salat: An End or a Means?

Although prayer was pivotal in cultivating certain inner dispositions that in turn facilitated its proper performance, this outcome was nonetheless never a goal in itself. As I was told persistently, prayer should enable the individual believer to adhere to ethical conduct in daily life. In Chapter 2, I discussed the link between knowledge and ethical action. *Salat* similarly appeared always to be intrinsically connected to ethical conduct. That is, the consolidation of faith through ritual prayer had to be translated into pious and ethical conduct. At the same time, prayer figured as one of the most important means to improve one's daily conduct. This fundamental link between prayer and ethical conduct was based on a Qur'anic principle, as Salwa pointed out during one of her *tafsir* classes:

> Only when you do it [the prayer] in a conscientious manner can you understand this Qur'anic verse: *inna a-salata tanha 'an al-fahsha'i wa l-munkar,* prayer moves [one] away from vice and what is reprehensible. *Fahsha'* is "vice" and *munkar,* "the reprehensible." If you take this really seriously, you know that prayer and doing something bad do not go together. In this sense, prayer is efficient.

Many women explained the power of the ritual prayer as coming from its organization, from its distribution throughout the day, which enabled it to work as a continuous reminder to survey one's own deeds. As one of the students at CERSI declared, "It [the prayer] is dispatched throughout the day in such a way to remind you every three hours. You are immersed in daily life and you face some trials, you encounter some temptations, and so on. So, it's always good to perform regular prayers to come back to God." It was hoped that prayer would eventually help to foster a state of mind that rendered ethical conduct more and more natural.

One day, when I was having lunch with Hanan in a fast-food restaurant in Aulnay-sous-Bois, a Parisian *banlieue* close to Hanan's home, she gave me an illustrative account of this process in her typically wry and humorous manner:

> In the beginning, you give yourself little limits; you say, I must not go beyond this particular limit because I pray. It would be a bit contradictory to do certain things and then say something else. Afterward, you integrate them into your state of mind. In the beginning, these limits—it's like cows who are locked in by these electric fences. . . . You set these barriers for yourself because you are scared of what you could be, you are scared of yourself; and afterward, these barriers that you have set, you don't even think of them anymore.

As Hanan's statement describes, praying several times a day in order to remember God should progressively create a mind-set in which the believer naturally does everything to please God. It is in this sense that prayer was often praised for its "protective function."[8] This logic is often taken by my respondents to contradict family and friends who claim—in response to my interlocutors' exhortation that they too begin practicing—that they are "not yet worthy" of praying. They reply that before they can begin to pray, they must first quit drinking alcohol, dating, and so on. In one of her lessons, Olfa, tackled this argument. She insisted that it was precisely the regular practice of prayer that helps to change negative habits, because prayer is the condition *sine qua non* for adopting an Islamic mode of life. According to this logic, a fashionably dressed young woman who did not wear the headscarf, with whom I got to chat at an Islamic conference, stated the following:

> It is through prayer that all the rest comes; well, for me, this is how I see it. Because before I began to pray I told myself, yes, I have to stop using makeup, I have to change my style of dress. And actually, if you try to eliminate all these little negative details before even starting to pray, you will never do it, because there are so many. And so, while praying, sometimes I feel like leaving some of them behind. You try to stick to it; sometimes you don't succeed and then you fall back, but well, that's how it goes.

This young woman clearly recognized that prayer had the capacity to strengthen the desire to conform to Islamic norms. However, she also acknowledged that this growing desire for a certain kind of conduct did not necessarily lead to its linear adoption. Old habits and former manners of self-presentation and body conduct could not be dropped so easily; changing them required a more sustained effort, this was never completely achieved. I heard again and again how important it was to remain vigilant in keeping watch over one's thoughts and actions, as well as to adopt a sincere, self-critical attitude, in order to interiorize ethical conduct. But because the *nafs* (lower self) was the "worst enemy of human beings," as Olfa persistently emphasized in her lessons, the individual was always tempted to succumb to his or her own weaknesses. This is why Olfa never tired of repeating that the *jihad al-nafs* "is always an obligation for the believer." The exigency of a life-long *jihad al-nafs* was corroborated by literally everyone with whom I spoke. Naima, for instance, who often talked about her inner struggles, told me the following in this regard:

> In the end, in your prayers, you know that you will meet *Allah subhanu wa ta'ala,* and this helps me tremendously to correct myself in daily life . . . in regard to my ego, because when someone attacks me [verbally], I feel like hitting back, and this is what is most difficult, to restrain yourself. . . . In my relationships with people, that's it; it's a work on the *nafs* that I do, and this is inseparable; it is linked [to the prayer].

All of these statements reveal an understanding of *salat* as an important technique for the broad effort of self-cultivation that is captured in the term *jihad al-nafs*. These women are clearly following classical traditions within Islam that define *'ibadat* (devotional practices) as integral to ethical character formation (Lapidus 1984). For al-Ghazali, prayer is one of the means given to humanity by God for struggling against vice and purifying the heart, which it will accomplish provided that it is performed with concentration and awareness (al-Ghazali 2001: 84).[9] This struggle against vice, as al-Ghazali recognizes, lasts a lifetime. It is this understanding that enabled my interlocutors to see their momentary failures to implement virtuous conduct not as due to the failure of prayer but rather as reflective of the inherent lifelong challenge that accompanies the project of pious self-cultivation.

Modest Dress

As I followed my veiled interlocutors on their diverse activities throughout the city, I often witnessed them looking at their mirror image in a shop window and adjusting their clothing, or hiding a strand of hair that had escaped from under their headscarf. If no "mirror" was available, they sometimes would ask me to make sure their clothes were in the right position and, if necessary, to adjust their clothing. From an outsider's perspective, wearing hijab appears to be a fully interiorized and uncomplicated practice. In fact, this is exactly what the women themselves suggested in our early conversations. Many of them initially tended to overemphasize the headscarf as taken for granted, as voluntary (a matter of "choice"), and as a simple practice.[10] Especially in France, these statements often had a defensive character that must be understood in the context of the passionate public debates over the headscarf that took place throughout my fieldwork.[11]

In her work on veiled women in Germany, German sociologist Sigrid Nökel (2002) has observed the same conscious caring that the women I interviewed enacted in regard to the headscarf. She explains in Foucaultian terms their will to conform themselves most rigorously to Islamic dress codes by identifying this practice as a technique of self-discipline, a "self-affirmation as a conscientious, self-disciplined individual, concerned about the perfect fulfillment of a self-imposed assignment" (2002: 95). She emphasizes the extent, similar to my own findings, to which this perfected exertion allowed these young women to distance themselves from the generation of their mothers—the generation that also often personifies, in their eyes, the uneducated, "traditional", nonreflexive, and pre-emancipated Muslim woman. As the first work on veiled Muslim women in Western Europe that analyzes the practice through a Foucaultian theoretical framework, Nökel's pioneering research enabled her to offer a more sensitive account of veiling than previous work had provided. Nonetheless, her observations, as well as my interlocutors' initial assertions, generally tell us only the (slightly simplified) *possible* end of the story, because quite often wearing hijab was the object of an intense and ongoing pedagogy. In that case, it was only through long-term, self-reflexive work and habituation that the headscarf could perhaps become "second nature," a habitus, so that women could make claims such as "it's a part of me" or "it became so very normal for me." But even this second nature was still not immune to potential disruption at certain junctures of these women's lives.

Before discussing the matter further, I first address how my interlocutors debate hijab in an extremely politicized context that constantly questions the legitimacy of that practice.

Debating Hijab

Generally speaking, within the circles I researched, women's obligation to wear the headscarf was beyond question. Everyone was clear on this point: there was sufficient textual proof in the fundamental Islamic sources—the Qur'an and the authenticated *hadith*—that women were, starting at puberty, obliged to cover their body and their hair. However, this has not always been the understanding of my interlocutors. Before embarking on their religious journey, most of these women were confronted with a variety of opinions about the hijab. Many had initially referred themselves to more liberal interpretations that claimed that the headscarf was not clearly a mandatory decree in the Qur'an. It was only after they had acquired Islamic knowledge in the revival circles that they learned the "correct" interpretation of the status and significance of the hijab. It was thus through the study of Islamic sciences in the Islamic centers that these women ultimately became aware that a fundamental source of Islamic jurisprudence is the authority vested in the consensus (*ijma'*) reached by Islamic jurists. They also learned who the recognized and respected Islamic scholars were, from whom to seek guidance. These scholars were then invoked to affirm that the obligation to wear the hijab was indeed an authentic Islamic requirement. Salwa (like Olfa) regularly pointed this out in her classes, espcially when newcomers who seemed to doubt this interpretation were present.

> So, it is a duty and there is no proof that it is not. It is one of the duties for which women will be held accountable. . . . It is very easy to figure out: people who say it is not a duty have nothing solid [as their argument]. There is a consensus among scholars about the headscarf. There are a lot of subjects where there is

no such consensus. But concerning the headscarf, there is a consensus, and no respectable scholar will say the headscarf is not necessary.

In spite of that consensus, the "pedagogies of persuasion" (Mahmood 2005) regarding the hijab that one could encounter in the revival circles varied. Some women referred to certain preachers who invoked a harsh divine punishment for those who neglected to meet that requirement. Others, however, took a more critical stance toward the virulence of these preachers. In our conversation that day at the fast-food place, Hanan, who did not wear a hijab, questioned precisely this kind of argument:

> For me, I am sure that it is obligatory. But there is a strange thing: they say the hijab is obligatory; if you don't wear it, a teacher told us, you don't even smell the perfume of paradise. I tell myself this is nevertheless a bit contradictory. On the one side, you say that if you do not wear hijab, you don't smell the taste of paradise, so all those who don't wear it will go to hell. On the other side, they say, in any case, if you do go to paradise, it is through God's mercy. So, afterward it is up to God to judge. For me, therefore, this is not an argument, if you don't put it on you will go to hell. Perhaps in the end I will have to take a trip there [*laughter*]; I would rather not, but I don't know.

Apart from trying to undramatize the consequences of her incapacity to cover her own head, Hanan's way of engaging the various discourses and arguments of the teachers and scholars she had heard was a quite typical approach among my interlocutors. Although she recognized the authority of those who had more knowledge than she did, she did not accept every statement without question. Because the discourse of the revival circles was not homogenous but often allowed for important variances, she was able to probe certain aspects that seemed to contradict other information she had learned. She was thus able to move within a larger space of reflection, weighing and comparing different elements of Islamic doctrine and their interpretation.

Whether veiled or not, everyone I talked to emphasized that the desire to wear the hijab increased after they began their religious journey. Yet for many women I encountered, the act of donning the headscarf was an immense difficulty. Their fear of the reactions of the majority society often caused them to postpone this act. I began my fieldwork in the immediate aftermath of 9/11 and it was during that time that stories of hostile reactions and aggressions toward headscarf-wearing women first emerged. In the years that followed, the political debates and legislations related to this practice rendered the step even more

outside opinion [handwritten marginal note]

difficult than before.[12] Some women hesitated for several years before adopting this religious requirement; others merely accepted their incapacity for the time being and projected this desire onto an unknown future. One unveiled woman admitted to me that her desire for the veil waxed and waned: "Well, there was a moment I really wanted to wear it, but I didn't feel capable of doing so. I still hope that I will wear it one day. It is one of my objectives. Right now I can't. I think it must be a lack of faith, but I still hope to wear it one day. When, I don't know; insha'Allah, soon."

I also gathered testimonies from covered women who revealed the conflict and remorse they suffered before they were finally able to make this decision. Such feelings were still present for many of my nonveiled interlocutors and, as they put it, what hindered them most was the lack of "courage" to face the majority society and to bear the practical social consequences. Although this reason for not wearing the hijab was the only one considered valid in the re-vival circles, acknowledgment of the "incapacity to veil" nevertheless points to a growing acceptance in this milieu of women not wearing the headscarf. This ac-ceptance was closely related to the pedagogy outlined earlier, which highlighted the intimate (love) relationship between the Divine and the individual believer. Following this logic, everyone insisted on the profound intimacy of this rela-tionship, which was why the decision to veil or not to veil took on a highly personalized dimension in spite of its public character. Although the move to don the hijab was encouraged and celebrated as "liberation" from fear of soci-ety's gaze, veiled women regularly urged understanding for those who had not (yet) succeeded in making that move. Gülden, for instance, when discussing the difficulties of wearing a headscarf in a secular, non-Muslim society, remarked:

> I think in Germany, and in general in a non-Muslim country, it is not always easy for people. You also have to look at other things regarding Islam. I am not say-ing [the headscarf] is not necessary, not that, but I understand people who don't behave as I do. . . . Even if in Islam the social aspect is very strong, you mustn't forget that religion is also a relationship between God and the human being.

Following this logic, my veiled interlocutors strongly contested any feelings of superiority felt by certain veiled women toward their nonveiled peers. Not-withstanding its normativity as defined by an orthodox reading of the Islamic tradition, the pedagogy sketched here emphasized the agency accorded to the individual believer to apply the tradition's rules and norms in a personalized manner. It also sought to integrate the notion of subjectivity and freedom into the revival circle's position on the "indisputable obligation of hijab." Even though in Islamic circles this obligation required reminders and encouragement, wearing the veil was conceived to be the result of choice and personal conviction. This is why some women vehemently criticized those who obliged their very young daughters to cover their heads. Salwa regularly talked about these issues in her classes and tackled them in her counseling work with Muslim parents. One afternoon, after finishing such a counseling session, she complained to me about Muslim parents who did not understand when the right time was to encourage their daughters to wear the veil. Highlighting the difference between these mostly "traditional" Muslims and "Islamically conscious" parents (like her own), she stated,

> If I could, I would have worn it at a very early age. When I was twelve or thirteen, I absolutely wanted to wear the headscarf. . . . For me, this represented being grown-up and being recognized as an adult, like a little girl who wants to wear her mother's high heels. My mum didn't allow me and I am still grateful to her today. When I see girls in primary school who pull this thing onto their head, I don't think this is reasonable. On the contrary, it is very destructive in terms of Islamic personality.

The conversations and statements about hijab that I recorded throughout my fieldwork point to a complex articulation of two seemingly contradictory principles: on the one hand, the uncontestable obligation to wear the headscarf, which seems to negate the autonomy of the individual's decision making; on the other hand, the affirmation of freedom contained in this act when it is a consequence of personal conviction. The notion of conviction—similar to the concept of sincerity—emerged as one of the key terms for expressing the experience of freedom within the practice of Islamic requirements, and with which the common association of Islamic practice with compulsion or lack of choice could be discursively refuted.[13]

Learning to Dress Modestly

For some women, dressing modestly seemed to be in continuity with their habits prior to their "conscious" turn to Islam. Especially for women whose parents had strongly emphasized the virtue of modesty in dress, a modest dress style was part of their early and more or less unconsciously shaped habitus, which they often expressed by asserting, "I'm modest by nature." For these women, the decision to don the veil did not seem to pose a problem to their self-image. If they hesitated, it was instead due to their fear of negative reactions from society at large. For other women, the adoption of a more covered style of dress represented a change, even a rupture with their past life. Not only had these women not previously given much thought to the Islamic legitimacy of their clothes, but they may even have viewed the prescription to wear the hijab with much contempt. Often this initial disdain was accompanied by a proclaimed passion for fashion and revealing clothes, which made the injunction to cover the entire body appear contrary to their personality. For these women, the adoption of a new dress code proved to be a difficult experience, and abandoning short or tight clothes and sophisticated makeup amounted to a genuine sacrifice. This change, however, was rarely effected straight away and became the object of an intense and long-lasting effort.

As my fieldwork progressed, I met more women who confessed the difficulties they encountered in enacting a modest dress code. Naima, again, was one of the most outspoken. Prior to wearing the headscarf, she claimed, she had dressed in the latest fashion. It had taken her a long time to give up that style, regardless of the fact that she had been practicing Islam for several years. Naima was very conscious of the struggle she had to wage; her "nature," as she put it, was opposed to this transformation. Significantly, she highlighted the necessity of *cultivating* her nature in a specific direction as prescribed by Islamic norms:

> The day before I took the headscarf, it was so difficult: one day you're wearing sunglasses, blond highlights, makeup, fashion, parties, and so on. It was really difficult, because from now on I would be unremarkable, whereas before I was so hip, had lots of cool friends. . . . And from one day to the next you are isolated, people look at you less, and your *nafs* suffers a blow. Each time I had doubts I told myself, OK, I have turned the page. If I wanted to live as I did before, I would drop everything, but what I found in return with *Allah ta'ala* is much better for me, and for that I am ready to make a lot of concessions. . . . It was very difficult. It was very difficult because my nature draws me in one direction and my principles draw me to something else. Yes, as they say, your *nafs* pulls you down and your spirit pulls you up toward Allah and you are torn between the two.

Accepting the hijab not only constituted a sacrifice of former habits, but at times it could also mean a complete reversal of one's personal convictions and certitudes concerning gender relations as defined by dominant liberal standards. I became aware of how intense this refashioning could be when I first met Hawwa. While spending an afternoon with Naima at the Mosquée de

Paris, we ran into her. Naima and Hawwa had known each other for several years and had watched each other grow on their Islamic path. Naima laughingly introduced Hawwa to me as a "difficult case" and encouraged her to tell me more about her journey into Islam. So Hawwa joined us and willingly related her struggles, many of which centered on the issue of hijab. Her *prise de conscience Islamique* (induction into an Islamic consciousness) had started with a temporary return during adolescence to her parents' hometown in Algeria, where she became acquainted with practicing Muslims who motivated her to pray. Concerning the hijab, however, she admitted to feeling a strong and long-lasting resistance and antipathy. Her account that day offered many interesting insights, which is why I reproduce a large portion of it here:

> Most of the young girls in Algeria wore hijab. I was one of the few who did not wear it. I said no, that's unjust. Why do we have to wear a headscarf? Why don't men too have to wear something on their head? I was a rather liberated girl, since I had lived in France until the age of fourteen. I had the ideas of a young girl from Europe; I didn't have the same mentality as these girls from the *bled.*[14] So, for me it was out of the question, and above all I was very coquettish. I loved to dress up. I hated this idea that the boys are the strong sex, the girls the weak sex; this is something I could never stand. So I thought that the girl who accepts the veil does so because she is weak. . . .
>
> When I returned to France after high school, I started to attend classes here at the mosque. My faith increased and I also began to fear God. And then I understood that Islam is not only about prohibitions. I understood that it was about living well, about happiness, and I was searching for happiness. I am very stubborn, I cannot stand proscriptions. But I then realized that, among these proscriptions, some were real, not just invented. The teacher explained to us why they were revealed, for what reason, and eventually I realized that if there are prohibitions, they are always in our best interest. Because Allah loves his servant, He loves us; God is generous and merciful, even if we have committed a sin. . . . So, I loved to be coquettish. I didn't want to cover my head until I understood. When you see how men flirt with you, how they look at you, even married men—I felt sullied by their gaze. So, I started to question myself. I am praying and at the same time I provoke men, because it's true, I loved to be coquettish, I loved makeup and taking care of myself. And it is true, men often turned around to look at me.
>
> So, the day I acquired that knowledge, thanks to the classes and the conferences—because I really learned my Islam here in France, not in Algeria, where

it is more a tradition—I understood that it was an order from God and that I should not disobey. And I felt that something was missing. I tried to practice. My faith had increased, I fasted during Ramadan, I prayed, and I know now why I practice. I do not need a person to survey me; the one who surveys me is God, whereas before I thought it was about people. Through this love, through this fear, I could not conceive of life without the headscarf anymore.

So, one day I prayed *fajr* and I was about to leave the house to go to work. I was not thinking anything in particular and I took a headscarf. No, I went to school that day and without thinking about it at all, I turned around and took this headscarf and I put it on my head. I went out like this and to this day I have not taken it off. It was an unconscious gesture. I did not understand why I put the scarf on my head. It was as if I had received a voice that morning. Someone came to me in a dream who said *Allahu akbar,* God is great, and I woke up that very moment. What is strange is that I walked out with my hair uncovered, I took just one step, and then I returned. I began to put on the headscarf just like that. It was an unconscious gesture, but there are no unconscious gestures, because God wanted me to do it. Sometimes you do not understand why you do certain things. But God wanted me to put it on that day.

Hawwa's account powerfully illustrates the many resistances that may be encountered by a practitioner before adopting hijab. It took her several years of attending Islamic classes, many inner battles and doubts, and much remorse before she was able to undo her beliefs and transcend her inclinations. It was only then that she became capable of desiring and then wearing the hijab, as well as of interiorizing the assumptions about gender relations that underlie the practice of hijab. But Hawwa's story adds another dimension that complicates the idea of the headscarf as a decision made through individual choice. Hawwa's description of her first moment of wearing the hijab—a description that was not at all unique among my interlocutors—demonstrates how ideas about conviction (and its specific affective economies), about sincerity and true understanding, about allowing for notions of choice, freedom, and agency—as opposed to the ideas of "traditional" Islam—stand in complex relationship with the recognition of God as the supreme agent. Though one might argue that Hawwa here denies herself some of her own agency and responsibility, we should not posit a too narrow understanding of agency in terms of consciousness and rationality. I treat this correlation more thoroughly in Chapter 6.

In spite of the centrality of the headscarf in modest Muslim female dress, it goes without saying that the conscious effort to adopt a modest appearance was also valid for those pious women who did not wear the headscarf. Most of the nonveiled women I encountered in the revival circles generally tried to adopt the same dress style as their covered coreligionists, which meant wearing (relatively) large, loose clothes with long sleeves. But what was crucial for both groups was that their efforts to conform to Islamic modesty requirements, as well as the resulting styles of dress, were not stable; nor did their development from less to more covering follow a linear path. Rather, the journey varied according to each personal biography and could evolve in either direction. Nonveiled women, for instance, related how in moments of more intense piety the desire to wear a headscarf deepened, which then led them (often only temporarily) to be more attentive to their style of dress and choose to wear ample clothing. Some veiled practitioners, on the other hand, at times found themselves confronted with their own declining concern for modest dress. Sevim, the language teacher and translator in Cologne whom I mentioned earlier, who has been wearing hijab for more than ten years, highlighted the potential instability of practicing modest dress:

> I have to say, in the beginning [of wearing the veil] I wore Islamic clothes according to traditional or conservative norms—only long skirts. At a certain point I became fed up and I started wearing trousers again. But the trousers got tighter and tighter, and if you also gain more and more weight, it is even worse [*laughter*]. . . . And sometimes the tunic also got a bit shorter. So you always have to check that you don't stray too far away from Islam. Allah gives you a limit and I have to be careful not to transgress that limit. Sometimes I feel that I have gone beyond this limit, and at the same time I realize that my *iman,* my faith, has decreased and that this edifying sensation is not there anymore. And then it makes no sense to wear a headscarf. The headscarf is really for yourself— also for your environment, but really for yourself. . . . I feel that the headscarf loses its sense if you don't do the other things: if you don't pray, if you don't read the Qur'an, then the headscarf doesn't make sense; it just becomes a rag.

Here Sevim expresses very clearly the extent to which dressing modestly required constant self-control. Even if this was not true to the same degree for all of my interlocutors, for Sevim and so many others, the practice of modesty continued to be an object of concern that never became simply "second nature." The other aspect of dressing modestly that Sevim brought up was the complex link she established between a bodily practice—her style of dress—and her interior attitude. Note that not only did the increase or decrease of her faith affect a particular corporal conduct—that is, her capacity to respect the dress norms she had imposed on herself—but also concrete bodily conduct—that is, an inappropriate dress style—influenced her inner state of mind, thereby causing a decrease in her faith (see also Mahmood 2005). I heard similar arguments from women in Paris who complained that their daily unveiling for work, which they were required to do, caused them "not to feel [their] faith anymore" (see Chapter 6). It was in relation to this impact that Sevim also emphasized—notwithstanding her acknowledgement of its social importance, most notably for regulating gender relations—the highly personal quality of the headscarf, as "only for yourself." Covering one's head was thus understood to indicate a particular relation of the self to itself, thereby fashioning a particular moral subject.[15]

At the same time, Sevim's statement also makes clear that the bodily practice of wearing hijab was not sufficient to render this outward conduct constitutive of a certain type of interiority. Only in conjunction with other techniques—various forms of worship—could this technique have a specific subject-fashioning effect. It was this combination that had the potential to transcend the mere materiality of the cloth, the "rag," and turn the wearing of this cloth into a self-discipline.

Modest Conduct

If dress was a central aspect of embodied modesty, it was generally insisted that dress alone was insufficient but had to be accompanied by modest conduct. Without such conduct, the hijab would lose all of its sense, as my interlocutors repeated time and again. This is what Salwa consistently emphasized in her *tafsir* class:

> The headscarf is only a detail; what counts is general behavior. If a woman wears a headscarf and is otherwise very coquettish—and unfortunately this exists—the headscarf is reduced to an absurdity. The headscarf is a detail, but you have to behave in a decent manner, adopt a certain morality in regard to the other sex. The headscarf is often viewed in an isolated fashion, and in this way one cannot apprehend its meaning. This is also what bothers me about the entire headscarf debate; the headscarf is merely regarded as a scarf on the head.[16]

In order to understand the relationship between the headscarf and modest conduct, it is helpful to look at how the women I encountered in the revival circles defined *modest* and decent conduct, or rather, at the attitudes they excluded from their understanding of that norm. What was particularly striking in this regard was their consistent and explicit refusal to associate modesty with any attitude of female submissiveness that they saw reflected in the "traditional" conduct of the preceding generation or of women in certain Muslim cultures. In the literature on Muslim women today, this modest conduct is often referred to with the Arabic term *haya'*, understood as "shame" or "shyness" (Weibel 2000, Mahmood 2005). Use of this term in this context implies a concept of the female body as framed by either honor or shame. This term was often discussed by my interlocutors, and they were all quite outspoken in their rejection of this interpretation. As they frequently insisted, modest and chaste conduct should not be linked to feelings of shame or shyness. On the contrary, by imposing a certain distance, a boundary they had defined for themselves in their social interactions with the other sex, they felt they were agents of this interaction. Lamia stressed this dimension very clearly: "My relation with men is like, it's in your own interest to respect me; otherwise, you'll be in trouble. So, as long as a person respects me as an individual, does not speak to me in a vulgar way, no misplaced comments, I have no problem." Indeed, the body language that I observed in these women when following them through their various activities at university, in the streets, or in different leisure settings, was geared to signal exactly that. They demonstrated self-confidence, assertiveness coupled with politeness, an attitude that was clearly more pronounced among veiled women.

Because this fine distinction—between chastity as conduct that defines and imposes limits and respect and chastity as conduct that indicates shyness and shame—was not always so evident, it was regularly discussed, often with reference to Qur'anic verses and *hadith*. Several interlocutors in France, for instance, invoked in this context a certain reading of the Qur'anic verse 24:31–32, "say to the believing women that they cast down their looks." They had all listened to a lecture by Tariq Ramadan regarding this issue, in which he allegedly interpreted this verse not as a general prohibition for women and men to look at each other, but as an injunction to avoid eye contact when confronted with a particularly (seductive) gaze.

One rainy Thursday afternoon in Salwa's *tafsir* class, a discussion of another Qur'anic passage proceeded in a similar direction. The day's session was devoted to the life and example of Prophet Moses (*Musa*) as revealed in the Qur'an and discussed in the *tafsir*. At one point during her lecture, Salwa mentioned the first encounter between Musa and his future wife. Her *haya'* was so strongly developed, Salwa related, that the young woman was hardly able to walk next to him; instead, she walked several meters behind him, with her head lowered.[17]

In her own commentary on this episode, however, Salwa did not uphold Musa's future wife as a model for Muslim women to emulate.[18] Rather, she insisted that "Islam does not demand such a degree of *haya*'," which according to her was due to the "Jewish context [of religion] in those days." To bolster her argument, Salwa referred to the example of Khadija, the Prophet Muhammad's first wife, who had requested herself that they be married. Salwa therefore concluded,

> Yes, you can talk normally to men, do activities together—as long as it respects
> certain limits. You can even propose to a man, if you want. And no, you do not
> need to walk several meters behind your husband, father, or son, as one can see
> here on the high streets when looking at certain Muslim families. This is totally
> not required. Islam wants proud and self-confident women.

Salwa's argument provoked laughter in the room and heads nodded in approval. Her comments gave rise to a vivid discussion in which the attendants shared and strongly critiqued their own experiences with certain expectations of modesty in terms of timidity.

All of these conversations reflected an effort to define the required Islamic chastity as neither imposed asymmetrically on women by demanding them to adopt a submissive attitude, nor as impeding "normal" social interaction between the sexes. These debates equally highlighted how common stereotypes—which generally read Islamic modesty codes as signs of gender inequality and female oppression—made it incumbent on Muslim women to position themselves loudly against this interpretation. Moreover, their reading of Islamic norms reflected to what extent these women who had been born and raised in Europe had been fashioned by the dominant discourses on gender relations and by many of their underlying ideals and modes of sociability. There was a clear effort to "ungender" certain notions of Islamic modesty and apply them in a more egalitarian fashion to men and women alike, thereby giving women more room to be the subject who determines the rules for how relations between the sexes should unfold. This effort was not uncontested. Numerous times, such as in the discussion following Nadia's lecture, I listened to bitter complaints about "traditional" Muslim men who insisted on placing the burden of modesty and chastity solely on women's shoulders.

These discussions all pointed to the broad field of what modesty—emphasized as something beyond the domain of female chastity—entailed in terms of restraint and reserve (see El-Guindi 1999). Jon W. Anderson (1982: 403, quoted in El-Guindi 1999: 92) rightly observes that "veiling refers actions to a paradigm of comportment in general rather than to chastity in particular."[19] This code of conduct, which has to be accompanied by a certain inner attitude, can best be captured by the term *adab,* which my interviewees frequently invoked. As mentioned in the previous chapter, *adab* aims to perfect the art of living in accordance with Islamic norms and requires a moral transformation of the person that is triggered by studying Islamic ethics (*akhlaq*).[20] Although *adab* was often articulated within a gendered logic, the ultimate model for Muslim men and women alike was the Prophet Muhammad. I often heard remarks like "the Prophet spoke with a soft voice" and "he never shouted," which again points to an effort to ungender, to the extent possible, the requirements for modesty so that the ideal of "restraint" becomes a paradigmatic virtue for men and women alike.

The Hijab Effect

Although everyone I spoke with insisted on the importance of modest conduct, it is nonetheless true that the veiled women were generally more consistent in their efforts to achieve this requirement in a scrupulous manner. This is not surprising given that they identified the headscarf as the principal catalyst for their induction into modest conduct. Therefore, even if they attributed more importance to modest conduct than to dress—meaning in particular the *hijab*—the latter was at the same time perceived as an indispensable instrument for fully realizing this conduct. Especially those who had not learned this type of conduct from their parents insisted on the difficulty of adopting such a demeanor. Sitting, walking, talking, or laughing in a modest fashion all became the object of conscious self-training. Often it was when the women were learning about the different Islamic norms and their related modes of conduct that their own lacunae in this regard were realized and they began to work on them. For hijab-wearing women, the headscarf played a significant role in this effort.

One of the arguments that the women put forward in favor of the headscarf's efficacy was that it functioned as a constant reminder. They described that they literally felt the cloth of the veil on their heads, and that they saw their headscarves in their reflections in shop windows when they walked down the street. *Seeing* and *feeling* themselves veiled caused them to experience themselves differently, which in turn affected the way they walked, talked, gesticulated, and so on. In particular, it made them more self-conscious and reflexive, as Naima expressed very clearly:

> Now I continuously remember because I have this thing on my head. Because it's true, *al-insan yansa,* as they say, . . . a human forgets. And the fact of know-

ing that I have this thing on my head—I assure you: before, I forgot, and now I continuously think about it. . . . Even physically, I see myself, I walk, I know that I'm a Muslim; this reminds me that . . . I have to maintain a certain comportment, and this helps.

Even though the women regularly insisted that the hijab should never be reduced to its materiality, Naima's comment clearly reveals that the hijab's material quality, with its inherent sensory effects, matters. It interestingly reminds us that subject formation through bodily practices often works in conjunction with material objects (in this case, clothes). This is precisely Jean-Pierre Warnier's (1999, 2001) argument. Warnier, a French anthropologist, draws on the *techniques du corps* of sociologist Marcel Mauss but criticizes him for overlooking that material objects are an inseparable part of most body techniques. Warnier's work investigates the "embodiment of the dynamic of material objects" in order to understand the body as a "dynamic synthesis of sensori-motricity in a given materiality" (2001: 7).[21] He furthermore emphasizes the necessity of articulating material culture in its relation to techniques of the self and processes of subjectivation: "We know that incorporated material culture reaches deep into the psyche of the subject because it reaches it not through abstract knowledge, but through sensori-motor experience. . . . It is through motricity and the experience of the senses that . . . subjectivity can be altered" (2001: 10).[22] As a bodily practice that incorporates the dynamics of a particular material object, the hijab reveals the extent to which material culture affects the subject "because it is immediately geared to emotions and psychic drives" (2001: 16).[23]

The phenomenological experience of hijab, then, helped these women to feel and to conduct themselves in a particular way. Experiencing hijab physically had a forceful impact on their inner dispositions and it was in this way that my interlocutors emphasized the hijab's "protective" function. But Naima's comment also pointed to the fact that this interiority was not easily "realized" once and for all; rather, it needed continuous outward stimulation. And as Sevim highlighted earlier, the hijab was only one element among a variety of other practices of cultivation. Moreover, there was no guarantee that the cultivated dispositions would remain permanently sedimented or naturalized within the subject.

A second aspect of wearing the veil that accounts for its strong impact on my respondent's experiences is the way in which the hijab tangibly and recognizably designates a female body as one of a practicing Muslim. It sends an unmistakable signal to the outside world and ideally prevents one's social contacts—especially male acquaintances—from enacting behavior deemed inappropriate by Islamic norms.[24] The women I talked to who had lived in an "in-between" situation before donning the veil felt they had not then been identifiable as practicing Muslim women in their social environment—an experience that nonveiled practitioners often cited to explain their desire for the headscarf. They felt that the "in-between" situation did not necessarily facilitate abandoning the secular lifestyle that they were used to. The hijab indicated a visible rupture with that previous life, and clearly assisted the woman wearing it in acting accordingly.

Let us return again to Naima. In the years following her initial "turn to Islam," she had begun praying regularly, fasting, learning the Qur'an, taking classes in the Islamic centers, and so on. But she had not succeeded in curtailing other mundane activities such as dancing, listening to music, and interacting spontaneously with the opposite sex. It was only after she donned the headscarf that she felt capable of doing so, as she told me one sunny Saturday morning as we set together in the courtyard of the Mosquée de Paris:

> It's true that wearing the hijab had brought me that aspect [modest conduct], which I certainly didn't have the way I do now. Before, as I said, I went out a lot, I was really attracted to music, dancing, etc. And everyone in my surroundings knew about it. But after I took the hijab, there are things I cannot do anymore. I set limits for myself in regard to others, in particular in regard to men. . . . My close relationships with my male friends progressively ended. They understood this on their own. Before, they came to greet me spontaneously with a kiss on the cheek. They understood now that I'm a Muslim, I have a different relationship [to men] now. Things like this gradually stopped.

Naima acknowledged that the headscarf promoted a certain type of conduct that had a direct impact on relations between the sexes. It facilitated this change particularly by signaling a barrier, a visible reminder of the principles to which the wearer of the headscarf adhered. As a clearly recognizable body language, it made verbal communication about the details of Islamic norms and etiquette less imperative, including with those who did not necessarily know all those details.

A third reason that was regularly provided to explain the headscarf as an efficient "technique of the self" was the "representative" role it embodied. Everyone was highly aware that a veiled women represents the entire Muslim community—and in this case, a diasporic community living in a context of marginality and stigmatization. Consequently, wearing a headscarf could become an opportunity either to positively represent the community or to further stigmatize it. Naima continued in this regard:

> It [the headscarf] helped me a lot in regard to *da'wa.*[25] Once I took the headscarf, I told myself that I represent Islam in front of other people. There are things I don't do anymore in the street; I used to cross the street running, eating, talking with friends, you know, shouting or laughing out loud, whereas after I started wearing the hijab—it's true, sometimes I still do it, I won't deny it. Recently I was walking in the street with my friend, we were laughing out loud, and afterward I thought, wait: we're wearing headscarves. So the headscarf helped me to change my everyday conduct. There were things I should not do anymore. . . . Before I didn't calculate; I did things naturally, whereas now I try to think about what I'm doing. I know that I represent an image, the image of Islam, and I am carrying this. On the day of the final judgment, I will be held responsible for this.

Naima's statement clearly indicates something frequently stressed by the pious practitioners. She has defined the duty of veiled women to represent Islam well, not only in terms of their social responsibility to their community, but also in terms of their moral commitment to God within an eschatological perspective. This duty renders the believer's obligation to excellence even more morally binding, requiring methodological life conduct, and to be realized only through continuous work on the self—but which, again, does not always guarantee success.[26]

Naima's two comments assemble all of the arguments highlighted by my interlocutors to explain the "hijab effect." They underscore the veil's power to shape emotional dispositions and to introduce a visible barrier and rupture between a former secular lifestyle and a later religious one, and they point to its representational impact, which generates specific moral obligations. Together these comments point out not only that the headscarf should be understood as both a signifying *and* an embodied practice (see Chapter 6), but also that a more thorough investigation into the complex articulation of these dual aspects is required. This assessment raises the question of how the disciplinary aspect of the headscarf as a technique of self-cultivation depends on and sustains itself through the particular meanings the headscarf conveys. Thus, the effect that the practice of wearing the hijab has on the habituation of the body, on shaping the interior self, cannot be easily disconnected from the various, at times, contextual meanings it signifies and represents.

Finally, in spite of Naima's insistence on the hijab's powerful efficacy, in her last comment she also alluded to the possibility of setbacks and failures in the effort to become a self-restrained, reserved female Muslim subject. Later on, in our conversation in the mosque's courtyard, Naima comically recounted, while animating her stories with vivid gestures, several other instances in which she had failed to embody that restraint and provoked some embarrassing situations. As we were enjoying some good laughs, a young man approached us timidly. He spoke in Arabic and introduced himself as an Algerian man looking for a Muslim woman to marry. The way he framed his question, by explicitly addressing it to Naima, suggested that he was interested in her. Naima did nothing to betray that she understood his intentions and kindly advised him to get in touch with the mosque's *imam*. When he left, she looked at me remorsefully and said, "You see, it just happened again. I should not have carried on like that. I was too noisy and made myself conspicuous. This still happens to me quite often." After a moment of reflection, she added mischievously, "Although in this case the guy is probably desperate to get papers [for residence in France] and asks after everyone." She nonetheless took this incident as an occasion to confess another of her shortcomings.

> You know, it's hard [*laughter*]. Until now there was always a desire for seduction within me; I see that clearly. I charm men without noticing; afterward I notice they write me a love letter or something like that. I often receive marriage requests or encounter men who want to date me. . . . I need to stop talking like that; I am too nice to them, I smile too much. . . . I try to fight it because I see the consequences, up to today. I have to work on this.

Naima's critical self-assessment of her own vanity (which simultaneously revealed that vanity) indicated that, for some women, the hijab's powerful effect cannot substitute for ongoing work on the self, and that the sedimentation of virtues such as modesty and reserve often remains a perpetual work in progress.

Modest Pedagogies

In the preceding discussion, the significance of the headscarf as a necessary tool for learning to conform to Islamic etiquette becomes more broadly clear. Subjectivities that had previously been fashioned to a large extent in secular contexts, with their particular ideals of liberty, sociability, and spontaneity, were consciously remade—reformed through disciplinary practices such as wearing the headscarf. However, the veil was not the only means to achieving modest conduct; nor did it guarantee its full realization. Like Naima, many other women provided me with anecdotes that illustrated the ups and downs involved in this learning process, and the important role of more advanced members of the community in correcting those forms of conduct considered improper according to orthodox standards of Islamic morality.

That the headscarf significantly facilitated the enactment of modest conduct but was not the exclusive condition for *striving* toward that demeanor became apparent when I listened to my nonveiled interlocutors, all of whom equally struggled to make progress in that regard. Nonetheless, these women often admitted how much more difficult it was to achieve success when they lacked a visible token of their intimate convictions and standards of modesty that could be recognized by those around them. This topic was frequently discussed in women's classes and informal meetings. I found these discussions particularly interesting because they provided lucid examples of the distinctive pedagogy enacted there, which the following exchange that took place in Salwa's *tafsir* course epitomizes.

The day's session had deviated from the initial theme as Salwa's lecture was waylaid, as so often, by a vivid question-and-answer session. The questions were centering on the difficulties of adhering to a modest comportment in everyday life when a young nonveiled woman raised her hand and asked how to deal with the greetings commonly exchanged between young people—involving hugs and kisses—when the opposite sex was involved. The woman acknowledged that such greetings between men and women were not appropriate from an Islamic point of view. She herself tried to forestall this type of physical contact by stretching out a firm hand—although she was a bit embarrassed to admit that this strategy did not always work. However, she also asked whether it was indeed necessary to shut down this mode of greeting, because it was widespread and hence a rather innocent and friendly social interaction without any ulterior motives.

In her answer, Salwa admitted first the importance of a sincere attitude; as she put it, "what counts for God is the heart." At the same time, she asserted that "purity" of intention was not enough: "The problem is the other side: How are you being understood? What are the feelings provoked on the other side?" But what Salwa deemed most important was the fact that this young woman had already started to engage in this reflection, motivated by the desire to comport herself modestly. Salwa continued: "This might seem insignificant to you, but this is a very crucial strategy. You tell yourself, I want to change this, I have to be careful . . . that no one will kiss me." While refusing to provide the young woman with a clear-cut solution, Salwa concluded that in time, by deepening her commitment to her religion and strengthening her faith, her desire to obey God would eventually grow. Solutions would emerge automatically from this desire.

After class, I discussed this episode with Salwa, expressing my appreciation of her leniency in her pedagogical approach, to which she answered:

> In our conversations I don't give so much concrete advice on how people should behave. Often these talks only aim at providing space for reflection so that the person might find her own opinion. . . . People find their own path as soon as they are ready. I believe that if you say this is *haram* [forbidden], you must not do this and that, you don't achieve anything. And then, this is not the beautiful relationship one has with God, and it won't be stable. It requires a process of maturation; once you feel such a love, your environment does not matter; you want to do things on your own. This is much more efficient than saying, *haram*, you'll be punished. I think this is a bad method, and it doesn't really take into account the relationship between a human being and God as intended by Islam.

Salwa's recommendations reflect a pedagogy built on the notion of self-initiated reform, in which the cultivation of certain emotions, particularly love, would render the believer *desirous* (and eventually capable) of enacting, consciously and voluntarily, the Islamic norms and rules. By articulating an approach that insisted on the personal relationship between the Divine and the believer as the central motor for pious conduct, Salwa was once again linking the desired self-transformation to a certain ideal of freedom and individual agency, and clearly distancing it from any expectation of *blindly* accepting socio-religious obligations.

Self-Cultivation Practices and the Virtuous Self

The different sections of this chapter offer a persistent reminder of the long-term character of the self-cultivation project enacted by my interlocutors. It was a project that did not unfold in a linear, one-dimensional manner, and it was rarely, if ever, completed. The women's awareness of this project's potential fragility, which required constant vigilance, remained strong, even though they did not deny the important transformation they had already undergone. Thus, at no point should the work and obstacles involved in refashioning the self and its habitus be taken for granted. In order to better grasp the kind of ethical self-discipline I am concerned with here, I return to Aristotle's ideas on virtuous practice. He developed an interesting model of the various states of mind involved in that practice, which can be productively interrogated for our case. In Book 7 of his *Nicomachian Ethics,* where he elaborates on different (mental and behavioral) states that lie between virtue and vice, Aristotle devotes much space to two types of individuals who struggle against the unruly desires within themselves. Whereas the *akrates* (weak-willed person) generally succumbs to his desires, the *enkrates* (strong-willed person) wins this struggle through the force of rational will. And though these two figures furnish a more nuanced analysis of the complexity of human action than had been provided by the philosophy of his age, one might be astonished, observes philosopher Carole Gould (1994), by the fact that he considers the two features as *hexeis* (dispositions) rather than as stages within a more complex developmental scheme.

This approach seems even more surprising in regard to the *enkrates.* If one follows through with Aristotle's praxeological account of virtue ethics as a matter of habituation and praxis, as does Gould, then one would imagine that a continual practice of *enkrateia* would eventually lead to the sedimentation of this potential, thereby not only enabling the individual to act well, but also instilling the *desire* to act well—because this is the crucial difference that Aristotle sees between the virtuous (*sophron*) and the *enkrates.* The former's desires are in harmony with his acts whereas the desires of the latter are in disharmony with his acts. Even if the *enkrates* is not capable of desiring to act well, he is at least capable of controlling his desires or passions so that the final result is, as for the *sophron* but unlike with the *akrates,* virtuous action. At no point, however, does Aristotle devote explicit consideration to the possibility of the *enkrates* becoming the *sophron,* and this is so because he considers both as *hexeis* formed at the stage of life when habituation and practice work best: at a youthful age.

Aristotle's account of ethical formation thus clearly differs from the traditional Islamic understanding of that process and from the ethnographic account offered here. Thus, neither his postulation of these clearly distinct states (*hexeis*) nor the idea of the paradigmatic *sophron* corresponds to my interlocutors' approach; to the contrary, according to their vision and their ontology of the subject, no one could ever pretend to reach such a state, for the simple reason that every human being harbors a *nafs* that is constantly prone to temptation by the negative powers of evil (*shaytan*). As I have shown throughout this chapter, the *jihad al-nafs,* which was so frequently invoked, did not constitute a stage that could eventually be transcended, but was an intrinsic part of the ethical work on the self and of the women's pious trajectory more generally. As Olfa indicated during a class in which she likened the succession of the various prophets to the gradual method of Islamic teachings, "The *jihad al-nafs* has to be done in a gradual way; one should never try to force change on the self in a hasty way. It is impossible and destructive to change habit all at once, because habit is our second nature. This is why we always start by emphasizing the effort rather than the result."

To be sure, progress could and should be made, according to their view, but it would be serious vainglory to assume that a state could be achieved in which vigilance and self-discipline become irrelevant and the inner desires were completely conformed to one's ethos. Because of this awareness and in accordance with their experiences of personal weakness, my interlocutors constantly expressed an astonishing wariness toward their own failures. Thus, the *enkrates* and the *akrates* should be considered stages, not in a linear developmental scheme but on a bumpy trajectory that is constantly haunted by the possibility of reverse. Conceptualized in this way, these concepts can help us to grasp analytically all the ordinary (micro) struggles that my interlocutors waged on a daily basis in order to become the pious self they aspired to be. They help us to account for their struggles against conflicting desires, for the rules and limits they imposed on themselves without wholeheartedly desiring them, and for the many times they acknowledged having succumbed to their (negative) passions, whether due to laziness, vanity, the lack of chaste restraint, or something else. It was also for this reason that all my interlocutors insisted on the importance of constant engagement with the Islamic sciences, in supplementary worship, and above all, in seeking out an Islamic environment and nurturing close relationships with other pious Muslims.

In this sense, the virtuous self is not a state but an ideal, and virtue is a practice that strives toward, rather than achieves, this ideal. In the eyes of my interlocutors, the term *sophron,* then, would probably be pertinent only for describing the Prophet Muhammad, considered the ultimate model of virtue to be emulated. Thus, ethical work must be understood within a theoretical framework that thinks of subject formation as an inherently unstable process, fragile, and constantly prone to turbulence—in this case caused by competing ethical paradigms or by disparate and conflicting desires and assumptions. Consequently, in this scheme, and contra Aristotle, the *enkrates* is virtuous, as Foucault (1985: 26) so clearly acknowledged when defining ethical work as concern for the "contradictory movements of the soul."

4 "MY LABEL IS NOT FEMINIST, IT IS SIMPLY MUSLIM"

Beyond Emancipation versus Submission

A GLIMPSE at the countless heated and polemical debates all over Europe targeting Muslim communities reveals that issues pertaining to Islam, gender, and sexuality are at the core of Europe's anxieties. These debates as well as the ensuing governmental practices "ethnicize" sexism (Ramm 2010), triumphantly claiming that sexism has been resolved in the West and remains exclusively a problem of migrant (Muslim) communities, thus making governmental interference necessary *only* within these communities.[1] The religious Muslim woman, in particular, figures persistently as the oppressed or alienated Other who, willingly or unwillingly, has given up on the possibility for emancipation offered by her liberal "host" society. In this context, social scientists have taken it upon themselves to deconstruct the dominant negative image circulating in these public debates. For more than a decade now, a growing body of work has demonstrated that the participation of many young, European-born Muslim women in the Islamic revival movement, far from being detrimental, can in fact foster emancipatory tendencies in these women, empowering them in relation to their at times restrictive family and community environments.[2]

One crucial factor that the academic literature often mentions in this regard is the positive outcomes of pious women's intensive efforts to acquire religious knowledge. These pious knowledgeable women are portrayed as thereby enabled to criticize the not-authentic Islamic customs, cultures, and traditions that they deem responsible for the inferior status of women in many Muslim communities worldwide. In conformity with the findings of other

outside gender judgment [handwritten annotation]

studies in the field, acquired knowledge empowered my interlocutors to defy what they called the cultural traditions and false interpretations that circulated at times in their family milieu. By invoking the Qur'an, authentic *hadith,* and the Sunna, they demanded rights from their kin and from the larger community, such as the right to choose their husband, to work, and so on. They also contested the marginalization of women in mosques and many Islamic associations. I heard numerous anecdotes about their struggle to claim space in mosques and prayer rooms that did not include a (decent) area for women, or to have their voices heard within male-dominated associations.[3] Historical examples of outstanding Muslim female figures distinguished by strength of character and independence were regularly invoked in order to construct the image of an authentic, active Muslim woman. Drawing on these types of observations, the above mentioned body of literature was relatively optimistic in judging the dynamics initiated by the revival movement as potentially liberating and emancipatory for women. Its authors claimed that the women participating in these circles should be understood as active and critical agents rather than as the oppressed victims described in public debates.

However, these authors' overall positive evaluations were occasionally complicated by statements coming from the subjects of their research, who persisted in acknowledging and validating a gendered division of labor, and in endorsing a differentiated attribution of rights and duties. From the perspective of several of these authors, these positions contradict their interlocutors' otherwise more "feminist" discourses. For example, Nadine Weibel, author of a book on veiled women in France, writes, "The totality of these traditional rather than innovative positions appear surprising from the mouth of these young, active women, who are in rupture with the patriarchal society model, which they reject" (Weibel 2000: 95). A similar remark is made by Sigrid Nökel, who explains the (surprising) "lack of critical debate" on gender issues in Islamic jurisprudence among women participating in the Islamic Revival by pointing to the "momentary priority" that women give to the defense of Islam in a hostile environment (Nökel 2002: 248). The puzzlement or unease among these authors that is provoked by some of their interlocutors' "traditionalist" statements reveals a certain taken-for-granted belief that once these women are proved to be critical agents in challenging patriarchal structures, they will contest all underlying patriarchal assumptions equally—a contestation that has not yet taken place. The emphasis on "not yet" (Chakrabarty 2000) suggests that these women, born and raised in the West (and hopefully guided by this Western

[handwritten margin note: marginalization in religion]

influence), will eventually outgrow their traditionalist positions and endorse values more in synch with the egalitarian ideas of modern, liberal culture.[4]

By raising this issue, I do not intend to diminish the important contributions made by these authors who, by unmasking the simplistic accounts promoted in public debates, offered new insights into the multifaceted life-worlds of these women. I also do not underestimate the political significance of an approach that highlights the potential for emancipation within Muslim religious circles in a discursive context in which this question has become a decisive factor for policymaking. However, it does seem to me that by investigating pious women's practices and discourses merely in regard to their emancipatory promise, one risks overlooking other important moments of practice, reasoning, and desire that are not necessarily fully captured by such language. Saba Mahmood (2005) makes a similar argument when she questions claims that posit autonomy and resistance to subordination as universal desires. She urges that attention instead be given to other possible motivations and desires, such as her interlocutors' desire to lead a pious life that reflects specific understandings of virtue and mo- rality (see also Bracke 2008; Hollywood 2004; Jacobsen 2011).

This approach has proved to be extremely useful for expanding our under- standing of female agency in the context of religious movements. Yet, in its focus on the desire for virtuousness and piety, it completely eclipses the desire for "empowerment" that features so centrally in the literature described previously. Mahmood (2005), for example, brackets her interlocutors' specific views on gen- der issues as secondary to her principle argument. This omission is untenable for my own research. In the contemporary European context, Muslim women's empowerment is a central feature of the issues that have come to render Islam a "problem-space" (David Scott 1999, 2004). Importantly, not only did the devout women of my fieldwork try to intervene critically in this discursive space, but they also were themselves partially shaped by it. This process unfolded in a sim- ilar manner for women in France and Germany. Their positions offer important insights into the struggle to articulate a language for women's dignity and em- powerment that was not only partially impacted by but also sought to distance itself from and compete with the language of individual rights and autonomy employed in public debates on Islam and gender. My interlocutors addressed liberal and feminist public discourses on Muslim women head on—in terms of piety *and* in terms of a different kind of empowerment—redefining the liberal terms even as they considered their own practices to be positioned squarely outside of liberal paradigms.

The following examination of the devout women's stances regarding gender issues reveals a complex interplay of several factors: the desire to prove the positive status of women within Islamic dogma, the struggle for the implementation of that status within the Muslim community, and a conscious cultivation of Islamic sensitivities and virtues that enable women to accept certain non-egalitarian principles, which were, however, connected in complicated ways to their own ideals about what constitutes the just society (see also Jouili 2011). On the basis of this material, I discuss the complex connections between my respondents' desire for virtue and piety and their reflections and aspirations on issues related to female empowerment and gender relations. This connection was so strong because, to these women, the cultivation of virtue and piety was crucially interwoven with a specific social ethics. By discussing the broader social implications of my interlocutors' conceptions of a virtuous life, this chapter seeks to shift the investigation from ethics as self-cultivation to ethics as obligation, responsibility, and care.

The "Woman Question":
Internal Debates, External Pressures

Within the institutions I attended, whether run by women or not, the theme of the status of women in Islam came up persistently. The broad salience that this topic had acquired in revival circles in Europe has to be considered within its political context and read against the backdrop of the politicization of the debate on Muslim women in European societies. The critique of these stigmatizing discourses and proposals for an alternative discourse had thus become important themes in the broader work of Islamic revival institutions. But their arguments were not merely critical reactions to public discourses on Islam; they were also responses partly fashioned and constricted by the broader discursive field in which these debates took place.

One central discursive strategy in these circles was the reversal of the dominant narrative that Europe's progressive linear temporality would culminate in the liberation of women and the establishment of sexual freedoms.[5] In numerous discussions, lectures, and classes, I saw this narrative contrasted with a different one: an Islamic temporality in which ultimate progress was epitomized in the first Islamic state in Medina, during the lifetime of the Prophet. It was at this time that women's liberation is understood to have been fully achieved through the implementation of women's rights as defined by the Qur'an. These rights were frequently enumerated and discussed by my interlocutors and then compared to a European history of women's rights. One of the arguments frequently advanced by my respondents as well as by various conference speakers was that women's financial autonomy was granted by the Qur'an. A remark by Emma, the French-Moroccan student mentioned earlier in the book, was highly representative in this regard: "In 1965, in France, women received the right to dispose of their own goods without the authorization of her husband. . . . We have had this for fourteen centuries, since the beginning of Islam."

This comparative perspective was meant to recall the problematic position of women in European history, both in more distant historical epochs as well as in the recent past and present—which is often occluded in the contemporary debates. According to my interlocutors' reading of history, female oppression in the European Christian past had been far more dramatic than in the Islamic past, which was quite often fairly idealized. The paradigmatic case most frequently invoked was the medieval witch hunt. Several lectures and discussion groups I attended took up this topic, providing historical details to bolster their argument. This evaluation was often complemented by a theological comparison between the Judeo-Christian foundational texts and the Qur'anic scriptures in regard to the status of women. Here again, numerous materials were gathered and presented to bolster the perspective of Islam as the religion more favorable toward women. Favorite examples that were frequently cited included, for instance, the argument that Islam positively endorsed sexuality versus Christianity's denial of its importance, or the issue of original sin, as associated with Eve, a woman. The women I interviewed insisted again and again that attributing blame for the fall from Paradise to a woman was a Christian rather than an Islamic teaching, because Islam does not hold the idea of original sin in the first place.[6]

Following their reversed comparative perspective on the woman question in both traditions, many women argued that the perceived "aggressiveness" of contemporary Western feminist movements resulted from a particularly misogynic Euro-Christian history. As they often put it, European women "had to fight for their rights." They carefully distinguished that kind of fight from their own struggle for gender justice, which for them consisted of fighting for the implementation of their already divinely given rights. Consider, for instance, Salwa's take on the matter. Although she considered the promotion of her students' "self-confidence" and "self-realization" as women and as Muslims to be the primary goal of her teaching mission, she nevertheless discouraged "feminist" interpretations of the Islamic scriptures. This became clear during a conversation with her about the interpretation of passages of the Qur'an that pertain to women. When she mentioned the dogma of original sin, which she rejected as a Christian reading of Genesis, I asked her what she thought of the work of Islamic feminists, who had made similar claims but also used the Qur'anic Creation story to argue for an ontological equality between the sexes.[7] Her answer reflected a skepticism shared by so many of my interlocutors:

> I am completely against transplanting discussions from Christian feminists, coming from a Christian context, into Islam. . . . This is a discussion which has a particular background, dating from the time when women were burnt as witches. There, you can understand that they are against everything; if you consider how the church has treated women, this was not very much in favor of women; they figure as the seducer of Adam and the reason for original sin, and whatever else there was. In this context, you can understand that there are sensitivities that result from Christian history.
>
> But you cannot transplant this to Islam, because Islam doesn't have the same history. And I totally don't care if I was created first and Adam was taken from my bones or if I was created from Adam's bones. This does not play any role in my daily life. And if I look at the Islamic sources that protect my life as a woman, that protect my rights as a woman . . . you have to look at it in a pragmatic way. This is a theoretical debate. If women have been oppressed for centuries in the name of the church, I can understand the passionate debates that are taking place right now.

Finally, in this comparative approach, the normative Islamic gender model and its materialization within Islamic jurisprudence were frequently contrasted to contemporary gendered norms of control and market productions of gender that they see as ubiquitous in the mainstream society around them. Again and again, my interlocutors accused the West of applying a double standard, for criticizing Islam while ignoring its own oppression of women through a materialist consumer culture that commodifies women's bodies and, even worse, falsely hails this commodification as liberating or emancipating. Similar critiques have been vehemently voiced by numerous Western feminists, but my interlocutors' assessment stands in the tradition of revival discourses in Muslim-majority contexts, which since the late 1970s have decried economic and cultural liberalization policies, as well as the subsequent increasing marketization of women's (uncovered) bodies (see, for instance, McLarney 2015). It was also in this context that the defense of Islamic ideals of modest dress was generally raised. Lamia's comment clearly conveys this logic:

> France is a society where women have very little value; the woman is an object— an object of satisfaction, an object to sell. It is funny, because they often say that the women in the West are free. No, I don't think so. As a woman you are not respected at all. You go for a job interview, you have to be almost in a miniskirt, you have to display décolleté [cleavage]. . . . To sell a forty-cent yogurt, to sell toilet paper, you need a naked woman to sell anything. So, often people tell me, your women are oppressed; no, we are not oppressed; we are free, but they are concretely oppressed [laughter].[8]

[margin handwriting: who is oppressed?]

As is clear in this account, the "West," "Christendom," and "Europe" figured in these discussions as omnipresent referents. In the sense that it emerged against this particular background, this "minor" or "subjugated" knowledge (Foucault 1980, 2003) was partly fashioned by that Western, Christian, European context: it was a concrete reaction to the dominant knowledges circulating in the public sphere of the majority society (as was evident in the comparative historical perspective or in the critique of what were perceived to be the dominant European gender models). Thus the particular historical discursive climate in Europe, or the "problem-space" that constitutes Islam and situates it within a specific power-knowledge nexus, gave new impetus to reviewing the Islamic sources and nurtured a debate within revival circles on how to take a position in this highly contested thematic field.[9]

However, notwithstanding the intense production and circulation of a "counter-discourse" (Amir-Moazami 2007) on the woman question, this "minor" knowledge faced serious difficulties in making itself heard outside revival circles. Because of the restrictive nature of the public sphere, which "is not equally" open to everyone" (Asad 1999), certain forms of knowledge of Islam are disbarred from being heard in that sphere. Thus, my interlocutors did not see any possibility of being recognized as legitimate speakers on this issue. This position was already occupied by other voices who had come to represent the authentic "insider" discourse to a European audience: secular (or ex-) Muslim women like Fadela Ammara in France, Neçla Celek in Germany, or Ayaan Hirsi Ali from the Netherlands (see, for instance, Amir-Moazami 2011; Chin 2010; Fernando 2009). It was for this reason that many of my interlocutors felt that the woman question is the principal battlefield in the "cultural war" that the West leads against the Muslim world, materializing most tangibly in the policies on Muslim minorities in Europe. To these women, the numerous public debates on the oppressed Muslim woman, the politics of "unveiling," and the celebration of liberated secular (ex-)Muslim women are clear proofs of that.

Incited by and reactive to this discursive context, the contours of discussion within the revival circles are equally determined by the moral languages provided by the Islamic discursive tradition. The Islamic gender model articulated here was always connected to central Islamic principles, ethics, notions of self and community, and structures of authority. Any debate on gender issues therefore cannot be disconnected from the overall aim of the revival movement, that is, to encourage a lifestyle pleasing to God (as defined by an orthodox reading). This specific understanding of the connection between piety and women's rights was apparent in the following remark that Naima made during a discussion we had about Islam and feminism:

> From the moment you say you are Muslim, you submit to God, you follow God's rules, you have complete satisfaction on every level. On a religious level, because it is a need, I need to adore my Lord, I need this connection with *Allah ta'ala*. He said, "Seek knowledge." He did not say, "Man, seek knowledge." He said, "Muslims seek knowledge." So, I need to search for knowledge. In this sense, I don't need to say I am a feminist, because I am Muslim; this implies everything. . . . Feminist, what does this mean? It means the struggle for the cause of women. And Islam, for me, it struggles for all the causes [of the oppressed].[10] As I said earlier regarding the Palestinians who are oppressed right now, the same for the Jews during the Second World War—for everyone who needs to fight for his rights, I am on their side because I am a Muslim. Now, when women are oppressed by the Taliban, what happens there is terrible; then I become an activist for their [the women's] cause. When you have to be feminist, you must do it; when you have to be antiracist, you must do it; you have to be against all injustices. But this does not mean I am a feminist, labeled as feminist; no, my label is simply Muslim.

As Naima made clear, living a God-pleasing life included the search for justice and the fight against the oppression of all human beings. It was in this regard that she defined herself (contextually) as someone pursuing a feminist cause. This type of statement, which I heard quite frequently, also pointed to a broader political awareness that characterizes many currents in the European revival movement. Islamic traditions that emphasize justice (*'adl*) and the ontological equality of all human beings, as well as a range of anticolonial and antiracist projects, have informed contemporary revival discourses in Europe in a variety of ways.[11] Thus, like Naima, many other diasporic revival Muslims seemed strongly committed to defending the "wretched of the earth"[12] (Fanon 2004).

My interlocutors navigated a difficult space here. They felt that it was incumbent upon them to respond to the dominant discourses—perceived as overwhelmingly negative—and to "talk back" (Bracke 2011) in order to rectify preconceived ideas. Thus, their discourse was embedded in a particular religious tradition but impacted and incited by dominant knowledges that—we should not forget—also fashioned my informants' positionalities to a considerable extent. On the other hand, they worked to cultivate their faith in response to specific ethical principles that did not necessarily accord with contemporary liberal understandings of gender equality. In this sense, "talking back" was not always easy, because the ethical languages in question did not neatly map onto the dominant discourse on rights, autonomy, and equality.

Knowledgeable Women and Religious Authorities

A growing body of literature examines female religious leadership in various Muslim settings. A central question that is regularly investigated in this literature is the relation between women's knowledge appropriation, transformations of religious authority in favor of women's participation in the production and circulation of religious discourse, and the promotion of greater gender equality.[13] One field of inquiry that literature is concerned with women's participation in Islamic networks and with their combined efforts in studying Islamic sciences and conducting grassroots work, with the object of empowering women. This activism has engendered a trend that has often been described with the term "Islamic feminism." Women engage critically with the sacred texts as well as with the larger corpus of scripture and claim the right to reinterpret those sources (see, for instance, Barlas 2002; Wadud 1999). They often break (in either modest or more radical ways) with past restrictions previously articulated in Islamic scholarship in order to rearrange the Islamic definition of gender relations to the advantage of women. In this sense, "Islamic feminism" challenges traditional religious authorities, not only by questioning their interpretations, but also by claiming authority for themselves, justified by their knowledge. However, although their interpretive work has at times had a tangible impact on legal debates within their specific national contexts, these groups remain rather marginalized and contested within many segments of the broader Muslim community.[14]

Studies on Muslim women in Europe have at times also highlighted the possibility of women's engagement with Islamic sources to produce more specifically feminized Islamic thought.[15] Interestingly, my respondents did not seem to hold Islamic feminists in very high esteem, mistrusting the idea of reinterpreting the texts through a female-centered perspective. One occasion that strongly highlighted this stance was provided by the much-reported mixed-gender prayer led by Muslim activist and scholar Amina Wadud in New York in 2005.[16] Because it was covered extensively by European as well as Arabic-language media and news channels, many of my respondents were aware of this event. During diverse conversations in both countries, most of my interviewees expressed skepticism toward or outright rejection of Wadud's undertaking, which was vehemently denounced by many renowned scholars as lacking in Islamic legitimacy—most notably by Egyptian Shaykh Yusuf al-Qaradawi (see Silvers and Elewa 2011).

In Cologne I encountered another case that illustrates the divergence between Islamic feminism and women adhering to mainstream revival Islam within the local scene. During conversations with my interlocutors, I learned about the Center for Islamic Women's Studies and Women's Promotion, or ZIF (Zentrum für Islamische Frauenforschung und -förderung). The members of ZIF are mainly women of Turkish descent and German converts, several of whom were closely affiliated through family ties with important figures in the Islamic revival movement in Germany and Turkey.[17] Notwithstanding these connections, ZIF's engagement with the sacred texts employs a "feminist" theology, which takes a highly critical stance toward the male-dominated orthodoxy.[18] Because their exegetical work is conducted in open opposition to the methods enshrined in the classical Islamic sciences of *tafsir* and *fiqh,* and to the established forms of religious authority, ZIF is quite marginalized within the Islamic sectors in Germany.[19] One could explain the marginalization of ZIF as resulting from a predominance of men in Islamic mainstream organizations in Germany, but their work did not appeal to the majority of the women I encountered in Cologne either. Those who knew of ZIF's work roundly denounced it for being "too radical" because it overstepped the bounds of the established Islamic orthodoxy.[20] Many women also described ZIF as "too feminist," which points to the more general skepticism toward feminism that prevails in most Islamic revival circles, where feminism tends to be associated with "Westernness" and a hostile attitude toward men, and therefore is construed as potentially anti-Islamic.[21] Although they were sensitive to gender issues, they all insisted that they did not want to "renew" or "reform" Islam, thus establishing a clear boundary between themselves and various forms of "liberal" or "progressive" Islam. Sevim, for instance, emphasized to me the difference between the work of the BFmF and the work of ZIF:

> They are feminists, a bit radical. In our center, we are women who want to do our thing too. We are Muslim and don't fall outside the frame of the Qur'an or of Islam. We say, OK, I am perhaps at the limit of this frame, but I am still within the frame. And we try to get along in society with this Islamic consciousness.

Sevim's statement reflected my respondents' concern to pursue their defense of women's interests within the limits of "authentic" or "true" Islam, defined very much by a specific relation to religious authority. They insisted that this boundary implied respecting the exclusive right of the *ulama* to interpret the texts. Teachers and conference speakers repeatedly cautioned their audience "not to engage in a personal *ijtihad*."[22] They stressed the need to acquire knowledge of the sacred texts, but at the same time underlined that this knowledge would not enable the individual lay believer to draw her own conclusions. According to this view, *ijtihad* was considered the prerogative of Islamic scholars. When advice was needed, one was to consult the trustworthy scholars.[23] This is also what Olfa and Salwa regularly emphasized, making clear that they themselves did not hold this position of authority.

In the women's approaches to studying Islam, the imperative for the individual believer to acquire knowledge and to understand it by using her own reason did not destabilize the authority of religious scholars in matters of interpretation. These women's growing understanding of the traditional Islamic sciences, which acquainted them with *usul al-fiqh* (the principles of Islamic jurisprudence), gave them a keen awareness of the *ulama*'s prerogative as interpreters, and that remaining within the Islamic consensus was part of religious dogma (*'aqida*). Their familiarity with the authoritative religious discourse also deepened their mistrust toward everything likely to be considered *bid'a* (unlawful innovation). Accordingly, when I discussed various Islamic injunctions with these women, they were always conscientious to emphasize that the opinions they circulated were "authorized" opinions and they regularly couched them in phrases such as "there is a consensus that. . . . " At the same time, many women did express their desire for more female scholars who had gone through rigorous training in the Islamic sciences so that they could eventually join the ranks of the "trustworthy" *'ulama*. They were aware that now, as well as throughout much of Islamic history, few women had made it into the category of respected scholars, and that the absence of female voices could indeed have an impact on how women's status was defined in the *fiqh* texts. But they clearly distinguished their wish for the emergence of such (orthodox) female scholars from the voices of "Islamic feminists," whom they did not credit with that legitimacy.

Indeed, the more conversant the women became in orthodox Islamic doctrine, the more they affirmed it. Yet this affirmation did not lead to simple conformism among them or to a homogeneous discourse. As illustrated in Chapter 2, they were strongly critical of the "traditional" emulation they perceived in the practices and attitudes of their parents' generation. In conformity to contemporary Islamic discourse that had been inspired by the reform movements, they rejected the notion of blind *taqlid* (imitation) and claimed their Islamic right and duty to consult the primary texts in order to weigh the opinions they heard.[24] They also tended to consult several scholarly opinions and compare them to each other. Additionally, it is important to note that the scholars to whom the women referred represented neither uniform nor stagnant opinions but responded in quite divergent ways to the minority condition of Muslims in Europe and to the various needs of the individual Muslim believer in the diasporic context.[25] Given the multitude of diverse and changing opinions within orthodox scholarship, women who were well-acquainted with the Islamic sciences were able to employ these differences to argue for a larger scope of action in their day-to-day lives. However, one cannot assume that these sources were deployed instrumentally to suit one's immediate practical interests. At times, when confronted with a variety of opinions, my interlocutors would choose to follow the more restrictive one.[26]

An exchange during one of the monthly women's brunches organized by Olfa at CERSI clearly exposed how my interlocutors could react very differently to that plurality of authoritative opinions. That day, the discussion turned to the issue of women's travel without a *mahram*, a man from among her closest kin, to whom she cannot get married. This question has been contentiously debated among Muslim scholars and opinions diverge widely, especially nowadays. Many women complained that, as unmarried women, they had few opportunities to enjoy vacations to distant destinations, given that their mostly working-class parents did not practice tourism. And if they traveled, they would, as my Maghrebi interlocutors put it, "just return each year to the *bled*" (their country of origin). Traveling with other, like-minded "sisters" was, they maintained, the only possible way for unmarried women to travel while guaranteeing a certain Islamic ethic. Indeed, many of my interlocutors habitually spent their vacations in this way. Others categorically rejected this practice as contradicting the obligation to travel with a *mahram*. Olfa too was not particularly eager to consent to this form of travel. Although she recognized divergent opinions, she held that the majority of scholars still required an unmarried woman to travel only in the company of men who fall into the category of *mahram*. She advised her students to respect this restriction for their own safety. Several women present contested this advice, however, and came up with an additional set of quotes from scholars who were considered respectable and who held that women were permitted to travel alone. One attendant quoted a *hadith* in which the Prophet declared, "One day the conditions for traveling will be so safe that women can travel alone."

Throughout this lively discussion, Olfa acknowledged the divergent opinion as "authentic" and considered it useful in an age of global mobility to enable women to move around for work or to visit their families without constantly depending on a *mahram*. Furthermore, she conceded that opinions like this one reflected Islam's flexibility and adaptability to different contexts (which she called a *rahma, or* "mercy"). Yet she also emphasized the necessity of not simply using opinions in an opportunistic manner while ignoring the rationale or wisdom (*hikma*) behind a contrasting opinion. These restrictions were meant not to hurt the Muslim woman but to protect her and to enable her to lead a life wholly pleasing in the eyes of God, which should always be the ultimate goal of any Muslim. She gave several examples of when tourism by "sisters" traveling alone to distant destinations had turned dangerous, and she recommended that her pupils stay on the safe side when confronted with a diversity of opinions. She concluded with the advice, "At least for young, unmarried sisters, I advise you to be more prudent. Once you are married, you have a different status, which gives you more freedom. But believe me, also in terms of reputation, this has an impact." At the end of the discussion, the women did not all agree with each other, but the Islamic legitimacy of both positions was upheld.

This debate illustrates, once again, how these women deployed the Islamic discursive tradition to resolve practical issues in a globalized world. This tradition delineates a broad discursive space in which a range of arguments and counterarguments are made with reference to the authoritative texts.[27] Although there is room for "strategic" use of these texts, this logic alone cannot account for the variety of ethical concerns involved in this engagement. As I elaborate in the following pages, the various issues that arise from the effort to ground one's life in orthodox readings of the Islamic scriptures need to be considered in connection with the overall struggle to lead an ethical life and the work of self-cultivation this entails.

Changing Regimes: From Autonomous Judgment to Submitting to Divine Wisdom

Much like other women who participated in Islamic revival movements in Europe, my interlocutors frequently expressed their adherence to an Islamic gender model that rejects notions of equality while upholding the idea of *equity*, a notion that often relies on a naturalized account of gender. In this section, I examine the ways in which these women reasoned through and enacted their adherence to these positions. I find their various modes of reasoning through this issue fruitful for thinking about different ways of situating oneself within a web of doubt, certainty, reflection, and confidence that does not correspond to modern ideals of the autonomous, rational, self-knowing self-ideals that are so strongly defended in public debates about the Islamic Other.

I should note here that addressing the topic of gender and Islam with my interlocutors was often a difficult task given the larger discursive context. However, in the course of our encounters, my interlocutors not only shared their (unfashionable) visions of naturalized gender differences, but quite a few of them also admitted that, prior to their conscious turn to Islam, they themselves had held negative opinions of their parents' religion, because of its alleged misogynist and patriarchal stances. This was the case with Maissa, a French-Algerian woman in her mid-twenties. Among my interlocutors, she was one who had been most estranged from Islam prior to embarking on her spiritual path (*cheminement spirituel*), having consciously rejected her parents' religion and been determined to live a secular life. She recalled:

> I was really rebellious, totally, because I thought the Muslim religion was a religion for guys. I thought there was too much injustice between men and women; this is what was transmitted by Arabs. For my parents, it was like, the guys can do what they like and the girls have to stay at home; they must not hang around with boys. I hated that; it did not suit me at all. And in the beginning, during adolescence, I had to fight to go out, but once I had my freedom, I took it, and had no limits anymore [*laughter*].

Many others recounted the difficulties they had faced in the past in order to come to terms with the gender vision they had progressively learned to appreciate as authentic within Islam. In the end, quite a few acknowledged that they still lacked a real understanding of certain highly gendered injunctions, especially of the rationale given to them by many of the Islamic scholars to whom they listened. The arguments with which they gave voice to their (former or ongoing) incomprehension revealed the degree to which these women had also been fashioned by modern ideals of autonomy and equality. What had happened to effect such a change of heart, from an endorsement of principles such as gender equality and autonomous selfhood to the rationalization of gender difference? Did women like Maissa simply abandon (their at times hard-won) freedom in order to submit to a restrictive system? Public discourses often explain these "reconversions" by saying that Muslim women have been manipulated by the teachings of Imams and other preachers. In this logic, they have given up on emancipation in order to adopt a *false* consciousness, and are therefore somehow regressing.

Obviously this is not the way I wish to read my interlocutors' changed views on gender issues. If one thinks of this adoption of different gender norms alongside the process of pious self-cultivation enacted by women in the Islamic revival movements in terms of changing disciplinary regimes (as discussed in Chapter 2) by which a different relation of self to self is established, one can escape the false dichotomy between freedom and unfreedom (as well as the problematic domination-resistance couplet).[28] From this perspective, subjects are always governed by certain kinds of power relations and discursive traditions, but they are also self-governing in the sense that they govern themselves according to the codes produced within these specific formations.

Following this line of thought, and against many taken-for-granted theories of freedom, Nikolas Rose (1999: 42) argues that freedom requires "the inculcation of particular kinds of relations that the human being has with itself," defined by notions of individual autonomy and choice (1999: 64). Rose demonstrates convincingly that freedom has become, not only in contemporary liberal rule but also within philosophical reflections on freedom, an "artefact of government," a "mode of organizing and regulation," and a "discipline" centered around responsible self-management. However, in that it builds the private conduct of free citizens on specific languages, self-disciplines, and forms of civility, freedom under liberal rule only sanctions a "certain way of understanding and exercising freedom" (1999: 62–68).[29] Individual freedom as a form of power is reshaped so that the individual freely desires to act in ways that are compatible with neoliberal governance. In this sense, individual autonomy cannot be assumed to be the opposite of, or limited to, neoliberal governance, but instead lies at the heart of its disciplinary control (McNay 2009).[30] In other words, specific self-understandings of autonomy and freedom are understood not as simply reflecting authentic autonomous and free individuals, but as *fashioned* by a specific *regime* of freedom.

In line with these reflections, I want to understand the trajectories of my interlocutors not in terms of abandonment of autonomy, but as a matter of moving from a disciplinary regime, one governed by the contemporary liberal norms and modes of self-fashioning that circulated in the public spheres of the majority society, to one informed by the Islamic traditions as they have been reworked in the revival circles of Europe, and that have clearly also been shaped by the liberal regime of freedom that the women intended to leave behind when they turned to Islam.

Let me illustrate this argument by investigating more thoroughly the pivotal moments in the process of "changing regimes." As discussed in Chapter 2, the intensified search for knowledge on Islam that occurred at the beginning of this process was often incited by public discourses on Islam and gender. Therefore, it became crucial for these women to learn more about their religion, to find out for themselves whether the basic assumptions conveyed in these discourses were true or not. The quest for religious knowledge supplied them with a range of arguments helpful not only to prove to mainstream society that women in Islam enjoy an advantageous status, but also to gain from kin and community the rights that had been denied to them at times. During classes and conferences, I frequently observed how enthusiastically female participants absorbed new knowledge about the different rights granted to women by the Islamic scriptures. But in the course of their quest for knowledge, they also encountered conceptions that clashed with modern notions of equality, such as the insistence on gender difference and the correspondingly differentiated distribution of legal rights and duties. I likewise witnessed confusion and unease when female students first learned about certain nonegalitarian provisions, which at times occasioned heated arguments.

Several interlocutors admitted openly that at the outset some of these principles had elicited feelings of discomfort in them. Nassira, a French-Algerian woman in her early thirties, was such a case. I met this young slender woman with large, gentle brown eyes at CERSI. It was through the classes at this center that she had started and progressed in her practice of Islam. In our conversations, she often insisted that it was initially difficult for her to act and feel according to the standards of Islamic morality defined in the revival circles she had begun to attend. It was hard for her to accept certain gender-specific legal injunctions, as well as certain gendered forms of social interaction that she witnessed between the pious Muslim men and women in her new environment. Their behavior stood very much in contradiction not only to the resolute nature that belied her fragile appearance, but also to the education she had received from her divorced, rather secular Algerian-Kabyle mother, whom she described as "very French." Her first years at CERSI had been fraught with arguments with teachers, which provoked tensions that even caused her at one point to drop out of the program. Nassira's troubles revealed the extent to which she had been fashioned by narratives on gender equality and autonomy—narratives that had produced and organized corresponding sensibilities and affects.

> When I started at the center [CERSI], in the beginning I never agreed, really. As a woman, you are not allowed to do everything [in Islam]. . . . What disturbed me back then [for example] was the idea of depending on the *mahram. Mahram,* this is dependency on a man. I said, no, I don't want to depend on a man. I manage on my own. A woman can do things on her own; she does not need a man [*laughter*]. The first year was very hard for me: everything shocked me.

However, as discussed in Chapter 2, the quest for knowledge is never simply a search for "facts" about religion, which would be a merely cognitive means of "knowing" Islam—in this case, of "knowing" what the Islamic scriptures say about gender relations. Even more important is the emotive or sensory effect of learning Islam. Here the acquisition of *'ilm* (knowledge) takes the form of "a self-technique for the cultivation and training of certain forms of will, desire, emotion and reason" (Hirschkind 2001a: 10), thus it enables Muslims to feel in accordance with standards of Islamic piety. Whereas for many women this affective knowledge grew out of their initial search for factual knowledge, others had already focused on that "affective knowledge" at the outset of their journey. Maissa, for instance, was shaken by her brother's death by overdose and exhausted by a series of unsuccessful relationships. She was merely looking for inner peace, and completely bracketed the gender issue. Her search focused on existential issues, such as divine love, mercy, forgiveness, and redemption:

> In the beginning I didn't dwell on these kinds of questions [gender issues]. Because I started to find answers to my existential questions, I pursued this approach. I really didn't try to understand the other things. And I didn't really

care. But in the course of attending lectures and classes, of course I also realized that the woman has a place in Islam, that after all she's not a dog you put in the kitchen, you know [*laughter*].

In all cases, it was the acquisition of affective knowledge that rendered these women capable of "feeling" or "sensing" the gender question differently, not only in order to relativize the importance of the topic, but also to look at the injunctions and provisions that regulate gender relations through the filter of a different set of virtues and emotional dispositions. A conversation with Salwa helped me to grasp the particular affective structures that repositioned prior modes of reasoning. One afternoon, we had just emerged from her "*Tafsir* and *Fiqh*" class, which had dealt with the centrality of *tawakkul,* the feeling of confidence in God; the preceding sentiment, *yaqin,* the certitude that God exists; and *taqwa,* God-consciousness, as the very pillars of Islamic piety. As so often happened, we continued chatting afterward in her office. During this exchange, we came back to the topic of the day's class, and Salwa said more about the significance of these sentiments in her own trajectory. She explained how these feelings had helped her to appreciate in a different light the importance of the legal provisions pertaining to gender, by putting her own capacity for judgment into perspective.

> In the beginning, when faith is still young and not very stabilized, you want to have answers for everything that are immediately comprehensible and logical. . . . At age 15, 16, I always had that fear that I will find an explanation, which seems to me completely inhuman and illogical; I had a fantasy that at this moment my faith will collapse. And then, at 16, 17, I had aggressive discussions for hours with my father about polygamy. Not that my dad thinks polygamy is great, but I always said, no, polygamy is a humiliation. And my dad said, no, you cannot talk like that; it was God's will to allow that and so you cannot say that this is unjust. So we had so many fights about that. Then I started to study Islam intensively, and now . . . there is a basic conviction which is so strong. . . . To submit to the will of God, that is what Islam means, that is now the priority. In the beginning I thought everything must be logical, I have to understand . . . and I felt that my logic, my feeling was the right one. Well, I grew up here and I was socialized here. With my German way of seeing things, influenced by Western thought, . . . this is how I saw things in the beginning. But now, when I see or hear things, for example, which I don't understand, I accept them because I feel that human reasoning is limited. . . . If I don't understand something, God, who created human beings, He understands how they function, He knows why.

Interestingly, Salwa recognized that the difficulty of developing confidence in God, with its attendant acknowledgement of man's limited reason, stems from a socialization in which the moral ideal invokes an autonomous, reasoning self. To undo one's learned modes of reasoning, affects, and modes of perception was (and still is for many) a laborious process. In this case, it could be done only through the willing and conscious cultivation of pious sentiments and virtues. The necessity of cultivating confidence in the Divine in order to accept its injunctions independently of one's capacity to understand was constantly emphasized in the teachings in the Islamic centers I attended.[31] This imperative corresponded to the idea that faith must be consciously cultivated by the believer. As everyone insisted to me, only by investing oneself in the Islamic sciences and worship practices could one hope to attain a superior degree of faith characterized by *yaqin* and *tawakkul*.

Even those of my interlocutors who were still not satisfied with certain explanations given to them in the Islamic books or in the classes they attended referred consistently to divine wisdom, thus accepting their own limited knowledge. I recurrently heard statements like this: "*Allahu a'lam* [God knows best], I don't know the exact *hikma* behind this specific word from Allah, I don't have the answer, but I always accept it. I know that Allah knows best." If they still expressed explicit doubt about a specific injunction (which only few did, and with visible discomfort), the same confidence and trust was invoked. Take, for instance, Saliha, a French-Tunisian woman in her early thirties, married, and a stay-at-home mother. She became interested in learning about Islam at the end of her high school days, shortly after which she began praying and wearing hijab. She had attended conferences by Tariq Ramadan, and those organized at the Mosquée Ad-Daʿwa on the rue de Tanger in Belleville, a Paris neighborhood, but she had also regularly participated in informal study circles with other "sisters." After her marriage, her involvement in these circles waned as she became increasingly critical of what she felt were their overly conservative stances. Speaking of her doubts regarding certain gendered legal injunctions, she made the following comment about the legal provisions on female witnesses:[32]

> I think this is not just [*laughter*], paradoxically, I am Muslim, practicing, but I
> think this is unjust, but I don't think that *rabbi subhanu ta'ala* [my Lord, glori-
> fied and exalted be He] is unjust. So, if he commanded this, there must have
> been a context. . . . Right now I don't really agree with this, I just live it like this.
> But the Qur'an, you cannot accept one part and reject another. Nonetheless, I

give myself this space inside myself where there must be an explanation, because I believe in God, I believe in what He commands, in what He does. Nothing He does is unjust.

If Saliha revealed more doubts than most other women, her approach nonetheless reflected a vision of the revelation that was quite representative. While
acknowledging that parts of the revelation, though logical and rational, were
not always accessible to human reason, believers still aspired to and actively
sought understanding. In the words of Werner Schiffauer (2000: 261), the "contradiction between revelation and discernment receives . . . the character of a
mystery. For the believer, to reflect on the sense of an enigmatic order becomes
an interesting intellectual challenge. Thus, it is important to emphasize that, for
the women I spoke with, evoking confidence in divine wisdom did not have to
constitute the end, but could potentially become the "starting point of a religious quest" (Schiffauer 2000: 261).

There is another aspect of Saliha's statement that is important to highlight
here. Even though she, unlike most women, was reservedly favorable to alternative (nonorthodox) interpretations of certain Qur'anic verses, she clearly
refused to select those aspects of the Islamic message that suited her. The phenomenon of picking one's own religious dogma according to the need of the
moment has been referred to as *bricolage* or *religion à la carte* (Dobbelaere
1999: 239). Many observers see this approach to religious tradition as characteristic of the contemporary age of "religious modernity" or "secularized religion,"
which is guided by the principle of the individualization of religious beliefs.[33]
It is important to note in this context that not only did all my interlocutors,
akin to Saliha, refuse this understanding of "religious modernity" implicitly
through their statements, but they also quite regularly formulated explicit critiques of contemporary European Christianity, which according to them had
been significantly weakened by such an "arbitrary" and "selective" use of religious doctrines.

Thus, by accepting the Islamic message as a whole and putting their trust
in the Divine, the women acknowledged the possibility that the answers might
not be available to human reason, given its limitations in relation to the Divine.
This position sits uncomfortably with the ideal of the autonomous, rational
subject, an ideal that these women had quite often endorsed in the past, and
still reflected in many other ways. Consequently, through the acquisition of
Islamic knowledge and the conscious cultivation of emotions that materialized
in certain dispositions and virtues, the women strove not only to detach them-

selves from these ideals, but also to change the aspirations and modes of conduct that result from these ideals. In this case, it involved changing how they related to the opposite sex and how they conducted themselves so that they would behave according to the gendered norms of Islamic modesty. Nassira again revealed the difficulties she experienced in this personal struggle to transform herself according to Islamic normativity:

> I worked a lot on my self. This was part of myself and it is difficult to change completely. But I did this work, and that implies that you have to touch on your education. . . . [For example], this former idea of mine, this feminism for dummies, you know, the woman is equal to the man—no, the woman has a place and the man has a place, the man needs the woman and the woman needs the man. It's interdependent. Of course there must not be any abuse. So, if you apply yourself, you change your habits, habits which are given to you by your education. The problem is that some behaviors are ingrained. This is difficult. Sometimes it still surfaces [in my conduct].

For Nassira, this change meant not only that she had to abandon what she called a highly independent lifestyle grounded in acceptance of "French" ideas of female autonomy (much to the distress of her brother whom she now wanted to recruit as her *wali*, a term she employed alternatively as protector or helper). It also meant that she had to develop a more restrained, controlled, and less spontaneous way of interacting with the opposite sex. However, she clearly recognized the limits of this work, the sheer impossibility of completely leaving behind the earlier-acquired habitus, which required constant and continuous monitoring of the self.

For these women, virtues like *tawakkul* and *yaqin* drive the ethical agency at the heart of the self-fashioning project they seek to enact. Yet the revival participants' emphasis on unflagging vigilance, on regular practice and inculcation, once more draws attention to the difficulty of always inhabiting these virtues, as well as to the fragility and incompleteness of this, or any, self-fashioning project. Nassira's statement clearly shows that even as they worked toward a "completed" self, these women recognized the impossibility of totally overcoming conflicting affects and sensibilities.

Individual Rights or Mutual Dependence?

Cultivating Islamic virtues such as *tawakkul* and *yaqin* enabled my interlocutors not only to distance themselves from (earlier) claims to autonomy, supremacy of human reason, and abstract equality, but also to affirm certain patriarchal assumptions that are integral to the orthodox Islamic tradition. One should not conclude, however, that these women simply shunned their initial convictions and social concerns with the help of certain "sentimentalized" feelings that they nurtured. Rather, the acquisition of virtues and emotions that are central to this kind of Islamic piety entailed the development of a novel set of corresponding convictions regarding concrete societal ideals and the common good. At the core of this social ethics was a belief in the primacy of duties and responsibilities. It is for this reason that they were highly wary of employing modern idioms of individual rights—notwithstanding their substantive struggles to enhance women's space for action, and their recurrent references to a language of "Islamic rights," which also points to a reconfiguration of the Islamic tradition as a result of the encounter with certain liberal languages. In order to understand this hesitancy, we have to dwell a bit further on these women's understanding of rights that are built on an Islamic base.

At the foundation of any concept of Islamic rights is the understanding that justice constitutes the essence of divine revelation and is codified within Islamic law. According to this belief, Islamic rights not only are cemented into a religious-moral framework of divine origin, but also are fundamentally linked to a certain ethical practice, the exercise of which results in the acquisition of virtue. If the abstract rights of the liberal tradition are, following Wendy Brown, "a paradoxical form of power insofar as they signify something like the permanent presence of an endangering power or violation" (1995: 12), then it becomes clear why my interlocutors are averse to using this language when it comes to the revelation. A language of power cannot account for the aspect of justice, or for the ethical impulse that practitioners see as inherent in all divine injunctions, including in the provisions governing gender relations.

It is on this basis that the women judged those Muslim men who "abused" certain Islamic legal injunctions. A positivist perspective would most likely evaluate laws not only for their capacity to guarantee an egalitarian application, but also by the room they leave open for abuse. If they open doors for abuse, they are considered less efficient (although it does not follow that in practice they will always be reformed accordingly). Such logic did not make sense to my interlocutors. According to them, Islamic legal injunctions could not be looked at from outside the context of piety and ethical self-cultivation, and in particular not from outside an omnipresent awareness of divine judgment. According to this logic, no truly pious Muslim man would misuse a prerogative simply because he potentially could. Listen, for instance, to Emna, the young French-Moroccan student introduced in Chapter 2. Her perspective clearly exposes the tension between the idea of a "perfect law" on the one hand and the possibility of abuse on the other. Like all my interlocutors, she resolves this tension by appealing to a broader ethical stance defined by God-consciousness:

> God is there, He hears and sees, *subhanu wa ta'ala* [glorified and exhalted be He], and those men [who abuse], all I can say is, I advise them to think of the day which awaits them, Judgment day. Because here you can twist and turn the law in any direction; even here in France you can use the law to your own advantage. This is what many politicians and the rich do. . . . Down here we can bring judges or *imams* on our side, but can we bring God on our side? OK there are all these laws, they are perfect, . . . but we have to be conscious of the fact that God is there . . . you need to know that God sees you.

The devout women I talked to adhered, then, to a vision of rights that could not be disconnected from the imperative of virtuous conduct. Central to this vision, with its emphasis on conduct, were notions of obligation, responsibility, and duty, and rights that should not be isolated from these highly interdependent concepts. Interestingly, I heard many women express the fear that by being highly reactive and defensive toward Western accusations of Islamic misogyny, Islamic discourse risked getting trapped in a logic that insisted too strongly on rights, especially when it came to women's issues. Emna, who provided me with numerous anecdotes about her battles with "patriarchal old men" during her struggles to increase women's avenues of participation and for space for women in her local mosque community, nevertheless complained:

> In the conferences and *khutbas* [sermons] I attend, I have heard so much of this valorization of women, more reminders of the rights of women and the duties of the husband toward his wife than vice versa. We always hear about that [women's rights]; I'd rather hear what duties we have. It's like we are always out to justify ourselves. I get tired of this. Well, OK, a woman has her rights, she has her duties, period. But we are always justifying ourselves, toward the feminists, toward the enemies of Islam. I am tired of this.

Emna's statement clearly conveyed the idea that it was the domain of duties that was most important for leading an ethical life. It is precisely this idea that Olfa hoped to get across in her classes. One day, after the Sunday brunch, I discussed with her an approach she had just outlined during the gathering. Whereas she generally acknowledged the importance for Muslim women of being aware of their "Islamic rights," that day she seemed rather skeptical of a rights-based perspective. A student had asked about women's rights in Islam, but she had strongly emphasized the realm of duties instead. Sometime later, in another conversation with Olfa, I came back to the argument she had made at the brunch and questioned her about her apparent refusal to talk about rights, and she explained to me her position:

> I want to alert the sisters that thinking in terms of, *voilà,* this is my right and this is my duty is a very first-degree understanding of Islam. If you dig a bit deeper, you understand that a conscious and rigorous Muslim who loves Allah and wants to please Him is more within the domain of duty, whatever the particular field, than in the domain of rights. This is the same for women: she should not say, I have rights; no, I have duties, and the man is in the same position. . . . If you see today, we are in a republican society that is defined in terms of rights. But you see that this can't work; the employer's right against the union's right, this can't work, because there is always one who will push the other. But if you are in the domain of duties, the duty of the employer is to respect his employee, the duty of the employee is to respect the employer, to do his job correctly; here we can find common ground.
>
> And this makes more sense: Where is the heart? Where is the *mahabba* [love]? Where is the goodness? When we talk about morals, we can only talk about duties: the woman, she has duties toward whom? First, toward Allah. If she has to satisfy her husband, it is because Allah has ordered it, not because she has to please her husband directly; it is always for Allah. And precisely when it comes to reforming the self, it starts with myself. I don't ask the other, I start with myself. This is what the big *jihad* [struggle] says: the effort over oneself, I start with myself and do what I have to do.
>
> So, concerning your question: today it is so fashionable to talk about how Islam has given women certain rights. I don't want to do as the others do. Because we are attacked in regard to the status of women, we have to show that we have rights? Everyone knows that women's rights are not always respected, even in France!
>
> This is my personal reflection, but perhaps you should talk to Hichème [El-Arafa, head of the the CERSI] in order to know what the scholars say on this question, with a more scholarly approach.

Both Emna's and Olfa's statements, in which they refuse the urge to defend Islam by focusing on Islamic women's rights, clearly point to a complex *relational* understanding of rights and duties that echoes the classical Islamic scheme of rights that asserts the primacy of responsibilities and obligations. Emna and Olfa consciously situated themselves in opposition to modern, liberal rights schemes, which usually postulate the primacy of individual rights over other concerns. The preference of rights in recent liberal theory has resulted in a highly explicit elaboration of rights, whereas corresponding duties have been poorly theorized (see, for instance, Morgan-Foster 2005). The concept of individual duty has strong historical roots in Western political thought as well, dating back to Greek philosophy, but from the Enlightenment on, this tradition of thought gradually eroded (Morgan-Foster 2005: 79).[34] In contemporary liberal political thought, the perceived tension between collective and individual interests has resulted in the prerogative given to the protection of individual freedom from collective sanctions and constraints.

Abdulaziz Othman Altwaijri (2000) claims that, from an Islamic perspective, individual duties "are not the intellectual result of a phase in the development of the human mind. . . . They are, in fact, duties of the faith, entrusted to the individual and the society" (quoted in Morgan-Foster 2005: 105). As S. H. Nasr (2002: 282) explains, the particular Islamic understanding of rights and obligations stems from the idea of a covenant concluded between humans and God: "Human beings have rights that are directly related to the responsibilities they have accepted as God's servants and vice-regents on earth." Obligations coming from the civil domain and those coming from the devotional domain are accorded the same moral status (Moosa 2000: 192).[35] The relationship between rights and duties is an interpersonal and correlative one, as Ebrahim Moosa (2000: 193) explains: "In the enforcement of a right jurists understand that one party has a claim to have a 'right' (*haqq*) and another 'obligation' (*wajib*) to honor a right: every right thus has a reciprocal obligation." In this sense, Islamic jurisprudence accounts for the right that God has over human beings, the right that the immortal soul has over the human individual, and the rights that others have over oneself, and so on (see Nasr 2002: 282). Thus, Nasr argues, it is less about the right to perform a particular act and more about leading a good life from a teleological perspective.

This understanding of the relationship between rights and duties explains my respondents' emphasis on their duties as mothers and wives within a gendered (but flexible and even constantly evolving) division of labor.[36] They discarded the idea of claiming rights "against" men, and rejected the thought that divine provisions potentially infringed upon their capacity for self-fulfillment. This is also one of the points of critique that they regularly leveled against what they understood as "feminist" tendencies predominant in European majority societies: the idea of a necessary struggle for women's autonomy and rights *against* men, which situated women structurally in opposition to men. It is from this perspective that we have to comprehend their insistence on the *complementarity* of the two sexes, and on the notion of *equity* as opposed to *equality*. This gender ideal defined by "complementarity" and "equity," which refuses to incline itself to actually existing power relations, is the prevalent approach maintained among participants in contemporary orthodox Islam (see, for example, Badawi 1995).

In the academic literature, the contemporary Islamic discourse on equity often appears as a somehow deficient reformulation of abstract equality, which is assumed to be the ideal.[37] It goes without saying that such a critical approach is reasonable in that it exposes different forms of gender discrimination that have been covered up by the term *equity* in various Muslim contexts.[38] For my interlocutors, however, this term circumscribes ideal gender relations as defined by mutuality, dependency, obligation, and care as an alternative to abstract equality and individual rights. And their recognition of specific gendered duties notwithstanding, they did not emphasize mutuality and dependency exclusively in the private domain of the family. In the comment by Olfa just quoted, she used the example of entrepreneurial life to dispute rights discourses and individualist notions of the sovereign, rights-bearing subject also within the realms of *public* life, even if the family was her main concern. Again and again, in classes and other discussions, I heard similar assessments, all of which critically depicted a society that suffered from an individualist attitude in every domain, including those of politics and the economy. So, although women's rights in Islam were being claimed and exercised, Olfa and the other women voiced strong skepticism toward an *exclusive* emphasis on rights and instead valorized the principle of interdependence of rights and duties, of obligations and mutuality.[39]

It is important to recall here that these assertions are not specifically Islamic concerns but rather are questions that have been broached frequently in political theory. Whether individual rights can be abstracted from any (substantial) vision of the good life was discussed particularly in the aftermath of the publication of John Rawls's work *A Theory of Justice* (1971). In the manner of Rawls, mainstream liberal thought has been reluctant to build into a theory of justice anything that belongs to a substantive conception of human flourishing. As communitarian and feminist thinkers alike have correctly pointed out, the liberal claim of the priority of the "right over the good" could be sustained only by an underlying ontological conception of the self as overly individualistic, existing prior to its ends, free and independent, unencumbered by prior moral ties, endowed with a voluntarist notion of agency, and standing at a certain distance from the interests it has (see, for instance, Brennan 1999; Nedelsky 1989; Sandel 1982; Taylor 1985; Young 1990).

This understanding, as its critics have pointed out, reinforces the divisive tendency to think of oneself as separate from and in conflict with others, and obscures the extent to which human beings are interdependent. A certain trend in feminist scholarship in particular has been concerned with the premise that such a self denies its own neediness, as well as its dependence on relations of love, care, and support (Brennan 1999; Kittay 1999; Noddings 1984). In such an overly individualist approach, these voices continue, considerations of the nature of human relations and the social and moral bonds that sustain them— whether love, care, or other forms of solidarity—are hastily rejected by liberal political thinkers as secondary issues, because they already fall into the realm of substantive conceptions of the good.[40] On the basis of these and similar lines of reasoning, a range of thinkers from different tendencies have argued against an overly individualistic conception of rights and in favor of a relational understanding of rights and duties.[41]

More specifically, within many tendencies of liberal thought, notions of mutuality and dependency were generally confined to the private sphere of the home, as has often been decried by feminist thinkers.[42] Notwithstanding the fact that Olfa and the other women did not question a gendered division of labor—which they insisted, however, should be applied in a flexible and contextual manner—they were also, as we have seen, highly critical of notions of autonomy in both the private *and* the public spheres. By pushing their interrogation of liberal rights into the public domain, my Muslim interlocutors' considerations resonate with other critiques of liberal doctrines that cite the inability of those doctrines to address need and mutual dependency in crucial domains of public life, reflecting the erosion and fragmentation of collective values and intersocial bonds (Brown 1995; Lynch, Baker, and Lyons 2009).[43]

This is not to obscure the significant difference between the epistemologies and teleologies that undergird those other critiques and the ones articulated by my Muslim interlocutors (which also accounts for the very different engagement with actually existing power relations). Though I do believe that it is politically significant to situate the revival participants' discussion within a larger critique of liberal values because it outlines possibilities for new forms of political solidarity, I am here especially interested in understanding the important consequences of the women's commitment to this Islamic notion of connectivity for their own investment in social relations, for their accomplishments in social roles, and for the various ways in which they put Islamic disciplines (of self-cultivation) into practice. It is the task of the next two chapters to investigate the precise impact that this commitment had on my interlocutors' day-to-day lives in mainstream society.

5 "A HOUSEWIFE WITH A DIPLOMA?"

Educated Women in the Family and the Workplace

ONE RAINY AFTERNOON in early fall, Aziza and I were sitting together in the cafeteria of the Centre Pompidou in Paris. Aziza generally spent her afternoons in the Centre's library doing her course work, which is why we met either there or in nearby cafés or restaurants. This afternoon, Aziza, as always, dressed in a carefully fashionable style and wearing delicate makeup, told me about her plans to study at the university and possible job options. The daughter of two university graduates, Aziza had grown up in a household where education was a central topic and where she was expected to pursue higher education. Furthermore, as the daughter of two active members of the Tunisian and later the French Islamic revival movement, her awareness of the significance of an academic education for both women and men had always been placed in an Islamic perspective:

> On the subject of knowledge, the search for knowledge, you know, the Arabic cultures where you have quite a lot of this backward mentality, not at all progressive, where you think, well, the woman does not need an education, only the man needs it, since he will work and all that. The woman, pfff, she has to educate the children, so it's not necessary. Again, this contradicts the spirit of Islam. All the *hadith,* all the Qur'anic verses that speak of searching for knowledge, science, and all that, they address themselves to humanity in general. There is no distinction between women and men. I quote, for instance, "search for knowledge from the cradle to the grave." Throughout life you study, you learn,

you pursue this knowledge [*savoir*], this science [*la science*]. And you need to know why, because knowledge is a fundamental duty for every Muslim—man, woman, without distinction. Knowledge is a duty, knowledge is light; this is also a *hadith*. There is another *hadith* which says, "search for knowledge even if it is in China," at a time where you didn't have airplanes, no sophisticated transport, only camels, so to go to China would take months—can you imagine? There are many other *hadith* like that; it's really important. This means that there is really urgency for women to be educated, as a duty toward the family and toward society. So, she really needs to live up to that education. Anyway, this really goes along with another Qur'anic verse which says, *bismillah ar-rahman, ar-rahim*—you might want to help me with that—*Allah la yughayru qawmin hatta yughayru ma-bi-anfusihim*—something like that, [which means] God does not change a people until it changes itself. And this means, how will it change? Through ignorance, through savagery? No, precisely through knowledge, you see? Again, it's always about knowledge, about science, and the woman plays a great role in this. Of course, the woman is not just good for teaching children, even if she is a great teacher. But before she teaches, she needs to educate herself. She has to achieve something herself before she helps those to whom she gives birth. You know, Jeanette, it would be interesting for your research to read the biographies of all these great women from the time of the Prophet and his companions. The wives of the companions, they were also companions themselves; they were *as-sahaba*.

While Aziza was speaking, she spotted a handsome Arab-looking young man at a table on the opposite side of the room. He had been observing her with visible interest. She cast the slightest smile in his direction, then continued:

So, education, for me, is what is most noble. Everything is based on education: education of the self, education of your children, education of society. There are a lot of girls who study, Muslim girls, *hamdulillah,* that's already good, who have an awareness of the value of study. But afterward, OK, they have a master's diploma, but then they do nothing. But we need people to see it through. We need attorneys, we need doctors—well, we have a lot of doctors, *hamdullilah*—but we need researchers, we need university professors, we need journalists. We need them in all domains of life, men as well as women. This is really important. We are a community; how can we talk of strength if we suppress our talents? Studying for three years is great, but the objective is, after having studied, to be useful to society, to the community, you see?

At that point, the young man had finished his coffee and walked over to our table. He greeted us politely with *Salam alaykum,* introduced himself as a Lebanese artist living in France, and handed Aziza his card, saying he would be happy to meet her for a coffee somewhere. She was visibly pleased but replied in a reserved, albeit friendly way that she would call him back, God willing: "insha'Allah." Then, turning her big, expressive eyes back to me, she seamlessly continued talking, without even mentioning the incident, about her ideas on marriage (in connection with career plans), including her support for marriage at a relatively early age and for birth control (especially for young couples).

Aziza's remarks before the young man's intervention touch on two interlinked themes that frame this chapter. First, they reveal the importance that contemporary Islamic discourse in Europe vests in education in general and in women's education in particular. Second, they highlight the significance attributed to the education of women for fulfilling specific roles within family and society. Neither observation is completely new and both find support in existing scholarship on Muslim women in Europe and beyond.[1] However, less attention had been paid to the potential conflict embedded in the twofold definition of women's roles—as service to the family and to the broader society—requiring not only a range of pragmatic negotiations but also, and even more noteworthy, yielding deep moral dilemmas. For the women, who quite often have reached an educational level beyond secondary school, erudite motherhood and a professional career became part of a broad but highly ambivalent ethical project defined by a multifarious web of (gendered) notions of duty, responsibility, and rights, and complicated even more by personal ambition and desire.

Because the idea of education as a duty for women was connected to my interlocutors' understanding of their specific social roles and obligations, we need to expand the scope of our analysis of ethical practice from technologies of the self (or care for the self) to care for others. Ethical work is here understood to be also profoundly ingrained in social interaction, characterized by a strong concern for others, and shaped by a structural and experiential relationality (Lambek 2010; Das 2010; Merlan 2010). It is the idea of ethical work as relational, and as social interaction, that I discuss further in this chapter. For my interlocutors, becoming the ethical subject they aspired to be implied as much a modification of the relation to oneself through self-discipline as it required a certain way of inhabiting social space and of assuming specific roles in that space. This social dimension complicated the ethical project in significant ways. Even if the enactment of a given self-discipline might cause personal conflict, the practice itself was generally not considered to be problematic. However, the women's understanding of their multiple (potentially conflicting) social roles in terms of moral obligations always implied a certain degree of dilemma, negotiation, and compromise.

Seeking Knowledge—"Even in China"

As discussed in Chapter 2, my interlocutors regarded the acquisition of religious knowledge as one of the most crucial preconditions for the development of a pious Islamic self. And as Aziza's statement clearly reflects, the Islamic requirement to search for knowledge was consistently extended into a general duty to learn, whether that learning was concerned with "religious" or "secular" knowledge—a binary that my interlocutors did not necessarily maintain. A typical feature of their discourse was to embrace a universalized understanding of what counts as Islamic knowledge. Many times I heard from the students in the Islamic institutions statements like the following: "Everything is important to learn; you can learn among Muslims and non-Muslims." And "If you invite me to a seminar about ecology, I think this is interesting, because for me, this is Islam, even if you don't call it Islam. I mean, to preserve the earth, this is Islam; to talk about health, it's Islam. It's all interconnected."

Indeed, there has been a proliferation of conferences organized or co-organized by Islamic organizations on the most diverse issues—from the environment to health issues to bioethics—at which (both Muslim and non-Muslim) experts and academics are invited to give presentations along with religious scholars, who explain the relevance of these topics for contemporary Muslims. During the time of my fieldwork in Paris, the Mosquée de la rue de Tanger was a highly popular site among young Muslims for initiating such broad-themed conference series (see, for instance, Amiraux 2011; Bowen 2010). Similar conferences were organized at many other institutes in both countries, and the BFmF's monthly Sunday conferences also reflect that trend.

Such a broadly defined understanding of Islamic knowledge furthermore aims to challenge tendencies within modern Western thought, which constructs religion—in particular the Islamic religion—as opposed to reason and rationality.[2] Enlightenment thought questioned religion's rationality in general, but from the colonial period onward, this discourse increasingly came to focus on Islam. Since the Islamic reform movement that began at the end of the nineteenth century, Muslim thinkers have tried to reject accusations made by Europeans that Islam's irrationality was the principle cause of the economic and scientific backwardness of the Muslim world (Carré 1990).[3] These arguments established the parameters for the contemporary Islamic revival discourse and were equally reflected in the ideas espoused by the women I encountered in the Islamic centers. At the same time, the women's arguments must be embedded in the specific discursive context of France and Germany. Schirin Amir-Moazami (2007: 214) noted in her study on veiled women in the two countries that this emphasis on Islam's compatibility with modern science is a counter-discursive strategy geared toward affecting public opinion, which continues to uphold the idea that Muslim religiosity reflects irrationality and backwardness (Amir-Moazami 2007). During my fieldwork years, this attitude was most famously epitomized by Pope Benedict's controversial lecture at the University of Regensburg in September 2006.[4]

My own interlocutors commonly responded to this discursive context by taking an inverted comparative approach in which Islam's rationality and its favorability toward the sciences, as exemplified in an idealized Islamic "Golden Age," was contrasted to the European Middle Ages, which were assumed to be dominated by a Catholic Church that resisted and delayed scientific discovery. Furthermore, numerous conferences and lectures that took place in the diverse spaces of the revival movement portray knowledge acquisition beyond religious knowledge strictly speaking as an activity conducive to increasing the believer's *iman* (faith). In the words of a young woman whom I met during one of the conferences organized at the cultural center of the Mosquée de la rue de Tanger in Paris:

> When it is said in the Qur'an, "read in the name of your Lord" . . . that does not refer only to Qur'anic and *hadith* knowledge, but to all knowledge. The Christian world was dogmatic at one moment, this is why they are against belief now, because they imposed on them something that they did not want to believe. And well, when Copernicus discovered that the Earth was round, they killed him. . . . In Islam it is different: the more you know, the more you believe, *subhan Allah* [Glory to God], in all the sciences.

According to this line of reasoning, scientific knowledge is credited with enabling believers to better grasp and then contemplate the wonders of divine Creation.

To be sure, my respondents' enthusiasm for knowledge and education should not be disconnected from their own educational trajectories. A large majority of them had had a successful school career and obtained at least a high school diploma; numerous women had pursued studies at professional schools or at the university level. In many instances, they constituted the first generation in their family to have done so. Moreover, in their pursuit of education they often had to overcome many obstacles caused by unfair treatment, discrimination, and the willful effort by teachers to orient them toward vocational tracks. I heard countless anecdotes about these types of struggles. Many of the women also indicated that they had been pushed by their parents to be successful in school and university, even though in many cases their parents had not had access to such education themselves. Even when their parents didn't particularly encourage them, success in their studies filled their parents with pride, because the migration project had been undertaken with the goal of granting their children a better future. All these trajectories indicate that in my interlocutors' environment there was quite often already an awareness of the importance of higher education and a clear desire for upward social mobility; and despite experiences of discrimination within the school system, they acknowledged education as the precondition for achieving success in society.

The valorization of knowledge couched in an Islamic idiom therefore seems to be almost in continuity with the women's own trajectories in the educational institutions of mainstream society. Yet it is equally important to consider those who developed this awareness only after they began frequenting the Islamic centers. I met many women there who had not had a successful school career, who had dropped out of school early on, discouraged by a social environment that did not value education or by a discriminatory school system. For these women, it was precisely their discovery of Islam's exhortation to seek knowledge, as well as the acquisition in the Islamic centers of a certain discipline in regard to reading and learning, that triggered a renewed interest in academic education. Several women I encountered in these centers recounted how they eventually returned to school to get their high school diplomas and in some cases even started university studies.

Therefore, I do not wish to suggest that, because women's appreciation of the importance of education often preceded their turn to revival Islam, their positions on Islam and education were merely derivative of their individual scholarly achievements. Rather, I hope to shed light on the intellectualist character of certain strands of contemporary Islamic revival discourses in Europe, and on the impact that these discourses had on the practitioners' larger life projects. In this respect, it was interesting to observe that often these women did not merely regard their pursuit of higher education as one of the perquisites of life in a Western society, but instead articulated it as a specific Islamic requirement.

In this sense, they attributed a quasi-religious and undoubtedly moral value to "secular" knowledge and education. In opposition to common ideas present in German and most notably in French discourses, in which school and university education are thought to guarantee successful assimilation,[5] my interlocutors often associated their academic education with their pious trajectories. According to them, not only was faith strengthened by knowledge acquisition of all sorts, but instruction and cultivation beyond the strictly religious domain also always fed into the project of pious self-reform, because it provided the believer with the skills to improve herself and to better contemplate the Islamic message. Moreover, beyond its significance for the individual believer, education was considered to constitute, in Islam, a *social* obligation: it enabled women (and men) to assume their various (gendered) social responsibilities.

Educated Mothers

One of the responsibilities that my interlocutors defined as most fundamental for women was child rearing. And as Aziza's earlier statement indicated, in order for that responsibility to be properly fulfilled, women must be educated beforehand. I mentioned previously that literature on women active in the European Islamic revival movements has observed the general acceptance of a somewhat vague notion of a gendered division of labor, which commonly reproduces a certain patriarchal order (Amir-Moazami 2007; Jacobsen 2011; Karakşoğlu-Aydin 2000). Contemporary mainstream Islamic discourse, which my interlocutors progressively appropriated, defines the first "natural" responsibility of women to be motherhood (see, for instance, Dif 2002 and El-Shabassy 1998. Aware of the negative connotations that any such naturalizing discourse provokes among feminist, progressive, and liberal sensibilities alike, my interlocutors sought to preempt such readings by giving additional and explicit value to that gendered task. One of the arguments I encountered frequently in this regard was the idea that the linking of women's nurturing nature to their procreative capacities vested them with one of the most essential of the divine qualities, namely *rahma* (compassion or mercy).[6] It was in this sense, for instance, that Naima, in one of our conversations, defended, against commonly held assumptions, the idea of female sensitivity in connection with maternity:

> She has a different behavior, because of her particularities, her sensitivity, her love, her *rahma*. This is why she has children. . . . this is why Paradise is under the feet of mothers; it's not for nothing, she has *rahma* compared to men, so you can't, it is contradictory to say that the man is superior; that's not it.

According to this conceptualization, men's duty was to earn money to provide for the family while the woman's first duty was to take care of the children.
Men are thus in charge of the family, which is considered their obligation under
the Qur'anic concept of *qiwama* (Dif 2002; El-Shabassy 1998).[7] In this view,
Muslim men and women will have to account on Judgment Day for the ways in
which they have succeeded or failed to accomplish their duties of motherhood
and *qiwama*. Naima continued her reflections:

> Because of her particularities, as I said, in regard to the family, for instance, for
> me, it's true, the man has an obligation to attend to the needs of the family, to
> work, this is his obligation. The woman, her status in the family is to take care of
> the family, as a priority. It is an obligation for her status in the family. . . . these
> are religious duties toward *Allah ta'ala*.

Not only discourses that naturalize gender but also the idea of a gendered
division of labor sit increasingly uneasily with many contemporary sensibilities
(even if such divisions of labor are still widely practiced). Aware of this discomfort, discussions by the pious practitioners about the Islamic gender model
generally already anticipated and invalidated possible critiques of this type of
gender regime, as did Naima's first comment quoted earlier. My interlocutors
also carefully calibrated their articulation of this division so as to preclude
excessively conservative and misogynic interpretations. Salwa, for instance,
when discussing the gendered duties in her "*Tafsir* and *Fiqh*" course, persistently emphasized that maternal duties were much more narrowly defined (and
therefore tied to other rights) than was commonly acknowledged even among
Muslims themselves. During one of these classes, when the topic came up once
again, Salwa replied as follows to a question from a participant:

> The first duty of a mother is to take care of her children, not the household.
> The household is not at all a duty for women. From an Islamic perspective, the
> woman is not obliged to cook, to wash for the man, or to clean for the man. She
> does all that out of generosity, if she wants. In Islam she is not obliged to do so.
> She is only obliged to take care of the education of her children, and this is a
> priority.

One of the most recurrent arguments in these defenses of motherhood as
an Islamic duty is the societal significance attributed to the task of child rearing.
In this perspective, the education of children plays a role in the construction of
both the Muslim community and the larger society. This viewpoint also raised

the question of education in that without it a woman cannot exercise her role effectively. Aziza too highlighted this point during our conversation that afternoon at the Centre Pompidou:

> Again, knowledge and education for women play an important role because she educates. So she has to be already educated, she herself has to succeed first. She educates the whole society, she is a school. . . . She needs to have access to education, to instruction, in order to educate a youth, a people, an entire civilization, you know.

The link between education and maternity is an important trope in contemporary Islamic discourse. The genealogy of this type of reasoning is rather recent, dating back only to the Islamic reform movement of the turn of the twentieth century. Whereas classical Islamic thought has treated the education of children, especially their religious and moral instruction, as part of the father's responsibility, toward the end of the nineteenth century a shift occurred, from the father to the mother, who then became the central figure in the education of children (Najmabadi 1998: 92; Baron 1994: 158–159).[8] This development took place within a broader redefinition of kinship, toward an idealized modern (bourgeois) Muslim family based on a monogamous and companionate relationship between the spouses (Asad 2003).[9] A wealth of literature documents how in many parts of the Muslim world, the nascent press, Islamic reformers, secular intellectuals, and women activists all began to promote a new image of the Muslim woman, for whom motherhood played a central role.

This novel maternalist rhetoric was embedded deeply in an emerging nationalist discourse.[10] The demands of nation building in countries that struggled against colonial rule made it imperative for the entire population to participate in the service of the future independent nation. For women, this task was henceforth defined in relation to their religious and national duty to become the mothers and educators of the future generations of the nation. Endorsing the idea that Muslim countries were developmentally (intellectually, economically, politically, and so on) inferior compared to the imperialist West, some reformers even identified the "ignorance" of mothers as the principle cause of this situation (Shakry 1998). They assumed that if mothers were instructed, they could better educate the new generations of sons who were needed to build a strong nation (Badran 1995; Najmabadi 1998; Shakry 1998). The stress on the educative role of mothers delineated and constructed a new autonomous domestic sphere. At the same time, however, the connection of maternity with national progress gave this domestic sphere a primordial social weight that blurred the boundaries of the private. The reformers proposed a number of measures to fulfill their project, most notably the establishment of new institutions designed to educate women.

Since that time, emphasis on the pivotal and "sacred" role of the educated woman in society has been a central feature in Arab nationalist as well as Islamic discourses. A pamphlet published by the Organization of the Muslim Brotherhood on the role of Muslim women in an Islamic society, for instance, reveals significant similarities with Aziza's last statement. It bolsters the idea of the family as the kernel of society, the primary provider of love, bonding, and affection, but also the ultimate source for building social cohesion on a national level: "Women make up half of society and they are responsible for the nurturing, guidance and reformation of the subsequent generations of men and women. It is the female who imbues principles and faith into the souls of the nation" (Muslim Brotherhood, 1994: 3) The same credo can also be found in the abundant literature on the status of Muslim women that is available in Islamic libraries all over Europe and often discussed during conferences on the subject.

I do not wish merely to state the similarities between reformist and global revival discourses (inherited by many Islamic institutions in Europe) and the discourse of my interlocutors. What is more interesting to me in this context is how my respondents made sense of but also reconfigured this maternalist discourse in light of their own life experiences and the social contexts in which they lived. If they assigned women as mothers a primary role in educating the next generation, they did so with awareness of their own minority condition. On the one hand, they saw this issue as a matter of cultural survival. Given their desire to transmit an Islamic lifestyle to their children, they posited that a thoroughly religious education in the family home, provided in particular by the (religiously knowledgeable) mother, was the only guarantee of the successful education of a new generation of European Muslims thoroughly rooted in their faith. On the other hand, in the context of their status as a racialized and economically disadvantaged group, they attributed a crucial role to the "educated mother" (educated in "secular" knowledge) in promoting their children's upward social mobility.[11]

This idea becomes most salient in view of women's own childhood memories of school. To recall, most of my interlocutors were from a working class background and their parents had little or no access to education and often did not have a fluent command of the national language, whether French or German. Consequently, they were not able to help their children with their scholarship, nor could they, when needed, interact with the teachers and defend their children's interests, such as when, for instance, the children had to choose their specializations or weigh their options for secondary education. As school children, these women depended largely on the goodwill of their teachers to acquaint them with the school system in a way that corresponded to their intellectual capabilities. They expressed that they often felt undervalued and discriminated against, which they related in abundant stories about their school years. These experiences shed new light on my interlocutors' pronounced understanding of the urgency of closely accompanying their children throughout their years of schooling, and of monitoring, guiding, and promoting their children's school careers. Olfa, a mother of three children, explained this to me one afternoon at CERSI during a conversation we had about the French school system and its weaknesses:

> I have a pretty critical view of the educational system in France, which is very discriminatory. Yesterday I heard a program on the radio and they were talking about the "French ghetto" showing that social mobility does not work anymore, the social escalator does not work anymore. And in any case, the first educators are the parents, so I don't see what I gain in terms of self-fulfillment if my children do not succeed. For me, their success is my priority. I know that, growing up in a *cité* [housing project], I suffered; I don't want my kids to live the same fate. So, I live in a rich neighborhood, the opposite of my childhood. I am very much invested in their schooling; I am involved in the parent-teacher associations. I am constantly in touch with the teachers. So, *hamdulillah,* the results are there. My kids are very good in school, not only in terms of conduct but also in terms of learning, and for me this is my priority.

Indeed, the mothers among my respondents were often very invested in supervising their children's homework, providing them with books, reading with them, and at times overseeing their practice of musical instruments. All that attention reflected a clear will to promote the social mobility of their children and to offer them a typical upper-middle-class environment. Furthermore, the mothers were equally devoted to nurturing close relations with their children's teachers. Like Olfa, they were frequently active in the parent-teacher association. They used their social, cultural, and linguistic skills to guarantee a position for their children in the school system, so that from the outset they would flourish. And here again I listened to numerous anecdotes from these mothers, about their struggles to contest a given teacher's unjustly negative evaluation of their child, which in their reading clearly reflected racial prejudice. In this sense, the maternalist discourse put forth by my interlocutors required their clear investment in the semipublic spheres of public institutions (in particular the school) through the exercise of specific representative functions, in order to combat stereotypes on behalf of their children. In the context of a decreasing faith in a state that would provide equal access to social and economic security to disadvantaged racialized minorities, a discourse that emphasizes the responsibility of the private realm, embodied by the mother-subject, seemed to make more sense than ever to these women.[12]

The Professional Muslim Woman:
Personal Aspiration and Social Utility

Even while reproducing a markedly maternalist discourse, a large majority of my interlocutors made strong statements about their desire to work, just as Aziza had. After all, they claimed, they didn't complete their university or professional studies to become "merely" knowledgeable mothers. Comments like "A housewife with diploma? No thanks" and "I didn't study in order to just do nothing" were extremely widespread. These women insisted regularly that the Islamic understanding of gendered responsibilities did not require them to abandon their professional objectives. As other studies have confirmed, everyone I talked to rejected as a complete misreading of the sacred texts the claim that the primacy of maternal duties would (or should) confine women to domesticity. According to their perspective, the Islamic division of labor encompassed a broad framework of religious duties that nevertheless allowed for a wide range of individual choices and preferences.[13] According to this logic, they generally defended the man's responsibility to support the family as an additional freedom for women, because ideally it allowed her to choose a profession out of interest and not merely out of economic necessity. This is what Rim, one of the teachers in the adult instruction program at the BFmF, explained to me during a coffee break at the center's cafeteria:

> There is a division of tasks; no, not a classical division of tasks as people here would imagine it, oh, the woman at home, etc. No, the positive thing is that the woman can choose; she can say, do I want to be a career woman or do I want to stay home and look after my children? There are women who do not want to be good at school, who say, I want to be a housewife, I want to make my husband

happy, I want to have kids; and there are women who say no, it's not enough for me, I need something else, etc. And that's the advantage in Islam: it does not prescribe anything to the wife; it leaves her several possibilities, and the option is there. . . . Of course you can abuse these things, but only if you misunderstand.

A similar position was articulated by Salwa in her class, just after she defined the woman's duties regarding motherhood:

The woman is not obliged to maintain anyone; she does not need to pay alimony. All the money that I earn is my money, and my husband is obliged to provide for me. No matter how much I earn, he cannot claim that, because it is his obligation. Most of the time, of course, this doesn't have much to do with everyday life, but one should take it like a security.

The women I interviewed, who more often than not had experienced difficult financial conditions during their childhoods, were clearly aware that in many instances employment for women is a harsh economic necessity. In line with the Islamic principle of *darura* (necessity), this obligation was taken as self-evident and did not require much debate. However, interestingly, discussions about the compatibility of women's professional aspirations with an Islamic ethical framework generally departed from the assumption of a condition of financial stability within the functioning (bourgeois) nuclear family. Arguments employed to defend the idea of women's work were twofold: they focused on rights and duties, and they always insisted on the interdependency of these two domains. When women invoked their "Islamic right" to work, they generally did so by referring to "authentic" Islam, and therefore to the example of the first *umma,* the Muslim community during the time of the Prophet.[14] This is what Naima highlighted during one of our many conversations at the Mosquée de Paris:

If you observe people, and from there you assume that this is Islam—the Afghan, the Taliban—they beat the women, and they prevent them from getting an education. How is this possible? The wives of the Prophet, *salla Allahu alayhi wa sallam* [May God honor him and grant him peace], they gave courses to men, they taught men; they were working. You have nurses *fi l-jihad:* they treated the wounded; there were teachers . . . and now there are some men who call themselves Muslims who say no, the woman must not work, we will hide her.

Women's "Islamic right to work" was frequently invoked along with complaints about potential marriage candidates who espoused erroneous "traditionalist" views. Numerous women related to me, often with a great sense of humor, stories illustrating this type of fruitless encounters. They were unanimous in their view that these candidates should be rejected immediately, even if they still tried to convince them [the candidates] that their understandings were erroneous. Like many others, Hanan had made several of these encounters, and even though she considered stopping or reducing her professional activity temporarily for the sake of her future children, any request from a suitor that she stop working after marriage would provoke her ire:

> There was this guy who told me, I don't want my wife to work because after work she will go out with her colleagues to have coffee with them. . . . Yes, I told you already about that one [*laughter*]. You see, you have a place which is assigned by God and, yes, you have obligations, of course, but you also have rights. When God accords you a right, it's your right. We have rights, but we still have to beg for them. I don't understand this; I don't understand why I should ask a man for my right, which has already been given to me: the right to work, the right to have your own money.

When, however, my interlocutors spoke of professional careers in terms of *duty*, they stressed most persistently their responsibility toward the community and the "social utility" aspect of work. Naima, in the course of our conversation, elaborated on this point in ways similar to Aziza's earlier comments:

> Of course it is an obligation for her, her status within the family, as I told you last time. But if she has time, she also has a responsibility in respect to the community. She has to offer her services to the community. Once she applies her religious duties toward *Allah ta'ala,* . . . her duties toward the family are also religious duties—then she has all the freedom to pursue other interests. So, it's important that women continue their studies and . . . specialize in certain disciplines. For instance, I am a nurse; we need people in this domain. We also need women in psychology, psychotherapy, teachers, doctors. We have to encourage young women and men to specialize in certain disciplines to respond to the needs of the community. There is this *hadith:* The best among you is the one who is most useful to the community.

Naima's statement weaves together in interesting ways the two familiar claims, that is, the idea of women's work as a right (or freedom) and as a duty. She begins by ranking maternal duties as "sacred," and situating work, which does not have equal merit, as a possible option. But then, somewhat belatedly, she connects this option (or right) to another duty: that of utility to the community. By invoking a *hadith* about the worth of being useful to society, she reevaluates work, linking it also to the struggle to live piously. I have heard this kind of argumentative scheme several times. If women's work was not in essence defined as part of the duty to utility, it became so contextually, in a social context where the community was understood to need women's professional skills as an additional resource.

Although revival discourses in Muslim majority contexts have taken up the question of women's work outside the home only marginally, and even then in an ambivalent or outright critical manner (see McLarney 2015), this discussion suggests that most of my interlocutors did accord this matter a more central place. For many of these women, professional work was connected to their commitment to social utility. Furthermore, this commitment corresponded to the general stress that the European revival circles placed on the individual's responsibility within the mainstream society. In France this was done by invoking the value of citizenship, whereas in the German circles, being "a part of society," and therefore "responsible," was not immediately connected to the question of citizenship, even though many women talked about the significance of citizenship.[15]

Yet it was especially in France that countless conferences were organized on the topic of citizenship and Islam. During a talk on this theme at the Annual Meetings of Muslims in France in Bourget in May 2006, for instance, the popular French-Moroccan preacher Hassan Iquioussen called on young Muslim men and women to pursue education and choose socially useful professional occupations. This, he claimed, was not only their duty as citizens, but also amounted to a religious duty for French Muslim citizens. He thereby coined the term *spiritualité sociale*, "social spirituality."[16] Notwithstanding significant differences, the notion of spirituality transferred to the professional world is reminiscent of the work ethos discussed by Max Weber ([1930] 1996), in which profession (*Beruf*) becomes vocation (*Berufung*)—an activity in the service of God that must also serve society.

According to this line of thought, my interlocutors considered women's access to higher education to be an "important resource for society." Not to make use of their skills and talents would be a "waste" of human resources; this was the main argument employed to emphasize the "Islamic right and duty" to work. It amounted to a "*jihad* [effort] in the path of God," according to Assia, a young dentist who had just opened her own practice in one of the many *cités* north of Paris. This young, unmarried woman was celebrated among her friends as a success story for professional Muslim women who wear the hijab. Even if *social utility* was defined in relation to society at large, my respondents most often explained this obligation with explicit reference to the local Muslim community, perceived as marginalized and in large segments impoverished, and therefore most urgently needing support.

Along with insisting on "socially useful" professions, conferences and courses offered by the Islamic associations commonly encouraged Muslims to avoid "morally questionable" professions. This category of employment referred but was not limited to activities that would contradict Islamic morals (such as conduct involving immoral gender relations in close proximity to forbidden activities such as alcohol consumption). Such concern was frequently related to employment in the corporate world, which was mistrusted by many pious practitioners because of its ruthless capitalism and exaggerated materialism. I heard several stories from women (especially in France) who had worked in this domain but, in the course of their religious trajectory, preferred to leave a world they had progressively come to view as immoral. Olfa's memories of her previous career crystallize these concerns:

> In my job as a commercial consultant in a credit institute, I saw brutality, I saw how people were destroyed. I saw it without even having preconceptions about the materialist society. I saw this with an attentive eye. I saw how we sold credit to poor people. When they couldn't pay, we treated them like less than nothing. . . . At the age of twenty-four, I realized that, OK, I knew how to do finance, I knew how to draw up a marketing plan, accounting, but I didn't know the meaning of my own life.

Disillusioned by the financial world, Olfa took her maternity leave after the birth of her second child as the occasion to quit her job definitively. For her, this traumatizing experience of work drove home the importance of operating in an ethical profession, a lesson that she frequently emphasized in her classes. Anything else, she insisted, was destructive not only to one's character, but also to one's *iman*.

A preference for "useful" professions often went in tandem with the voluntary work that many of my interviewees had already done, from their teenage years onward, in charity associations, in after-school structures to help younger students with their homework, and in associations that provided literacy classes for migrants. Moreover, all these activities familiarized them with the range of social problems that haunt the Muslim community, as well as other minority groups. This awareness generally coaxed them to extend their concern to other impoverished migrant communities. It was their practical knowledge and experience of the precarious conditions of these communities that so strongly subtended their reasoning in framing their career plans in terms of "social utility." Many women I spoke with expressed their concern for the socioeconomic problems that affected this category of the population. It therefore comes as no surprise that many of them worked or aspired to work in social services geared to these communities. The "useful" professions that my interlocutors spoke of were thus usually situated in the social, educative, and medical fields.[17] Lamia's still rather vague career plans clearly followed this approach:

> You know, for me, working means working on my faith. The ideal would be to work in the social sector because, for me, working in the social sector amounts to lifting my faith, advancing toward Allah. I would love to work in an institution geared toward youth, or toward [disadvantaged] neighborhoods [les quartiers], to educate. . . . Thereby, I could build up a lot of things, give people back an ethics, a meaning to their lives, because so many youngsters are lost, don't have meaning in their lives anymore, no hope. I don't have real career ambition, I just want to do something humane. I would not like to work for the sake of working, but to work to transmit the message, without talking about Islam at all. Because for me, if I talk to youngsters, I can talk about Islam without talking about Islam, you know what I mean? Just teaching them ethics, good manners, to motivate them.

Lamia's reflections are important for understanding how many of my interlocutors defined female work: as an activity "in the service of God" or as a "social spirituality," it is not primarily connected to wage labor, and especially not to the accumulation of wealth, but it constitutes another domain, where Islamic virtues could be exercised and taught (see also Deeb 2006).

In numerous classes and conferences, women were encouraged to pursue careers in the social domain, also because such careers corresponded to the idea of women's "caretaking nature," a theme prevalent in the discourse of the revival circles.[18] Malika Dif, for instance, a French convert and one of the most important female figures in the Islamic revival scene in France, promoted such an understanding in several talks I happened to attend.[19] The mobilization of women's maternal qualities in the service of society carries interesting similarities to what Pnina Werbner (1999) has called "political motherhood," a concept that seeks to fortify the maternalist discourse discussed here with a stronger social and political activism.[20] *Political motherhood* is a useful term for identifying some common threads in different strands of "first-wave feminism" beyond that of the West. The notion also aptly teases out several of the concerns that my interlocutors advanced in this respect. However, my aim here is not to postulate that these women merely reflect an older trend of feminist activism (thereby situating them at an earlier stage within a linear progressive history of feminism). Their various arguments and modes of reasoning were crucially embedded in a larger economy of rights and duties within an overarching concern for living a life pleasing to God, but they were also informed by and responding to a number of discourses and social realities that cannot be neatly subsumed into that timeline.[21]

Yet the idea of "socially useful work" was not always linked to specific professional (gendered) domains. Whenever my interlocutors laid stress on the omnipresent question of *representation,* the specific field became secondary. Any professional activity with a certain level of qualification was suitable to present the Muslim woman in a valorizing way, as a role model to other female members of her own community and as something akin to an ambassador for her community within the larger society. A statement by a young student of biochemistry in France was typical of this line of argument:

> I don't just want to study for nothing, I want to work. But my goal is not simply to earn money, but to have a place in society *as* a Muslim woman. And also, you know, I want to be active in society so that other Muslims will follow me. This is very important. Because, here [in France] it's not really the Muslims who study hard. So, it's really also to motivate others. This is my objective.

Pursuing higher education was clearly valorized, similarly to this woman's logic, within the circles I attended, as an important means to contribute to uplifting the community. Promoting upward social mobility for the community as a whole was not only considered a crucial objective given the precarious social status of many of its members, but was also viewed as one of the preconditions for improving the community's image in mainstream society. Following this second logic, many women also located the usefulness of their professional objectives in how they would positively represent Muslims in general and Muslim women in particular. Aziza summed up this point succinctly during our conversation at the Centre Pompidou, quoted early in this chapter. She hoped for the emergence of an elite class within the Muslim community, not only to help the community escape its marginalized status, but also to empower it to define its own "image" through voices that take part and become audible in the public debate.

Several respondents were influenced in their professional choices by this type of consideration. As journalists, lawyers, and university professors, they wanted to use their voices to defend their religion and community, which they perceived to be subjected to caricatures and unjustly negative depictions by the media and public discourse (see also Chapter 6). Most of the women I talked to, whether they worked in these "discourse-making" professions or were simply present in skilled employment, regarded the workplace as a central arena for counteracting negative stereotypes of Muslim women that they felt were *prevalent* in French and German society. Take, for instance, Ilknur, a German-Turkish woman in her early thirties and a regular attendee of the BFmF classes, who was preparing to take her final exams for a law degree when I met her and who, by the end of my fieldwork, had established her own law firm. As one of the few veiled lawyers in Germany, she was highly aware of the symbolic value of her position. And though motherhood had decreased her passion for her job, she considered it important to continue, for precisely this reason—which was not unalloyed with a very personal pride:

> If I still want to work, it is for my ego. And of course because you are responsible as a Muslim woman to make something out of yourself, so that society looks at you accordingly. In this sense, it is a highly symbolic thing for me, to show that there are Muslim women who have achieved something.

Like Ilknur, the daughters of mostly unskilled immigrant workers hoped to pursue higher education and skilled professional training in order to escape the fatality of social reproduction.[22] Highly aware of how class, culture, gender, and race converge in common assumptions about the status of (veiled) Muslim women (imagined as either housewives or cleaners), most of the women I talked to seemed very eager to carry the "burden of representation" (Mercer 1990). The simple act of working, of maintaining a visible presence in key fields of the public sphere, such as the professional world, was identified as a contestatory practice. Statements like "I wanted to say: here I am, a Muslim woman, independent, and I can be anything I want" revealed how group identity and personal identity converge. Embodying the success of "Muslim women" collectively thus also becomes a personal success. It is for this reason that the women I talked with often experienced this representative work as "self-fulfillment."

Hence, collective concerns and personal aspirations were articulated in intrinsically interconnected ways.

The deployment of *da'wa* in this particular effort to improve public perceptions of Islam indicates one of the important shifts that this term has undergone in the context of the European diaspora. When the pursuit of socially valorized professional careers was articulated as *representational da'wa*, not only professional excellence and discursive skills were required, but so was the adoption of a commendable demeanor in everyday conduct. Thus, it was generally insisted that especially those who were visibly marked as Muslims, such as women wearing hijab, needed to adopt an exemplary attitude in their professional environment and in their daily face-to-face engagements with the non-Muslim Other. To be polite, punctual, and helpful were the qualities required, because every movement, every word—when issued from a minority body—potentially attains representative status. And everyone acknowledged that such a comportment necessitated continual and arduous work on the self. Naima invoked the difficulties that this representational burden entails in day-to-day life as a nurse:

> I work essentially with non-Muslims. I tell myself every day before going out, if *Allah ta'ala* has brought me there, it means that there is a reason. Our duty as Muslims is to bear a message. And, well, today, I tell myself, I have a duty toward *da'wa*, without saying proselytism and all that, or that I'm going to talk about *din*—no, not at all. I'm there, I have to conduct myself in a certain way; this includes work upon my *nafs*. If I feel like getting furious—and it's true, this happens on a daily base: aggressive people, people who complain, who yell at me because I come in late—I assure you, I want to talk back.

Similar to other ethical practices, representational *da'wa* (which, as Naima pointed out, must be clearly distinguished from proselytism) requires self-discipline, involving mastery over one's passions and the cultivation of specific qualities, such as punctuality and professionalism, but also patience, composure, and empathy.

The strong sense of duty that these arguments display when the question of female work is invoked does not obliterate the fact that many women just simply have a strong *personal* desire to work. And part of this desire is expressed as the need for "self-actualization." In this context, the term *self-actualization* is very much a tribute to modern ideals of authenticity (Taylor 1991). In spite of how they valorized their occupation as (potential) mothers by calling it "the most gracious work," many of my interlocutors equally acknowledged that motherhood alone was not likely to give them a sense of having "achieved their full potential." Statements like "if you have a [professional] occupation, you give yourself self-esteem" or "it's not just for the money but for self-fulfillment; you do something that is for yourself" were typical and clearly reflect their individual aspirations. But interestingly, this very personal project of "self-fulfillment" was never considered fully sufficient in itself. Again, it had to be embedded in a larger moral justification that transcends the scope of the individual. In my respondents' estimation, then, self-fulfillment also became a prerequisite for better accomplishing their responsibilities toward their family. In Naima's words, "Someone who just stays at home becomes frustrated, and well, you need to invest yourself elsewhere. And then it's something positive for the community, for the woman herself, and for her married life."

This "frustration" was precisely what happened to some of my interlocutors, who at some point during my fieldwork were full-time mothers, not only because they had young children, but also due to the difficulty of finding work wearing the hijab (see Chapter 6). Maissa's story elucidates that point. Recall her religious trajectory from the previous chapter, which brought about a significant change in her lifestyle. During a long conversation at her home, she admitted that she found her status as a stay-at-home mom depressing at times (which is why, she said while pointing remorsefully to the cigarette in her hand, she had fallen back on her former habit of smoking):

> I didn't grow up in this kind of atmosphere, always staying at home, only taking care of the kids, the house, and all that. So this is really hard for me, and he [her husband] sees that; he would also prefer that I work, so that I get out of this depression and so that I can develop myself again.

For many women, then, being circumscribed to the domestic space was seen as an impediment to their personal growth. In their eyes, the full development of one's character could take place only through professional participation in public life.

I have pointed out repeatedly, in line with recent literature on Muslim subjectivities in Europe, that the ideals of freedom, autonomy, and self-realization have informed the reasoning and desires of these young pious Muslims, which in turn affects the ways in which pious practitioners rearticulate the Islamic traditions to which they adhere. In this context, however, it is not sufficient merely to identify these "secular" desires in Muslim discourses of piety. Instead, the ethical consequences and implications for these practitioners must be examined. Women like Ilknur, Rim, Naima, or Maissa were quite aware of the influence that modern ideals wielded over their personal ambitions and desires. But because they also wished to lead ethical lives, as defined by a certain Islamic ethos, modern notions such as "self-fulfillment" needed to be reordered so that they could become part of their ethical life-plan. Only if these goods were reasonably inscribed into the larger ethical project could they become legitimate and justifiable. Thus, I abstain from considering the religious or moral renderings of these desires as mere justificatory techniques to cover up or legitimize their "true" desires. If one takes these modes of ethical reasoning seriously, one realizes that the larger ethical project is not simply challenged or contradicted by (potentially conflicting) desires but rendered more complicated and complex, and may potentially even be nourished by these divergent desires. I substantiate this argument in the remainder of this chapter.

Negotiating Divergent Commitments of Care

In this chapter, I have outlined two distinct argumentative strands advanced by the female participants in the revival circles to argue in favor of women's work. Especially noteworthy here is how my interlocutors delineated these different roles within a distinct "ethics of care": care for the family, for the Muslim community, for impoverished migrant communities, and for society at large.[23] Once we acknowledge that practices of care form a crucial ethical realm for these women, we can also grasp more fully the moral dilemmas provoked when conflicting commitments emerge within this realm. By defining women's social obligations in terms of motherhood and professional career, my interlocutors were confronted with a set of demands that are potentially contradictory. Indeed, the educative duty of the mother, as most of the women conceived it, requires an important presence at home, whereas a professional career most often demands precisely the opposite. The ideal of a mother passionately dedicated to the education of her children complicated the idea of professional activity ("if I still have time left"). It was therefore not surprising that, when discussing employment and motherhood together, my interlocutors often articulated a strong critique of working mothers' full dependence on child-care facilities while their children were still very young.

It is noteworthy to observe the distinct ways in which my respondents in Germany and France situated their views on motherhood and child-care services in relation to the practices of the mainstream society. For the women in France, their understanding of motherhood became another argumentative strand by which they distinguished themselves from French (or Western) society. Public day-care facilities in France are much more developed than those in Germany, which is why the practice of placing children in these structures from the age of four months is more generalized in France. My French interlocutors often interpreted this practice as a consequence of excessive individualism, which for them was causally connected to a unilateral emphasis on rights (see Chapter 4). This is what Lamia and Hanan had to say about the issue:

> Lamia: I don't see myself working and dumping my infant at 7:00 a.m. at X so that I can go to work.
>
> Hanan: This issue of equality, I see today, women work thirty-five hours like men, they do everything like men, and what you see then is that the family is breaking up. Actually, equality between the sexes is more about an individualist politics; women are playing on their rights and forget that they also have duties. Men do as well, but here, in this context, concerning the education of children, it is primarily the women who leave them, who say, I want to work, I want to go out with my friends. Of course you can; I also want to work and go out with my friends, but not in such a selfish manner, not for my own pleasure while leaving the children behind.

Compare this to the attitude taken by my respondents in Germany. Although they too emphasized the desire to care for their young children, this task was generally not embedded in a logic of distinction. Barbara Vinken (2001), who has studied the development of German discourses on motherhood, suggests that in contemporary Germany, in contrast to neighboring countries, motherhood is much more strongly defined as a priority for women.[24] This definition has also been inscribed in the nation's family politics, that is, in the absence of adequate child-care structures. Although Vinken is highly critical of this discourse, it nevertheless resonated with my respondents' arguments, which might explain why the women I encountered in Germany often defended their ideas by stressing perceived similarities with their non-Muslim peers. They thus understood motherhood as a reality they shared with other German women. Sevim had not yet fulfilled her desire to have children, but she clearly emphasized this understanding:

> Here there are also German women who say, if I have a child, I want my husband to work, and these are modern women. . . . We also pretend that we want to be modern and equal in rights, but at the end of the day, if we have a child,

we want our peace and we want financial security. . . . Look at Steffi Graf: she
has become a housewife. And no one tells her, you are behind your husband; to
Muslim women they have to say it, because for them, it's proof.

In the final analysis, does the care-giving function of mothers leave any
time to commit to socially useful professional work? I indeed encountered
considerable tension and unresolved questions regarding this question. One
of the ways in which I gauged these very ambiguous positions was through my
own maternity, which happened over the course of my fieldwork. My preg-
nancy at an early stage of the research turned out to be a large advantage, because my interlocutors were eager to be supportive; and in my new position as
a mother, I felt my status rise in the eyes of these women. Their benevolent attitude did not decrease much once my one-year old son started day care. I had
to field a flurry of (skeptical and critical) inquiries about my decision to make
(full-time) use of a public day-care structure, about how I would juggle the
"double burden" of career and child care, and especially about how I would
make it up to my son after our daily separation, but my responses seemed to
satisfy them fairly often. In fact, I regularly got approval (especially from my
younger interlocutors) for apparently managing to handle motherhood while
doing academic research that investigates Muslim women's lives (which was
perceived as a much more noble activity than any merely moneymaking profession). And when they introduced me to acquaintances from their circles,
these introductions frequently highlighted my commendable "double" career.
The many discussions I had about my maternity and professional ambitions
were highly revelatory of the women's own very conflicting ambitions, desires,
and anxieties concerning their different possible roles in society.

A moment that dramatically revealed the sometimes irresolvable tensions
that surrounded this contentious question emerged during one of the Saturday
women's brunches at CERSI in St. Denis. As always, Olfa had designated a specific topic to address that day; this time, it was the issue of stay-at-home versus
working mother. Recall that, regardless of the fact that she taught at CERSI
on the weekends and did other volunteer work, Olfa identified as a full-time
mother dedicated to the education of her children. In this meeting, she criticized a trend that she observed among many of the practicing Muslim women
around her, whom she accused of trying to emulate Western ideals of female
emancipation. She mentioned that these women closely connected the pursuit
of a professional career to the notion of "self-fulfillment." Although she did
not question the pursuit of a professional career for women without children,

nor for women who worked out of financial necessity, she took issue with the very idea of wage work as the ultimate locus of self-fulfillment. Such a conception would often motivate women to pursue their careers without interruption, even after they became mothers. In conformity with widespread Islamic revival narratives about the authentic Muslim family and their critique of "working mothers," Olfa conjured a bleak picture of the "burden" of working outside the home, a burden in which the mother was torn between career and children and constantly overworked, and in which the children were neglected.[25] At this meeting, she wanted to take the opportunity to initiate a new self-understanding of the pious, modern, (and implicitly bourgeois) Muslim mother. Her exposé, as well as the answer it elicited, reveals how much the effort to find a proper contemporary definition of Islamic womanhood was connected to an ongoing and unresolved debate within the revival circles about what constitutes authentic (yet modern) Islamic principles and comportment:[26]

> We are educated women, intelligent, but we are proud to be *only* mothers, without any complex toward other professional women. Why can't we tell them, yes, we are 100 percent mothers and housewives and maintained by our husbands— so what? We must create our own ideal, our own model, and change the way this model is perceived.

Olfa's position, which was clearly the minority view in the room, met with vivid and passionate opposition. Many women started to talk at the same time, throwing the discussion into momentary chaos. Olfa's severe critique of working mothers was not easily digested by the participants. When everyone calmed down, those who opposed Olfa spoke in turn. One young woman was visibly upset by Olfa's judgment:

> I am really disappointed to hear this, especially from you. You, who always encourages us to study, to choose careers that are useful for society, and to be strong Muslim women. We have so many difficulties with traditionalist Muslim men, who always throw a wrench into the wheel. And now you're doing it too!

Another woman spoke more calmly. She recognized the importance of being there for her children, and she also recognized that it was not always easy to reconcile her maternal duties with her professional requirements. And whereas for her, a divorced mother, working was not a choice but a necessity, she nevertheless insisted, similarly to the arguments spelled out in the previous section of this chapter, on the significance of Muslim women's contributions in

traditional role (handwritten marginal note)

the professional sphere, especially in terms of representation and social utility. She gave some concrete examples of what she had accomplished through her work at a center that helped migrant women receive professional training, but also recounted in detail how her presence, as the only Muslim employee in the workplace (where her colleagues were mainly *français de souche,* that is, native French) had opened up a space for interfaith dialogue with them. Although Olfa did not want to diminish the good intentions and achievements of these working women, in her response she remained nonetheless skeptical toward the idea of representing Muslim women through professional work:

> We have fallen into the trap of trying to counteract stereotypes against us by complying with Western standards of what is "modern." But I suggest that we have to establish our own standards of modernity. And I think that this is more authentically Islamic, because it permits the Muslim woman to fully accomplish her sacred duties. And I'm not asking you to just sit at home; on the contrary. I want you to be useful to society. I rarely ever sit at home when my children are in school. I am very active, in parent-teacher associations; I do volunteer work in various associations, but I have the flexibility to make decisions regarding my own time, and I am not under threat of losing my position because I spend too much time with my kids.

Olfa fretted over Muslim women's imitation of Western ideals in a way akin to the arguments prevalent in Islamic revival literature. And she wanted, similarly to other contemporary feminine voices of the Islamic revival, to free Muslim women from the inferiority complex induced by Western ideals of female emancipation through employment.[27] Accordingly, she criticized the "persistent glorification of work" (promoted not only by both Rightist and Leftist political orientations, but also by second-wave liberal feminism), which assumes that work is "an essential source of individual growth, self-worth, and social status" (Weeks 2009). For Olfa, this critique, in conformity with dominant revival discourses, led to a revalorization of the traditional family model, which reversed, however, the logic of dominant capitalist valorization processes: here women's affective and caring labor was posited as (ethically) superior to but also more personally rewarding than paid work (see also McLarney 2015). At the same time, Olfa acknowledged that (unpaid) volunteer work was a strategy to escape the rigidity of work rhythms and to better control one's personal time, thereby making space for family and sociability. Her insistence that unpaid volunteer social work was fully equivalent to "useful work" does not merely reflect a (neoliberal) citizens' ethos that valorizes volunteer activism; rather, it is also very much informed by the concrete recognition of the importance of voluntary work within diasporic communities that are structurally neglected and disadvantaged within the state.[28]

In spite of Olfa's proximity to mainstream revival narratives and arguments, many women remained unconvinced, and the discussion was followed by moments of uncomfortable silence before someone eventually brought up a less contentious topic. I found this debate illuminating in various regards. To begin with, the unease triggered by that discussion powerfully reveals how an Islamic discourse developed in and geared toward conditions in the majority society (where opposing models of development vie with each other) does not necessarily succeed in responding fully to the needs and aspirations of pious practitioners in the diaspora. For many women present, it seemed neither easy nor desirable to merely throw off the "burden of representation" and develop a model of self-presentation that does not immediately seek to counter and dispel common (mis)representations of Muslim women and their capacities. The exchange just presented therefore also points to the ambivalences and ambiguities that inhere the struggles of the Islamic revival movement in Europe to make ethical sense of new and conflicting perceptions, sensibilities, and ideals that have become so persistent among its participants. In such a context, Asad (1993) reminds us, "discursive coherence" becomes increasingly difficult to maintain.[29] Finally, the open and challenging way in which the participants responded to Olfa reflected the mode of deliberation that characterized the Islamic institutions where I performed my research. As mentioned in Chapter 2, the exchanges that took place there did not follow traditional standards of respect toward religious teachers but commonly unfolded instead as open, unstructured, highly informal, democratic conversations. The teacher was respected for her or his knowledge, yet did not place her- or himself among the authoritative religious scholars. This is why the women did not hesitate to challenge Olfa's statement, or at least to claim space for alternative interpretations.[30]

Regardless of how intense these controversies may appear, they are nonetheless provoked by a *shared* ambition to participate in a "common moral project" (Hirschkind 2006: 110) embedded in an Islamic framework. This moral project posed concrete practical questions about how to decide what was the right thing to do in the face of competing and potentially opposing moral commitments. How should one act within this only roughly and often ambiguously delineated moral space that is heir to a complex history of Islamic traditions that have successively been reread in contexts of colonialism, modernization, neoliberal politics, and diasporic conditions? What priorities should be established?

The modes of reasoning enacted by my interlocutors in their efforts to maintain that rather delicate balance between competing moral commitments, all of which were considered consequential for an ethically fulfilled life, invite us to revisit Aristotle's notion of *phronesis*. As explained in the introductory chapter, *phronesis* is a mode of ethical action (*praxis*) based on the disposition to do the right thing when a conflict presents itself. This concept, as Michael Lambek (2002b) elaborates, does not posit an antagonistic relationship between the instrumental or the interested and the high-minded or disinterested, but rather strikes a balance among these domains. It also refuses to draw any rigid distinction between materialist and idealist conceptions of truth and falsehood, action and passion, freedom and necessity (2002b: 16). As Lambek (2002a: 36) claims, "To argue that people are political, desirous or ambivalent subjects does not preclude them from being moral subjects, living virtuously or seeking the means by which they do so." *Phronesis* can help us to grapple with the intricacies of daily life, with conflict, ambiguity, and inconsistency; at the same time, it forces us to acknowledge that these conflicts do not necessarily jeopardize the attempt to live one's life according to a specific moral project and its (ethical) ideals, but are very much a part of any such attempt. And significantly, it requires from those who study religiously minded people, like the participants in the Islamic revival movements in Europe, to take seriously the ways in which they read and negotiate these inconsistencies through their model of religious virtue.[31]

Let us return to my interlocutors and the practical ways in which they negotiated these two ethical commitments, motherhood and professional career, which turned out to be not so dissimilar to strategies adopted by other women of their generation. For many of my respondents, the question is purely theoretical because they do not yet have children of their own. This is not merely a coincidence. The literature on young Muslim women in Europe observes that one of the strategies that Muslim women use to achieve their professional aspirations is to delay marriage or motherhood or both (Jacobsen 2011; Nökel 2002; Weibel 2000). I was told many times that a woman should achieve a satisfying professional career before her first child arrives. Some of the women (such as Olfa) came to place such a priority on motherhood that they put their professional careers on hold indefinitely. In Olfa's case, this decision was perhaps eased by the fact that her work ceased to be satisfying at a certain point, ethically and otherwise. However, choosing to be a stay-at-home mom did not prevent these women from engaging in public life through other kinds of voluntary and informal activities, both within and outside of Islamic institutions.

Other women sought to reconcile motherhood and professional life: some contemplated a one- to three-year leave from work after childbirth, followed by reduced work hours; this is a quite common option pursued by mothers in Germany more generally. Independent or liberal professions were popular career goals among such women, because they allowed for a certain flexibility in the work schedule. Being a schoolteacher was another sought-after career, again especially in Germany, where the school day generally ends in the early afternoon.[32] Furthermore, many interlocutors could lean on a family support system. They were, for the most part, enmeshed in solid and extended family ties and could therefore recruit their parents and in-laws to perform child care, which these women often considered to be a more appropriate option for young children, given that they understood infant education as a family affair rather than as a matter for public institutions.

Their conception of children's education as a *family* duty also allowed my interlocutors to emphasize the educative role of the father. Notwithstanding their insistence on the caretaking duties of the mother and the division of tasks along gendered lines, many women maintained that the father played an important role in their children's education. Fatma, a woman of Turkish background in her late twenties, was adamant in this regard. I met her at the Islamic Student Union at the University of Cologne, where she was an active member, and I ran into her several times at the cafeteria of the main library. Fatma was about to finish her MBA; she was married, mother of a little boy, and pregnant with a second child. In spite of her insistence on her primary role as mother, her husband as well as her parents were very much invested in the children's education:

> My son is three and a half, and our next child is on the way. I will have to stay at home for one year, during which I will send out job applications until I find a job. . . . When my daughter is two years old, and since my parents are also there, I can go and work. My husband works in the evenings, so he is there in the mornings. So, we can collaborate. If my husband didn't participate, as in the typical Turkish couple—very macho, where the men do nothing—I could not work, of course, because the children come first. If we make a mistake in their education, we cannot correct it afterward. That's very important for me. He [the husband]

is also very aware of this. He is a teacher, he also knows this. And we both try to invest in this, if we have time, to use this time exclusively for our children.

Many of the unmarried women adopted similar views, expressing their desire for a supportive husband who would help with the children's education so that they could be professionally active. I also heard numerous complaints about "traditional Muslim men" (who abounded on the marriage market, much to the chagrin of my interlocutors) who were not willing to share such tasks—which was also a primary reason for the many divorces that occurred in the scene I studied. Indeed, the perceived unwillingness or incapacity of many Muslim men to commit to child-rearing activities recently led the BFmF to establish an entire pedagogical program for Muslim fathers.[33]

As these complaints already suggest, in real life things often turned out different than the women initially imagined. Earlier in this chapter, I mentioned Maissa, the young woman who quit her job in order to raise her young children (and because of problems related to the hijab). Like many other women, at a certain point unhappy in her unemployment and searching for a way out of this dilemma, she began to regret this decision. For other women, premarital promises by their husbands to help with child rearing did not materialize, whether because of unwillingness or out of necessity (due to time constraints imposed by their husbands' work). In addition to divorce or early widowhood, unemployed or minimum-wage-earning husbands (who hardly lived up to the bourgeois ideal upheld in the Islamic circles) made it incumbent upon many women to earn a living themselves; if they succeeded in finding a job in an ever-tightening (and discriminating) job market, it was frequently not the type of work that bestowed upon them a sense of self-fulfillment. In this case, their employment would not always allow them to dedicate as much time to their children as they had initially hoped. Working part-time often led to complications as well, because many careers did not accomodate such a schedule. Therefore, my interlocutors had to adapt, to revise their initial aspirations and dreams. Many times in the course of my fieldwork, most notably when reconnecting with women I had not seen for a year or so, I witnessed how reality had forced them to make painful concessions.

Conceiving of motherhood and career as embedded in a specific "ethics of care" entailed many negotiations, difficult choices, and especially compromises. Regardless of the outcome of their decisions, I argue, it is through a kind of phronetic reasoning that these women addressed the dilemmas, ambiguities, and ambivalences of life, which they sought to resolve within the contours of a (roughly) delineated Islamic ethical framework. This mode of moral reasoning is crucially defined by a particular *telos,* or higher good. The *telos* is, however, "never achieved and often only vaguely defined, yet activates the phronetic and interactive capacity of the individual" (Salvatore 2007: 41).

The postulation that people who belong to a particular tradition share a *telos* (such as, for instance, my interlocutors' ultimate desire to lead a life pleasing to God within an eschatological perspective) and endeavor to build dispositions that enable them to live their lives according to this *telos* does not imply the absence of conflict, ambivalence, or ambiguity. Nor does it deny the impact of opposing *teloi* on the followers of that tradition. Rather, the *telos* is "individually interpreted in different or even in conflicting ways" (Salvatore 2007: 38).[34] This dynamic explains conflicts between practitioners who differed significantly in how they weighed their various ethical obligations and expectations, as epitomized in the debate at the CERSI. Following the same rationale, an individual practitioner may come to very divergent conclusions at different moments of her life. She may even regret an earlier decision, or reverse it completely. *Phronesis* does not necessarily guarantee that "the right thing" will always be done "in the right moment," nor does it guarantee success. However, what it does promise is that the ethical agent strains to resolve a conflicting situation as best she can by taking all aspects into account and by aspiring to order the goods in a reasonable way. This includes consideration of religious norms, the common good, and personal interests. And within traditions of Islamic ethical reasoning, it also always attends to harsher situations of necessity (*darura*). What unites the divergent decisions that are made is the awareness that one's acts are accountable to a divine authority.

6 VISIBLY MUSLIM

Negotiating Presence in Public Spheres

ONE EVENING IN LATE OCTOBER, Nassira and I decided to go out for dinner. We met at a subway station in the 10th *arrondissement* right after Nassira got off work. When she walked up to me, I did not immediately recognize her. We had met before she donned the headscarf, but I had since gotten used to her Islamic attire and did not expect to see her without it. When she approached me wearing a fashionable white coat and a woolen beret of the same color, she resembled any other young, trendy Parisian woman. After I greeted her and commented on her appearance, she laughed and told me that this was her "professional look." She was unable to work in her headscarf, so she went to work wearing a beret, which she took off when she entered the office building. None of her colleagues knew that she wore the headscarf. On our way to the restaurant, we chatted about various topics, from the difficulties caused by her daily unveiling and her reflections on how she might manage to introduce her veil into the office, to her yoga class the day before. She took me to a Pakistani *halal* restaurant, assuring me that this was one place where one could trust the meat was indeed *halal* (permissible according to Islamic law), so she was not limited to the vegetarian dishes, which she usually stuck to at other restaurants. Once we arrived, she did not immediately sit down at our table but informed me that she wanted to "change first," after which she headed to the restroom. When she came back, she had replaced her beret with a regular headscarf. She exhaled deeply and smiled at me. Now the evening could begin.

This short episode introduces the main concern of this chapter, which is to investigate how religious Muslim women like Nassira inhabit on a day-to-day basis the often hostile secular spaces of French—and German—societies. This inquiry involves not only exploring how these women try to enact (or not enact) quotidian pious practices such as prayer and embodied modesty in the context of numerous constraints. Moreover, it examines how the women reason and give meaning to their particular bodily investments and disinvestments, visibilities and invisibilities, in the different spaces of mainstream society.

In many Western European societies, especially since 9/11, visible Islamic practices such as prayer and Islamic dress provoke increasingly inimical reactions. In this environment, my interlocutors oscillated between higher and lower degrees of visibility in the enactment of their pious practices, depending on how they thought they could best challenge or counteract Muslims' poor public image and ultimately to gain recognition from the French or German society. Thus, the first part of this chapter investigates how Islamic ritual practices and other forms of embodied pious conduct, once they are enacted in secular public spheres, get entangled in considerations of representation and recognition (see also Jouili 2011). Here I investigate the complex interlacing of self-cultivation and (re)signification practices, which is implicit in my interlocutors' everyday struggles to pursue their Islamic mode of life (whether visibly or not) within the different spaces of (secular) society. By being attentive to questions about the everyday, to embodiment, and to space, I also respond to cultural geographers' (and especially feminist geographers') plea that we extend our study of everyday practices to include everyday *lived* spaces (Gökariksel 2012; Smith 1992; Staeheli, Kofman, and Peake 2004).[1] Such an approach is also highly relevant for better understanding the workings of (and the intertwining of) secular and religious power. As Banu Gökariksel (2012: 5) notes,

> The continuous defining and governance of the "secular" and the "religious" are place-based, meaning that they are formed through the specific set of political and social relations, ideologies, and practices in particular sites. But they are also productive of places, in the sense that the particular ideas and practices of the secular and the religious produce space—from the body to city spaces.

When thinking about space in connection with secularity, Gökariksel implicitly raises the question of the relation between space and time. Indeed, as will become clear, the possibilities for my interlocutors to dwell or not dwell in certain spaces are conditioned by a secular-modern ideology of time, which defines the normative contours of the public sphere.[2]

The second part of the chapter investigates how this representational impulse, prompted by the enactment of pious Islamic practices within the secular public sphere, sparks a new set of ethical questions that these women have to tackle. In this context, these practices are not only concerned with the self but they take a broader social dimension that transcends the individual. Here I inquire into the ethical quandaries raised by these day-to-day negotiations, embodied practices, and modes of inhabiting space and time. As anthropologists of ethics suggest, paying attention to "ordinary ethics" can expose the ethical consequentialness of everyday interactions, conversations, and the minute adjustments that occur therein (Lambek 2010). In its concern to extend the study of Muslim ethical practices from the individual's practice of self-cultivation to a more capacious approach that emphasizes the intersubjective character of ethical action, this section builds on and continues the reflections in the previous chapter.

Pious Female Bodies in Everyday (Secular) Spaces

Searching or "Sacred" Time: The Predicament of Salat

As discussed in Chapter 3, the regular and punctual exercise of the five ritual prayers (*salat*) was of crucial importance to my interlocutors, all of whom expressed great concern about praying in the different spheres of their active lives (such as at university or work). As a very bodily practice—a "mobile corporal technique" (Henkel 2005: 305)—*salat* allows the practitioner to maintain continuity across her diverse life spaces while creating intimate, Islamic spheres around her individual body.[3] However, the regular and punctual performance of *salat* also marks an experience of time that does not fit neatly into homogeneous, secular time. This mode of temporality, which Elizabeth Freeman (2010) so aptly calls "chrononormativity," has become naturalized and seemingly self-evident, but it is in fact the result of specific regimes of power that have been converted into "bodily tempos and routines" (2010: 3). Although other temporalities have not been completely abolished, they are equally regulated so that they fit into the larger chrononormative regime. Regarding "religious practice," one could say that it is relegated to specific periodic and seasonal moments on the calendar, as well as to specific spaces.

Hence, *salat*, if performed in places that follow "work time," constitutes an intrusion (if not legally defined then at least viscerally sensed) that threatens the naturalized articulation of space and time that lies at the heart of the "social imaginary" (Taylor 2003) in secular societies. Furthermore, ritual prayer is likely to represent, for the secular gaze, a "dramatic gesture of submission"

(Henkel 2005: 487).[4] Watch, for instance, the images regularly screened on European television in which praying Muslims are shown in a bowing position—the embodied performance of submission—filmed from the back. Such pictures are most often stripped of any aesthetic qualities (Schiffer 2005). When practiced by second-generation Muslims, prayer is at times cast as an indicator of incomplete integration, or even a turn toward fundamentalism.[5] In contexts where Islamic ritual prayer creates all kinds of phantasmagorias, demanding a prayer space in public or professional institutions becomes potentially a quite unsettling form of claims-making.

My interlocutors only rarely dared to request spatial accommodation for their prayers at the workplace. At the university, however, they were more assertive. Many women imagined the university—one of the ultimate symbols of upward social mobility for these daughters of mainly labor migrants—to be a space of (newfound) freedoms: they had the opportunity to organize Muslim student associations, and generally expected to be able to pursue their Islamic lifestyle more visibly. For my interlocutors in Germany, in spite of certain setbacks, this expectation was generally met. Most German universities accommodate the need for prayer rooms, and religious Muslim students generally do not hesitate to occupy any empty classroom they can find if a nearby prayer space is not available. I witnessed this myself when spending time with Muslim students at the University of Cologne. Rim, the Palestinian-German English teacher at the BFmF, recalls her student years:

> At university, . . . sometimes we went to pray in the department of Islamic studies. We asked a professor if we could have a room; sometimes we just took any room and prayed there. We were aware that people could see us, but that didn't disturb us. We were adults by now. In school it was rather like, oh, people can see me pray, they will ridicule me. There was not yet that self-confidence.

Rim's testimony established a link between the ability to practice "in public" and self-confidence. This link was frequently highlighted to me. Self-confidence appeared to become increasingly important for maintaining one's religious practice in daily life, because it provided the strength to confront the Other's gaze. (I return to this topic later in the chapter). And even if at times the nonofficial nature of certain space appropriations provoked minor incidents, during my fieldwork in Cologne I never heard of significant problems.

In the Paris region, however, not only did I frequently learn about the difficulties involved in wearing hijab at university, but I also heard about conflicts resulting from prayer at university, which disappointed hopes of discovering a new space of freedom after having finally "escaped" *laïque* (secular) public school.[6] Hanan was one of many women who shared with me her negative experiences from her student years:

> We used to pray under the staircase, outside the building. But to bother us, the secretaries walked their dogs there to soil the place. My brother told me that they prayed in a room in the basement of his university, but when the janitors found out, they closed the room. The students decided to pray in the hall in front of everyone. Finally the administrators preferred to reopen the room. There were a lot of stories like that.

This testimony reveals how Islamic prayer in secular spaces becomes a "spatial practice"—in Henri Lefebvre's (1991) understanding of the term, a site of struggle for the ideological definition of space (and I would add, of time). In other words, as a spatio-temporal practice, *salat* disrupts, contests, and potentially transforms the dominant definition of the secular public sphere. Notwithstanding the importance of understanding ritual practices in their subject-fashioning role, these cases suggest the need to explore additional layers of meaning that are contextual and contingent. When Muslims visibly pray in a non-Muslim social environment, the ritual gets invested with meanings not related to the enacted practice as such. Employing Judith Butler's (1997) locution, one could say that, when confronted with a hostile and wary Other, *salat* is "de-contextualized" and potentially emerges as a "site of contestation."[7] However, in the context of Muslims praying while visible to the gaze of passersbys in public spaces such as a university, decontextualized *salat* challenges not the norms they "cite" but norms external to itself; thus, it openly contests seldom-questioned secular-religious dichotomies and exposes the contingency of secular understandings of (chrononormative) time and space.

Yet many women feared that such an overt contestation could engender situations that were too difficult and conflict-ridden to risk, especially in France (but also in Germany when it came to the workplace). Furthermore, they felt that praying in this atmosphere was detrimental to the spiritual well-being sought through prayer. For this reason, many women searched for mosques or prayer rooms near their university or workplace. Students wearing backpacks, as well as young men and women in professional attire, are commonly seen converging on the Mosquée de Paris, for instance, around and during prayer times. Those of my interlocutors who studied nearby would go there as well.

If there was no mosque close to their university or workplace, many women searched for a secluded place to pray without fear of detection. Venturing into and exploring unfamiliar contexts could lead to the discovery of empty spaces in storage rooms or basements. Several times I found myself accompanying my interlocutors on these searches (most notably in libraries and university buildings) and assisting them as a guard on the lookout for anyone approaching their hiding place. But even this "secret" prayer induced in some women the fear of being discovered, especially at work. Hence, praying in a still position has become, in particular in France, another much appreciated option.

I first learned of this "technique" during one of Olfa's "Islamic Morals" classes at the CERSI. She brought up this option during another discussion about how best to reconcile the duties of worship—in particular, *salat*—with an active life in French society. Although she provided some positive examples, demonstrating that the accommodation of Muslim practice in France was possible, she nonetheless remained, on the whole, pessimistic and considered it imprudent to voice these claims in the current political climate. As she put it, "Mentalities are not yet prepared for it; there is too much manipulation, so for me, I know that in most cases the result is zero." She therefore preferred to provide students with alternatives that would allow them to practice in spite of the harsh constraints. She emphasized the "flexibility of Islamic law," which permits numerous "adjustments."

Olfa suggested combining noon and afternoon prayer (*zuhr* and *'asr,*), as well as evening and night prayer (*maghrib* and *'isha'*). This would mean that only one prayer session would be required during the daytime. A second option was to pray in a seated rather than prostrate position. Students in the class who had already been informed about this method shared their own experiences. They recounted how they had prayed in this manner at work, in the library, in the car, in class, or on a public bench. If this option was still not possible, Olfa insisted that one must always keep the prayer time in mind so that, at the moment of the call to prayer (*idhan*), one could at least make an invocation (*du'a'*) asking God to ease the accomplishment of *salat*. She also commented that similar facilitations (*taysir*) could be made for ablutions (*wudu'*, the ritual purifications that precede *salat*), and went on to explain her pedagogy:

> In Islam, what counts—it is not about being perfect, that is, God ordered us to do this and that and that's it. . . . What He asks us is, according to your history, your path, that you made some efforts to satisfy him. . . . So, I make efforts; when I have this lucidity in the face of the situation, I tell myself, *hamdulillah*

'ala kulli hal [In any case, praise God], I can't do it [the prayer], but I did my best to satisfy Him. . . . It is not the result that counts but your intention. I really like this approach because it doesn't overpower you, it facilitates. It is an approach of facilitation; we try to find reassurance in facilitation.

Olfa's argument echoes the pedagogy that was so typical for the revival circles in which I worked; while promoting a specific disciplinary regime with the goal of self-reform, it equally accounted for the specific diasporic context, which does not easily accommodate Islamic practices. Furthermore, Olfa's comment also raised the idea that Islam is an "easy" religion that does not hinder the believer's complete participation in modern (Western) society. This trope, which I heard often, countered the idea commonly articulated in French and German media debates that Islam is incompatible with modern life. But the discourse about Islam being an "easy" religion also reflected a certain current of reformist thought that sees *taysir* as one of the essential principles of Islam. Thinkers close to the Muslim Brotherhood, whose opinions are highly influential in these centers, have equally claimed this tradition as their heritage.[8] On the basis of these discourses, participants regularly stressed that *taysir* should not become an easy excuse for one's own deficient practice. Instead, one must never diminish the effort to fulfill one's religious obligations in the most rigorous way. Olfa's emphasis on the idea of "effort" taking priority over "results," which she asserted in regard to the ritual prayer and the hijab, must also be read in this context. Olfa's reasoning again invoked a tradition within Islamic ethical thought that judges acts not only in themselves but also according to the intention (*niyya*) behind them. At times that tradition even prioritized this dimension by arguing that an incorrect or absent intention could invalidate an (otherwise virtuous) act.

Ablutions rendered the difficulties of praying outside of a Muslim environment even more acute. Islamic law prescribes ritual purification as a condition for valid prayer. Like *salat, wudu'* is an inherent corporal practice in which parts of the head and of the body's extremities have to be moistened with water. Everyone I spoke with about this admitted that being caught by a non-Muslim while performing *wudu'* created a strong sense of unease and even shame in the practitioner, as conveyed in this statement by a German-Turkish student in Cologne who abstains from praying at university:

At the university, it [the prayer] is very complicated, because of the ablutions. You can't go to the restroom and wash yourself there because people will just give you strange looks. Like, what, doesn't she have water at home? Is she tak-ing her shower here? Why does she wash herself? That's embarrassing and you try to avoid this.

As this statement suggests, the feeling of embarrassment about performing *wudu'* in public bathrooms is joined by another fear, linked to one's racialized class status. Thus, "to wash yourself" in a public place was not only a strange practice, but also became, when linked to a racialized body, a sign of poverty, and possibly dirt. All of my interlocutors emphasized that they avoided being seen when doing their ablutions. Sevim recalled jokingly, "I used to spend half of the day at university with my prayers, not because of the prayer in itself, but [because of] preparation, the *wudu'*." Many women identified the restrooms reserved for disabled people as the ideal place for accomplishing this task, be-cause they often contained a private sink. Other women mentioned the pos-sibility of *tayammum*, dry ablutions that could be carried out using any natural substance, such as dust, sand, earth, or stones, as a welcome alternative to the "hassle" linked to *wudu'*. Women who practiced this alternative method usually carry a medium-sized stone in their bag.

These discussions all made it clear that the effort to perform *salat* in a punc-tual and regular manner heavily impacted the daily life of pious practitioners. It required much of their attention, even as they remained mostly invisible to the external observer. Together these practices constructed a specific micro-topography of everyday (orthodox) Muslim piety within secular urban spaces. To secretly accomplish *salat* in localities such as the university or the workplace demanded not only a certain level of Islamic knowledge (in particular, *fiqh al-'ibadat*) in order to know the rules for facilitating devotional practice, but also familiarity with the places where one dwelled, and finally, a fair amount of creativity. In situations in which one felt unable to claim a prayer space, certain "tactics" (Certeau 1984) allowed one to inhabit restrictive secular spaces in ac-cordance with one's own needs, while visibly respecting the unwritten rules of the majority society.[9]

These micropractices, which appear so banal that they are easily over-looked, nevertheless "manipulate space" in significant ways. Michel de Certeau (1984) analyzes the "creative" ways in which individuals consume the domi-nant cultural, economic, technocratic, and spatial orders of society in every-day life, thereby individualizing constricted social structures. These practices are, he writes, "the microbe-like operations proliferating within technocratic structures and deflecting their functioning by means of a multitude of 'tactics'

articulated in the details of everyday life" (1984: xiv).[10] Regarding spatial practices, then, one discerns a discrepancy between the dominant mode of managing space and the individual mode of reappropriating it. However, though
these tactics are clearly subversive, Certeau acknowledges that they are far
from independent from power. In our case, their subversive character emerges
exactly where they purport to obey the normative secular structures.

Finally, these micropractices also remind us that even though prayer can
take on different meanings according to specific social contexts (Bowen 1989)—
here, for instance, it could mean defiance of secular norms—it should never be
reduced to these ancillary meanings. It remains first and foremost concerned
with enacting a religious duty that is understood to generate and maintain certain pious sensibilities. But whereas anthropologists studying the Islamic prayer
ritual have generally highlighted its fundamental embodied and spatial character, *qua* bodily and spatial presence, they have rarely imagined the possibility of
disembodying and despatializing it. Although doing so was the result of compromise in a hostile context, rather than a process that followed secular scripts
of interiorizing religion, it nonetheless requires us to think of *salat* in connection to different possible modes of bodily and spatial presence or absence.

To Veil or Not to Veil: Confrontations and Modes of Passing

The participants in the circles I studied, whether they wore the headscarf or
not, almost unanimously considered covering the hair to be mandatory for
Muslim women. A third of my interlocutors did not wear a headscarf, but this
fact was never advocated in a way that led to any substantial questioning of
the headscarf's obligatory character—at least in principle. All of the women
I spoke with wished to wear it, but they feared the reaction it might provoke
from society at large, especially the possibly negative consequences for their
professional life.[11] The successive debates on the headscarf in both France and
Germany have not only officially proscribed the headscarf in specific places
and on certain female bodies (pupils in French public secondary schools,
teachers, and other civil servants in German schools), but they have also fostered a broad hostile climate that reinforces long-established representations of
"veiled" Muslim women.[12]

In such a context, many Muslim women linked their inability to wear a
headscarf with their lack of courage to confront the majority society. Overcoming one's fear and becoming capable of wearing the headscarf publicly was often
described as "liberating" oneself from the gaze of the Other.[13] In this sense,

wearing the veil in key institutions of the public sphere (such as in school, at university, or in the workplace), similar to claiming a prayer space, was increasingly understood as an act of autonomy vis-à-vis the majority society, an act of self-confidence, and a refusal to let the majority society's negative perception of Islam determine one's own conduct and impede the exercise of one's religious duties. Thus, many conferences and classes I attended sought to encourage Muslim women's "Islamic self-confidence." It seems that the cultivation of self-confidence or pride—qualities not specifically grounded in the Islamic ethical tradition but in this context more connected to expressions from contemporary minority groups' "identity politics"—has become one of the explicitly acknowledged conditions for being able to live piously according to Islamic norms in a context of diaspora and alterity.

Nonetheless, pride and self-confidence were not sufficient responses to the structural constraints faced by pious Muslims in secular public spheres. In many instances in France, not only schools but also universities turned out to be hostile toward the headscarf. Many interlocutors in Paris spoke of the difficulty they experienced at certain universities trying to enroll or to sit for exams while wearing their hijab. And for women in both countries, wearing a headscarf severely reduced opportunities for professional employment outside Islamic institutions.[14] Therefore, everyone I spoke with carefully considered the question of the visibility of their sartorial practices. When examining this issue, one cannot simplistically oppose "Islamic dress" (being veiled) to "un-Islamic dress" (being unveiled). Being "covered" of course refers to more than headgear. Not wearing the headscarf does not excuse pious practitioners from "covering" themselves: they wear clothes that conceal the body and are large and loose enough not to accentuate the female figure. Also, wearing and not wearing the headscarf were not two different stable and fixed states; I observed several intermediate states, which often alternated. These different ways in which my correspondents wore the headscarf were as follows: veiled only for prayer or when inside an Islamic association; veiled when outside the workplace (as illustrated by Nassira in this chapter's introductory vignette) but reducing their temporary "openness" to a minimum by wearing turtleneck shirts and tying their hair back in a strict fashion; veiled like Aziza and Emna by wearing "discreet" headgear such as a beret or a scarf tied at the back of the neck (a covering that is not immediately recognizable as Islamic but that tends to signify "ethnic" fashion); veiled by wearing a discreet head covering during work or at university and a "conventional" hijab outside these spaces—which is what Naima did; and finally, wearing a conventional headscarf full-time. Although this last option significantly reduced job opportunities to employment inside Islamic structures or self-employment, a few of my interlocutors in Germany who dressed that way succeeded in finding employment in other sectors. Sevim, for instance, who wore a conventional hijab, opened her own translation agency but was also employed part-time as an English teacher in a business company as well as at the BFmF.

Therefore, the dichotomy between visible and invisible was diluted by the multiple and changing ways of covering one's head. The women found myriad "ways of doing" (Certeau 1984) that constituted, once again, "tactics" aimed at maintaining modest dress in spaces where doing so was perceived to be extremely difficult. Whereas for some women, the "discreet" hijab in the form of a beret or a scarf tied behind the head was merely a compromise, somehow deficient in comparison to the "real" hijab, others took much pleasure in that kind of fashion and considered it a fully equivalent dress style. At times these strategies succeeded (momentarily or for the long term) in subverting the interdiction of the headscarf. Consider, for example, Aziza's remark about her experience from her high school days:

> Well, actually, I didn't wear it, I took it off at the entrance [of the school building]. At one point I started to wear it like this, like a turban, but only in the front, you see; in the back it was open, and it was pretty. Most of my teachers didn't really notice; they thought it was only a style, except one teacher, my history teacher. You know, most of the history teachers are hardline atheists. The first day of school, he had already detected me.[15]

Aziza's story conveyed neatly how the efforts of some women in France to increase the size of their head covering became a play of inches, in which a few too many inches of cloth could bring down the entire scheme, exposing the "true" meaning of a regular fashion item.[16]

The different strategies that my interlocutors adopted to obfuscate a clear reading of the "marked" Muslim female body bear some resemblance to the notion of "passing," a simulation of the "unmarked" body that is widely discussed in queer, feminist and postcolonial theory. These theories employ the term to reveal the constructed and contingent nature of fixed identities and their signifiers, and to open up possibilities for subverting normative categories, the boundaries between female and male, white and black, colonizer and colonized (Butler 1993; Tylor 1994). However, the "passing" I describe here did not aim to blur identities, nor did it question or deconstruct the moral project itself, that is, the goal of living a normative Islamic life. Rather, passing was a strategy for creating space for particular ways of life not tolerated according to dominant definitions of the public sphere, which are increasingly articulated in terms of normative sexual conduct (Amir-Moazami 2011; Ewing 2008; Joan W. Scott 2007). In this context, strategies of passing also directly challenge the state's effort to govern Muslim populations through the regulation of the female body.

For some women, veiling "part-time" was a temporary solution that became unbearable at a certain point. Given my interlocutors' approach to the headscarf as a practice essential to shaping a pious subjectivity, several of them complained that the daily unveiling had precipitated a "decrease of faith." Others suffered from the lack of correspondence between their inner feelings and their outward appearance, a situation they considered "hypocritical." Yet for women like Nassira and Aysel, a high school teacher I met in Cologne at the BFmF, wearing the veil part-time seemed to have evolved into a permanent situation. When they did not feel (or no longer felt) capable of bearing the social consequences of wearing the headscarf—most notably in the form of professional marginalization—the possibility of taking it off during work hours allowed them to continue engaging in that particular pious practice while also pursuing a professional career, in spite of the suffering and humiliation that daily unveiling often entailed. But these different perceptions and assessments were also subject to significant change, depending on each woman's life history.

Take, for instance, Saliha. As mentioned in Chapter 4, when I met her she was a stay-at-home mom. Her decision to do this was due not primarily to her understanding of motherhood but to the emotional difficulties that resulted from daily unveiling at the workplace. "I was in the middle of a crisis. I took it off, and I put it on, off, on; it was schizophrenic. I was not feeling well. I even started to question my Islam." However, after a couple of years without employment, she came to view her position differently. Although she had been very active in associational life (in groups fighting anti-Muslim racism and in parent-teacher associations), she nonetheless felt increasingly dissatisfied with her role and desired to be professionally active again, for all the reasons discussed in the previous chapter. Simultaneously, she went through a process in which she grew increasingly critical of the revival circles' discourses on hijab, which according to her "presented hijab as the sixth pillar of Islam." After discovering a text written by an Egyptian Islamic thinker that questions the hijab's obligatory character,[17] she began feeling more comfortable with the idea of taking off the headscarf for work, and eventually did so.[18]

One aspect key to various strategies of introducing the hijab into the public sphere, from passing to more assertive approaches, concerns the aesthetics of the head covering. In my earlier "typology" of hijab techniques, as well as in Aziza's comment about her high school experience, the aestheticization of the headscarf was linked to an effort to make the hijab appear less disturbing, less conspicuous, and therefore more acceptable to society. A growing body of literature has recognized the importance that veiled women give to their outward appearance and examined the divergent sartorial practices related to fashion in modest dress (Balasescu 2003; Lewis 2007; Moors 2007; Moors and Tarlo 2007; Tarlo 2010).

According to many pious practitioners, wearing the headscarf "differently"—that is, aestheticizing it by combining it with fashionable but modest Western clothes—signifies that wearing the headscarf is the result of "personal choice" and "self-confidence." It should therefore also express the capacity to be a reflexive and autonomous actor. As we have seen in Chapter 3, women constantly claimed to wear the hijab out of "choice." Moreover, a distinctive style is meant to signal individuality and originality—other qualities often denied to veiled women. Thus, the different meanings that women attached to fashionable Islamic dress must be read as attempts to bridge the commonly perceived *temporal* gap between Europe and Islam that is epitomized by the headscarf. By signifying a certain type of modern interiority (a subjectivity characterized by the capacity for choice and reflexivity) and by including Muslim dress in the rhythm of fashion, the now fashionable headscarf seeks to situate itself within a modern temporality, thereby turning it into a contemporaneous practice.[19] The integration of Islamic dress into the "temporality of fashion," though doubtlessly a growing trend, was still regarded by some of my interlocutors with a skeptical and cautious eye. Because for most women hijab and Islamic dress also signaled a critique of the dictates of the fashion industry and commodifying impact on the female body, Islamic fashion exposed an inherent tension that continued to incite debates and contestation.[20]

However, regardless of the specific sartorial practices employed, wearing hijab was never understood as sufficient in itself; rather, it needed to be accompanied by conduct that signaled simultaneously both restraint and openness, and that radiated both self-assurance and politeness. In this communication project, language skills play a crucial role, because lack of fluency is the first mark of the stranger, with whom the veiled woman was frequently identified.

The very fashionable, charming and self-confident Aziza, who usually tied her scarf "discreetly" at the back of her neck, talked to me at length about the importance of visual communication:

> You speak good French, you are young, . . . and then, I mean, you're not ugly, you don't try to hide yourself out of a complex. . . . Well, you know how to value yourself. In addition, you are a smiling person, you're outgoing, you match your headscarf with your clothes. This shows that you wear it out of choice, with pleasure, out of conviction; you see that this person is flourishing. . . . So, after all, communication is very important, your conduct is important, your look, the relationship you have with people, *al-islam din al-mu'amalat* [Islam is the religion of social relations].

Aziza's statement clearly reveals how a practice initially concerned with cultivating a particular kind of virtuous self could turn into a work of resignification. This resignification was enacted through everyday micropolitics, conscious and reflexive actions that became constitutive elements in the struggle for gaining recognition as pious but fully French or German Muslim women.

When looking at the way in which women like Aziza tried to resignify the headscarf, I am required to pay closer attention to the complicated relationship between a practice of self-cultivation related to a material object (hijab) and its capacity to signify. Webb Keane's work is particularly illuminating in this context. On the one hand, he is wary of any intellectual tradition (which he considers a substantial element of the narrative of modernity) "that treats signs as if they were merely the clothing of meaning, meaning that, it would seem, must be stripped bare" (Keane 2005: 2–3).[21] This tradition of thought, he claims, "dematerializes" signs and thereby "privileges meaning over actions, consequences and possibilities" (2005: 3). Nonetheless, he cautions us not to merely reverse this privilege, which in his eyes would reproduce the dichotomy. Building on the notion of "semiotic ideology" (see Chapter 2), Keane grapples with this conundrum so as to be able to grasp the semiotic principles in the study of the relation of material objects to human practices without reiterating familiar, problematic "modernist" assumptions. It is in this way that he analyzes, for instance, how clothes matter. While recognizing the sensuous qualities of clothes, their material impact on the body, the cluster of habits they entail, and their possible disciplinary effects, he in particular wants to understand "what are the conditions under which cloth does or does not come into view as a bearer of iconography, with meanings that can be treated as texts?" (2005: 12).[22] Keane claims that the indexicality of an object is a potentiality that might be realized depending on the specific historical context. He thus urges us to pay attention to the historicity of semiotic practices.

One of the explanations that Keane offers elsewhere (2008) is that this potentiality can become open to signification when the semiotic ideologies in which these material practices are embedded change. These practices thereby become "objectified" and develop into objects of reflection for the practitioner or outside observer.[23] Keane's discussion indicates that, because of a mismatch in semiotic ideologies, embodied practices can turn into disturbing signifying practices, which then become occasions for larger discursive struggles beyond the particular group of practitioners. And it is in this context that resignification can potentially occur. However, resignification, while possible, does not happen in an arbitrary way and is not freely chosen by the practitioner. Rather, it is structurally linked to specific semiotic ideologies, and thereby also to long-standing discursive traditions. Keane's reflections on processes of (re)signification are informed by his interest in practices related to material culture and language in the context of colonial encounters, especially the Protestant missionary endeavor on the Indonesian island of Sumba. His thoughts are extremely helpful when thinking about how embodied material practices like wearing the headscarf become "a bearer of iconography" and, consequently, entangled in (re)signification struggles.

Such an approach can powerfully reveal how my interloctors fine-tuned contested practices—in complicated and fragmented ways—to a dominant semiotic ideology that promoted individual autonomy (and by which the practitioners were also fashioned). However, the self-cultivating aspect and the representational aspect of hijab should not be considered side-by-side in an isolated and conflicting manner. The women's effort to resignify the stigmatized headscarf through a certain type of conduct was embedded, as Aziza's comment reveals, in a discourse of Islamic ideals of social conduct. Although a veiled woman's "good conduct" has a representational function, it also requires practicing certain embodied virtues. The women acknowledged the difficulty of living up to the irreproachable social conduct required of them; Naima, for instance, spoke repeatedly of this challenge. All the veiled women insisted that their representative position as *visible* Muslims constituted an important motivation to live up to these ideals. Because the headscarf was not only a self-fashioning practice *but also* a representational practice, we have to attend to the complex articulation of both dimensions. It also begs the question of the extent to which the self-cultivating aspect of the headscarf sustains itself through the particular meanings it conveys in specific, historically contingent contexts. Consequently, the effect of this practice on the habituation of the body and the shaping of the self cannot easily be disconnected from the meaning it signifies at particular times.

Modest Conduct in "Indecent" Places

The desire to dress modestly significantly affects Muslim women's presence in the German and French public spheres. So does their modest conduct. As discussed in Chapter 3, the Islamic injunction to conduct oneself with modesty not only implied the regulation of relations between the sexes, but also more generally an embodied attitude of "polite reserve," "self-restraint," and "respect" (El-Guindi 1999: 88). Just as this conduct defined the modalities of these women's social interaction, it equally shaped how they selected and appropriated public and semipublic space. Thus, modest conduct is inherently a bodily and spatial practice that defines what posture a body adopts, as well as where and how it moves. French and German secular public spheres are usually seen as enabling free interaction between men and women, as open to individual spontaneity and desire. As Katherine Ewing (2008: 3) argues for Germany (and which is applicable to France), "the culturally specific aspects of gender and the organization of public spaces are confounded in public discourses . . . with what are generally agreed to be universally applicable ideas of human rights and democracy in a kind of logical or rhetorical slippage." Ewing (2008: 192–195) shows how, in Germany, the ideal of free mixed-gender interaction is nourished by a nineteenth-century *Körperkultur* (body culture) tradition that valorizes nudity, associating it with openness, purity, and healthy sexuality. In France, the insistence on *mixité* as a core value of republican *laïcité* is a rather recent development (see Bracke 2013).[24] Nonetheless, while articulated and justified in specific national idioms, the critiques in both countries of the modesty ideals endorsed by religious Muslims are equally vehement, because they associate these ideals with female segregation, gender inequality, and an oppressive sexual regime. In mixed spaces, Muslim women not only have to take into consideration non-Muslim males' possible ignorance of the Islamic rules of interaction, but also the negative connotations that these rules might provoke among outsiders.

One of the most common problems in this context stems from differences in modes of greeting involving physical contact. In an orthodox reading, Islamic etiquette proscribes any physical contact between women and men outside their closest family (*mahram*). When women greeted friends or colleagues,

direct physical contact was always a concern. In the inflammatory public debates about Muslim practices that have taken place in Western Europe, shaking
hands is considered not only a common gesture but also a highly politicized
act.[25] Not surprisingly, this gesture has now turned into another signifier of
Western civility. It is for this reason that my interlocutors generally accepted
that mode of greeting from non-Muslim men, even though they considered
it illicit from an Islamic point of view. They feared that a refusal to return this
salutation might provoke misunderstanding among their male counterparts,
thereby confirming stereotypes about the inhibited and "secluded" Muslim
woman. Sevim's explanations of her own attempts to develop a practical position on the handshake neatly convey this approach:

> At the beginning I wanted to do everything hypercorrectly, and I thought, oh
> God, now I must not shake hands anymore. And this was really difficult with
> my family, the family of my husband. They always shake hands, and of course
> they kiss all the time [*laughter*]! In the beginning I absolutely refused to shake
> hands, and I received very aggressive reactions from my family. But I was not
> very consistent. Sometimes I did it, sometimes not. I was still in the phase of
> finding myself. I was not very diplomatic back then. And then, I did not explain
> it to them, and this was wrong.
>
> Nowadays, when I have contacts at the company, mostly with men, I shake
> hands. I accept handshakes from German men more easily than with Turkish
> and other Muslim men. It also feels different with German and Turkish men;
> they don't do it because they want physical contact. The Muslims, they should
> know. With the Germans, it is also difficult to explain each time, and if they
> don't understand, they will feel insulted and say, ah, this Muslim woman. I don't
> want that, but it's tricky.

Another concern to which Sevim alluded is cheek kissing. Almost everyone
I spoke to disapproved of this greeting, when performed with non-*mahram*
men, as a form of illegitimate intimacy—even if this was widely practiced in
their own (non-orthodox) family environments. In the mainstream society, because of the signal the headscarf sends, veiled women can easily avoid the cheek
kiss. Not so for unveiled women: many times I heard about the difficulties they
encountered in imposing limits on this practice (see also Chapter 3), precisely
because of the invisibility of their Islamic values and norms. The negotiations
and hesitations of these "invisible" Muslims regarding handshaking were similar to those employed by headscarf-wearing women. In all these cases, when

negotiating Islamic modesty codes in relation to European norms of civility, women constantly worried about not creating situations that might "damage the image of Islam" and thereby thwart their desire to be seen as active, independent women, especially in professional environments. I come back to the broader ethical implications of this concern toward the end of this chapter.

Participation in semipublic spaces, such as in the university or workplace, where regular daily contact establishes more solid personal relations than simple stranger sociability, posed another problem. In these spaces, the question arose not only about how to greet but also about how to manage increasingly familiar relations yet maintain a required distance. Once again, bearing in mind "the burden of representation," my interlocutors insisted that "modesty" should not be mistaken for either "segregation" or "auto-exclusion." In this sense, friendly relations with colleagues or fellow students became proof that Muslim women were capable of maintaining "normal" relations with the other sex. On many occasions I witnessed the balancing act between these two requirements, especially while spending time with my interlocutors at the University of Cologne. There they socialized with non-Muslim male students, studied together, ate together, or simply bridged time from one class to another at a cafeteria. Spontaneous interaction, laughing, joking, and warm and friendly relations were clearly established. At the same time, I often felt a certain sense of being on the lookout, of attentiveness. One of the women at the university who I thought was particularly good at mastering this balancing act was Shayma, a German-Moroccan student in education sciences. A petite woman with a straightforward manner, she always came across as kind, and calm but firm. She explained:

> I don't have problems with my male fellow students when I'm at university or the library. In my leisure time, I don't have contact with them or with other men. But I also don't avoid them. At the university cafeteria, I eat with them, I talk with them about everything. Sometimes we joke. . . . That's not a problem for me. If every Muslim woman avoids them, I imagine that this would reinforce their imaginations. . . . And a lot of them who know me say that they can't believe that this is a woman who wears hijab. It's an educational labor that I'm doing.

In these day-to-day relationships, which are imbued with a certain degree of familiarity, the required restraint could, however, be easily forgotten by one or both sides. Several women described such relationships that led to stronger feelings on the part of their male friends, which generally was not acceptable to them. In other instances, the increasingly spontaneous interaction that resulted from such familiarity made it harder for the women themselves to maintain the required restraint. Sevim again provided me with numerous (quite funny) anecdotes about this kind of problem that recall that the practice of virtue (in this case, the learning and enacting of reserve and restraint) is not only an ever uncompleted work in progress, but is not always so easily defined.

> In one of my English classes, for example, the men always make vulgar jokes. That's quite typical for German men. And I laugh with them, and then I think, *astaghfirullah* [I ask forgiveness from God], I have to pay attention to not falling into the same genre. . . . My God, you are not very Islamic anymore. So, I try to pay attention at my place of work, with the headscarf, to be Islamic and not just to pretend. It's difficult in the beginning, when you still lack experience; you're really stuck to it. But afterward, at some point you just relax and you become a bit more laid-back in your conduct. We even joke about Islam. This must not degenerate. You have to stay on the middle path, toward Allah; that's important.

Comparable consideration was given to where, when, and how to dwell in different leisure-related spaces. Even though Islamic-oriented restaurants and leisure activities proliferate in France and Germany (as in Muslim communities elsewhere), many women did not want to restrict themselves to these spaces.[26] Early on in my encounters, I came to realize that the concern for an appropriate way of inhabiting these spaces produced a range of quite divergent individual strategies. When planning our first appointments, women would often immediately raise their specific ideas and concerns about the appropriate places to meet. Some told me they did not frequent cafés or restaurants that serve alcohol, which is why many women in France proposed instead to meet in fast-food restaurants, because they generally do not serve alcohol (although they often preferred French chains because, as they pointed out to me, they boycotted American chains).[27] Other women, like Aziza, suggested stylish but "respectable" and "not too noisy" cafés or restaurants, where they seemingly felt comfortable. Similarly, in Cologne, when we did not meet at the BFmF or at university, we got together at Turkish fast-food restaurants or, when meeting with university students, in a quiet café on a popular street near the university that was filled with cafés, bars, and restaurants.

I also noticed that the time of day could be equally significant in deciding the appropriateness of a meeting location. For instance, Afaf, a young French-

Moroccan woman in her mid-twenties, proposed that we get together in a café in the 14th arrondissement, because there she could conveniently make a bus connection to her home in a nearby *banlieue*. We met at about two o'clock in the afternoon and got carried away by our animated conversation. It was only a bit after five o'clock when she pointed out that the clientele had changed and we should leave the place. At that moment I realized that the clientele had indeed shifted from a majority of afternoon coffee consumers to customers having their after-work (alcoholic) drink, with a significant number gathering around the bar. Afaf no longer felt comfortable in this environment.

In addition to meeting in cafés and restaurants, I had several opportunities to accompany my interlocutors on different leisure-time activities such as to movie theaters, ice skating rinks, and other sports activities. Again, they would consciously select the place so as not to flout Islamic standards of morality and modesty. For instance, when considering going to a movie theater, everyone insisted on avoiding films judged to be too "free" or "vulgar." They generally tried to know in advance which "appropriate" movies were currently being screened. Some women were more demanding about what they deemed "appropriate" and thus only rarely went to the movies, "because there is at least one love scene in every movie." Others, however, dealt with these scenes on the spot: "when we are confronted with such a scene, I try to chat a bit with my friend sitting next to me and eat some popcorn until the scene is over." And though many preferred to participate in sports in an exclusively female (Muslim) environment, others accommodated themselves to existing mixed-gender venues. Naima, who spoke extensively of the difficulties she faced in progressively abandoning her various hobbies—including dancing, clubbing, and hip-hop music—did not, however, stop pursuing her sports activities. The classes at her fitness club are now also substitutes for her former hobbies, providing her with a welcome occasion to listen and move to music. But these classes were not disconnected from her "modest" way of making use of the fitness club's facilities:

> Well, there is the room with the fitness equipment and the rooms where classes take place, where they do stretching, aerobics, etc. I put on a headscarf and wear something large and loose. . . . It's true that in the room where the courses take place, the majority are women, perhaps one or two are men, because they prefer the room with the machines. I don't go into the rooms with the machines anymore; before I went, but now I feel embarrassed [*laughter*].[28]

Sports seemed to be another terrain in which Muslim women could power-fully demonstrate their participation in society and dispute the accusation of self-segregation. A veiled student in Cologne brought this up in regard to her kickboxing class:

> During the class, I tie the headscarf in the back, because you sweat quite a lot. People don't recognize that I wear a headscarf because it looks fashionable. When I change in the dressing room and I tie my headscarf, people say, oh, you wear a headscarf. And they say, I think it's great that you are doing this despite your headscarf, and that you don't exclude yourself."

For these devout women, enacting Islamic norms of female modesty while actively participating in spheres of mainstream society (and thereby hopefully challenging certain common representations of themselves that are prevalent in that society) entailed a whole range of (often invisible) microtactics. Like every-one else of their generation, they were urban consumers within a society of mass consumption and had been fashioned by its very structures, which was palpable in, for instance, the desire for entertainment, fashion commodities, fitness, well-ness, and so on. But their way of selecting and employing these products was not unilaterally imposed by an abstract dominant order. Rather, they "manipulated" them quite differently, in the sense that Certeau has given the term.[29] However, while Certeau insists on a highly individualized way of manipulating, in this context one has to understand it as guided by a specific reading and application of the Islamic tradition. Beyond being merely a "tactic" for circumventing secu-lar constraints, this "art of the everyday" also points to how these pious women made themselves *at home* within the dominant, secular spheres; how they nego-tiated and created their spaces of belonging, selectively reassembling practices, objects, images, and sounds connected to their various (social) locations and histories. This "making home" is therefore also a deeply embodied experience involving bodily sensations and emotive responses, and constructing specific but constantly shifting "sensuous geographies" (Fortier 2006: 15).

But the representational dimension of their presence and the various mes-sages that their presence signals can also have the opposite effect and provoke unfavorable reactions. Take, once more, Saliha. We became friends during the course of my fieldwork in Paris and, having emphasized her pleasure in going out to fashionable cafés, she joined me on several occasions for drinks with friends. During most of my research she was a full-time mom, so she particu-larly enjoyed "getting out of the house," as she liked to put it. Noticing the at times surprised and at times reprimanding looks she received the first time I entered a café with her, I raised the issue with her on a later occasion. Saliha, aware of these reactions, complained:

> This happens all the time. But whenever I go out, like with my husband to the Quartier Latin [an area of the 5th and 6th arrondissements known for its restaurants], it's not only Muslims who are closed up; the people from the restaurant, even those who are eating there, when I pass by, they always look at me like this [grimace]. Oh, a veiled woman has entered the restaurant. That's so annoying.

Comparable reactions are encountered in Cologne. Nasreen, a young German-Turkish computer science student, recounts similar experiences:

> Me and my husband, we like to go to restaurants. In the beginning it was difficult to sit down in a restaurant, because you have all the eyes on you. I was so embarrassed. But with time I got used to it. Sometimes I look at them too. There was once a woman who stared at me—you know, if looks could kill. I snapped at her, "What do you want from me?" She was scared! [*laughter*] Now I have learned to manage that quite well.

Saliha's and Nasreen's testimonies illustrate the curiosity, discomfort, and anxiety about the veiled Muslim female body that is evidenced in places that represent the *savoir-vivre* of the German and French middle class. This racialized, classed, and gendered pious body seems to appear here from out of time, as an illegitimate invader appropriating the symbolic spaces of a lifestyle that "distinguishes," in a Bourdieusian sense (Bourdieu 1977), a privileged social class. Through these cultural practices—visiting a stylish restaurant, a "hip" café, a theater, or a museum—these unfashionably devout women manifested a taste and a capacity to manage time in ways that reveal their proximity to European middle class society. The sight of the veiled body (often fashionable and therefore strangely "modern" while still evoking for its non-Muslim audiences a past temporality) disturbs, even shocks, because of its ambivalence and the outsider's resulting difficulty in deciphering it (see Göle 2001). It can be successfully excluded from certain public spaces, such as the workplace, but many spaces for leisure activities are, in principle, open to everyone who can financially afford to be there. The display of not only a certain cultural taste but also a financial capacity imposes this proximity even more forcefully. As Göle (2001: 67–68) has observed, it is the imposed "proximity" of the hijab of young, European-born Muslim women that seems so disturbing: "because the stigmatized comes closer to her opponent while at the same time claiming her difference, that is, because she disrupts the categories of domination. Basically, it is this proximity with the Other that triggers fear, rejection and visceral reactions."

Representing the Muslim Female Body

In public debates, the naming of the religious Muslim female subject is defined by the impossibility of imagining (and thus naming) her through characteristics that are part of European meta-values and self-descriptions, such as freedom or autonomy, which are widely understood to manifest themselves through certain modes of sociability and aesthetic appreciation. Religious Muslims are thereby excluded from Europe's hegemonic temporality of progress. Practices such as the prayers, the hijab, and embodied modesty more generally signify precisely the opposite—the premodern temporality in its midst that Europe anxiously wants to forget.[30] These practices have thereby come to define an abjected, uninhabitable zone (Butler 1993) that constitutes a threat not only to the definition of the public sphere, but also to the secular subject's very sense of (temporal) being.[31] A range of authors have pointed to the visceral feelings of unease, dislike, and even disgust that are expressed in public debates about Muslim practices connected to the management of gender relations (Amir-Moazami 2007; Bowen 2007; Ewing 2008; Göle 2001; Moors 2009; Joan W. Scott 2010; El-Tayeb 2011). As Sara Ahmed (2004: 82ff.) has argued, affectively charged discourses of disgust work powerfully to bind together those who express these feelings and to effectively exclude those who become the object of these discourses.

In such a charged context, when some of my interlocutors tried to resignify the religious Muslim female body, they also sought to enable a reading of these practices that makes sense according to the dominant "semiotic ideology."[32] In addition to connecting these practices (albeit in ambivalent ways) to choice and autonomy and thereby to a modern temporality, the women also linked them to other social attributes that generally construct European self-descriptions from which they have been excluded.[33] This response, however, is not to be situated exclusively within the norms enunciated by a prior injurious address (Butler 1997). The specific recognition project in which many of these women engage is meant to prove their compatibility with European modernity not *in spite of* but *because of* their Muslimness. Therefore, the response enacted by them is also clearly embedded in a specific deployment of Islamic traditions (and Islam's semiotic ideologies). Being "civil," "professional, "refined," and "aesthetic" are then considered not exclusively European attributes but also authentic Islamic qualities for which textual evidence can be provided. Those who talk about the necessity of an aestheticized mode of dress, for instance, often refer to the *hadith* "God is beautiful and He loves beauty." When insisting on the importance of manners, they will talk about *adab* (etiquette; see Chapters 2 and 3); and when reflecting on their professional ambitions and work ethic, they will mention the virtue of *ihsan* (excellence). In this way, the modern temporality pursued is integrated into a *timeless* modernity, which is what, for my interlocutors, the Islamic tradition, if understood correctly, stands for.

Once again, all of this discussion points to the ways in which Islamic traditions are reconfigured through a set of ideals, affects, and sensibilities that are in part fashioned by European civilizational discourses and self-descriptions. Devout women (and men) reinterpret the traditions and resignify the practices using the vocabularies at their disposal.[34] They therefore also hope to strip from their mode of life and its related practices an increasingly politicized identification with seemingly wrong "background assumptions about the world" (Keane 2008: 14). This is also clearly a response to a context in which citizenship in the "new Europe" has become increasingly "culturalized," thereby connecting it to specific national norms, values, and even modes of conduct (such as gender mixing, civility, greetings, and so on).[35] In this sense, my interlocutors' (re)signification struggles are negotiations of these ever more heavy requirements, partly accommodating them, partly resisting or circumventing them.

The performance of (embodied) Islamic practices discussed here occurs at the nexus between the increasingly exclusionary regulatory regimes of the German and French secular public spheres, along with the specific semiotic ideologies they display, *and* the disciplinary regimes of evolving Islamic traditions. Within this "field of enabling constraints," (Butler 1997: 16) the performance of these practices does possess a quality of *poeisis:* they can be read as creative employment of body, space, and time, as subverting in multiple ways the constraints of secular public spheres that seem to render impossible the public exercise of "illegitimate" religious practices. Yet these creative tactics also often encompass hard decisions involving significant and painful sacrifices. The most obvious example would be the question of whether or not to wear a headscarf in public. If the decision is answered in the affirmative, the pious practitioner often has to accept severe sanctions (in professional life, for example); however, resolving to take off one's headscarf at work, for instance, often provokes equally intense feelings of humiliation or guilt. Thus, the tactics employed here to make up a specific public performance are answers not only to harshly unequal power relations but also to deeply felt moral dilemmas that involve reasoning, interpretation, and deliberation, which are not directly accessible through theories of resignification. I address these ethical entailments in the remainder of this chapter.

Negotiating Pious Practices as Moral Reasoning

Notwithstanding the ease with which my interlocutors repeatedly made statements like "We need to fight for our right to wear the hijab, to practice our religion freely"—statements that reflect, evoke, and imply languages of individual rights and modern recognition discourses—this type of language constituted only one aspect of a much more complicated approach to the restrictions and exclusions they encountered. Just as in Chapter 4, in regard to gendered social relations, the women were suspicious of a pure rights discourse that was unaccompanied by notions of responsibility or obligation. Similarly, claims for the "right" to practice Islam freely were never made in isolation, but rather were embedded in a complex web of other moral commitments, most notably the commitment to properly represent the community. In the various ways in which these women negotiated prayer, the hijab, and modest conduct, one could often see that the repercussions of individual practice on the community weighed at least as much as, if not more than, the fulfillment of an individual's religious duty. It was the conjunction of these different concerns that determined the modalities of appearance of pious Muslim women in secular public spheres, and whether or not specific claims were maintained.

This is of course not a novel observation. John Bowen (2007: 81), for instance, has pointed to how the introduction of such practices as wearing the headscarf involved "negotiations, anticipations, and weighing of benefits and costs . . . a subtle dance among convictions and constraints." However, what these types of arguments have generally not considered fully is the extent to which all these minute adjustments, negotiations, and modes of reasoning allude to ethical labor. If dilemmas could arise on a daily basis, as we have seen, in regard to prayer and embodied modesty (such as handshaking) that all potentially pose ethical challenges, for my interlocutors, the most thorny and painful dilemma generally emerged in relation to wearing the hijab, and most notably at work. Two different trajectories shed light on the ethical dimension of these negotiations and modes of reasoning.

Mariam, a young woman of Tunisian background in her late twenties and a PhD candidate in psychology, was the first person in her family to achieve that educational level. Her father, a factory worker, had passed away while she was still in school. The family had faced economic difficulties from that time onward, and now she had to support herself financially. Throughout her teenage years she had studied Islam in a program offered by the Institut Europeen des Sciences Humaines of the Union des Organisations Islamiques de France, and she had worn the hijab since high school and throughout her time at university. But since she had started the PhD program, she strongly felt she was being left out by her professors. As she told me, all of the students in the program had been offered teaching positions except her. She feared that her PhD would not produce the university career to which she aspired if she continued wearing the hijab. A personal emotional crisis followed, which she described as very painful and full of doubts and uncertainty. At the end of this period, she decided to abandon her headscarf. This was her reasoning:

> Because, this is the struggle, to show the real face of Islam and not only the one you see on TV. . . . It bothered me that I could not continue, to show that Muslims are capable of doing something too. . . . That's not it: the men make war and the women are oppressed at home. To me, this is not Islam. And so I wanted to show that we are capable of achieving things too. We have to participate in French social life, in French political life; this is very important. And this has to happen with our generation. . . . Already during my master's, I saw the injustices and the difficulties. . . . So, after mature reflection—at least I hope so—I was able to resign myself to take it [the headscarf] off. . . . This is my own reflection, God is the only judge. Some of my Muslim friends did not really approve of that, certain of them I saw less and less afterward. But I feel that I made the right choice, because I believe that we have a task to accomplish here; this is my type of *jihad* [struggle], my personal way to do it.[36]

Sihem was also a young PhD student, in political science, in her early thirties, married, and the mother of a young child. Her parents had come to Germany as students from Syria and had been influenced by the Syrian Islamic revival movement. Sihem had therefore received a rather comprehensive Islamic education from her upper-middle-class parents. I used to meet her at the BFmF, where she occasionally gave lectures at the monthly Sunday seminars.

She had worn the headscarf since adolescence. Having ambitious career plans equal to Mariam's, she nonetheless stayed intransigent about her hijab and about the idea of "sacrificing" it for her work:

> My goal is to teach at university. I think we must not give in. We have to work hard to achieve this. We are not bad for society and we should not let ourselves be convinced to take off our headscarves. I have a friend who wore the headscarf until recently. She is a doctor. She had an offer to work in a big, prestigious hospital where you have great career opportunities. But they told her, as they had told many others before, we would love to take you, you have an excellent education, you would be qualified for the job. But we have a problem with the headscarf and that would damage the reputation of our clinic. You have to take it off. In the end she assented to take it off.
>
> I could not live with such a bad conscience vis-à-vis God. And I also think that society must understand that it is not the women who are wrong but society overreacting, which associates us with a symbolism and with political ideologies that we don't endorse at all, these extremist positions. They link this to the headscarf and we have to oppose this association. For me, this is most important, more important than having a job.

Both stories suggest that the decision to take off the hijab is not only a painful step for the individual believer but can also elicit disapproval from her peers. And even though, as mentioned in Chapter 3, there seems to be a growing acceptance of women without hijab in the revival circles, the tension between the indisputable religious obligation of the hijab and a more pragmatic approach connected to an understanding of the difficulties of its implementation remains unresolved. It is in this context that women like Mariam cautiously expressed that they thought the revival circles may have placed too much emphasis on the hijab rather than focusing on what they define as the number one priority, that is, to lift the Muslim community out of its precarious economic and social status. A few women have, in private conversations, also expressed their dissatisfaction that too many women used the hijab as an "excuse" for not working, for not being professionally ambitious. Hanan, who made such an argument, defended her own decision not to don the hijab in order to avoid not being able to realize her professional goal: "I am fed up with always being the last in society. If you put on the hijab and you stop working, it is only for yourself and the family; but if you work, you can change society." In her view, once Muslims had succeeded in attaining a certain economic and social weight, they could start making specific claims about their religious practice.

By pointing to the various approaches defended among my interlocutors, I do not wish merely to point to the tensions and unresolved conflicts over the hijab that still exist in the revival circles. What I find even more interesting are the important *similarities* in these divergent forms of reasoning. Beyond the idiosyncratic decision, there is consistently a deep concern for what the individual's place is within society and for the specific responsibilities that follow from there. Both Mariam and Sihem are deeply worried, not only about the individual eschatological consequences but also about the social entailments of their personal acts. In similar ways, both women saw their social obligations as closely connected to questions about representing Islam and Muslims.

Sihem considered that abandoning her headscarf would send the wrong signal to a society that seeks to exclude veiled Muslim women from participating fully in that society. This exclusion, she reasoned, was premised on erroneous assumptions, which could not be challenged if one complied with the regulations that follow from these assumptions. For Sihem, the struggle consisted precisely in contesting these suppositions by demonstrating that veiled women can be "modern," moderate, and professionally active; neither an illiterate housewife nor a "fanatic." Mariam too wants to challenge the negative representation of Islam in French society. However, according to her line of thought, most important was the impact that she, a Muslim woman and descendent of working class immigrants, might have, the difference she could make, in a professional position that had not yet accommodated women of her background. Being denied that position because of the headscarf, and therefore being denied the chance for her voice to be heard in the larger public sphere, she felt it was incumbent upon her to pursue the struggle without the headscarf:

> My PhD, I work on French converts to Islam, so [*laughter*] I push the doors a bit and take this as an opportunity to talk about Islam, and about myself, yes. I am Muslim, I live in this way, I believe this and that. And it's true that people listen to me more carefully since I don't wear the veil anymore. They acknowledge that I dress like everyone else, and at the same time I don't drink alcohol, I don't eat pork, while at the same time a Halima or a Fatima might drink. So, I explain, no I don't drink; yes, I am a practicing Muslim. And people started listening to me in a different way than when I wore the headscarf.

In this persistent struggle to represent Islam and Muslims positively, my interlocutors would frequently employ the notion of *da'wa* (invitation, call). Yet, although the term *da'wa* is embedded in a broader Islamic lexicon, in order for the broadening of its meaning in the diasporic context (as "representational *da'wa*") to be effective, it has to take into account definitions of modernity, progressiveness, and female emancipation that were defended by the majority society. The difficulty lay in deciding to what extent this form of *da'wa* was still in line with the most essential Islamic norms and modes of conduct, and at what point it would lead to an impermissible departure from them.

The conclusions drawn in that balancing act could diverge significantly, yet they all stemmed from the same understanding of the individual's responsibility for the greater common good. The idea of a common good (in Arabic, *maslaha*) had been theorized in certain traditions of Islamic legal thought and then was rediscovered in late nineteenth and early twentieth century reform discourses and contemporary revival discourses. Indeed, this notion was recurrently addressed and discussed in the classes and conferences I attended in the different Islamic centers (for France, see also Bowen 2010).[37] Armando Salvatore (2007) argues that *istislah* (the search for *maslaha*) shares important structural similarities with the Greek ethical category of *phronesis* (see Chapters 1 and 5). *Istislah* is a mode of reasoning that is less text-bound and more context-friendly than other methods of jurisprudence (such as consensus, *ijma'*).[38] Within Islamic legal thought, *istislah* is a particular instantiation of *ijtihad,* a method of jurisprudence that relies on independent judgment in the absence of clear textual guidance.[39] As a case of *ijtihad* with a specific view toward the common good, *istislah* also differs from a sheer utilitarian approach because its considerations are not limited to this world and its goods but apply also to the hereafter (Salvatore 2007: 156–157). In this respect, *maslaha* has to be distinguished from a relativistic approach and from the mere pursuit of particularistic interests, personal preferences, and passionate desires (2007: 162). At the same time, this tradition does not oppose the pursuit of self-interest as such; when the pursuit of personal interest serves the *maslaha,* then it is "not only . . . legitimate, but . . . necessary for common welfare" (2007: 166).[40]

The particular tradition of Islamic legal reasoning studied by Salvatore extended *istislah* to enable laypersons to deal with the complexity of the social world, which is defined by a tension between "goods and ills [that] are not found in a pure form . . . , on the one hand, and the moral command of the *shari'a* to do good and prohibit evil, on the other" (2007: 161). In other words, although this approach was initiated by and linked to a legal command, it also confirms that phronetic reasoning can never be defined exclusively by command or authority (2007:159). *Istislah,* Salvatore argues, therefore delineates "an ongoing process of agential and relational responsibility for authoring and authorizing the kind of social practice that defines the common good" (2007: 170).[41] In Mariam's and Sihem's mode of reasoning, a resonance with the ethical tradition of *maslaha* is apparent. After carefully scrutinizing their own intentions, they connected their own interests and desires to a broader, common interest. They took scripture seriously, but did not constrain their reasoning purely to scripture ("command"); they reflected on the possible consequences of their various actions. It was only from there that they made their decisions.

I also find helpful Salvatore's discussion of *phronesis* within this particular Islamic tradition, because he clearly shows how this modality of moral reasoning avoids "over-subjectifying" the agent by defining the deeply *relational* character of phronetic reasoning. Important in this understanding of reasoning is that it is not rooted in the "pure volition of a virtuous subject" but instead emerges through interaction and is therefore "intrinsically intersubjective" (Salvatore 2007: 162). This relational quality builds on the social interaction between *ego* and *alter,* but is not limited to it, because God as another possible agent is always included in this interaction. This tradition, Salvatore writes, reflects

> the view of the actor not as a "subject" of virtuous or vicious conduct or simply
> of rights and duties, but as a genuinely relational agent, who discharges duties
> incumbent on him/her, whose origin and justification are firmly inscribed in the
> . . . triangular relationship between ego, alter, and God. (2007: 166).

This tradition accounts for individual agency without overemphasizing it, and I would argue that it can accommodate other modes of ethical practice and reasoning that include the prospect of "being acted upon" (Lambek 2010; see also Mittermaier 2012). Such an account of *phronesis* does not, therefore, necessarily depend on a "unity of consciousness" and on a "rational basis of ethical judgment" based on the idea of an "'unaltered' or pure and unitary state of mind," a notion criticized by Michael Lambek (2010: 722–723) as reflective of a dominant Western model of mind. It does not endorse the purification and compartmentalization that are so persistent in much Enlightenment thought, but rather takes a holistic approach, as also advocated by Lambek's (2002) use of *phronesis* (see Chapter 5). It thus attributes to thought a broad range of moral sources and resources beyond those grounded in human reason, and encourages us not to oppose the subject's intentionality to inputs coming from other agents, such as the Divine (or spirits and witchcraft), because the concept precisely acknowledges an inherent relation between ego, alter, and Alter (however the latter might actually be defined). Going beyond human reason and intentionality does not defer ethical practice but, on the contrary, has important ethical consequences and redefines significantly the way we conceive of ethical practice.

Although my pious practitioners' acknowledgement of agency "from Elsewhere" (Mittermaier 2012) alludes most often to less esoteric practices than the spirit possession discussed in Lambek (2002, 2010) or the dream visions examined in Mittermaier (2012), the mode of reasoning that accompanied their acknowledgment still revealed quite forcefully the limitation of an account that links ethical reasoning to "rational" or detached "observational" reason. Women's deeply felt sense of divine agency interfering in this world, not only as a motivation for their acts but also as producing these acts in the first place, yields a quite different type of ethical reasoning than one built on such notions as the agency of the intentional, reasoning, and knowing subject. Listen to Sihem as she continues her account:

> For me, religion comes first, and I could not live with such a conflict of conscience. Because for me it is something complete and perfect. And if I am really conscious of this, and I have a choice and yet I still choose the wrong priorities, then it is against religion. This is beyond doubt; I have confidence that if one wants to follow the path of God, God supports you. God is with his believers and He helps them. . . . Because in urgent situations I have always prayed a lot and I do this for God, and I do it with the knowledge that He'll help me, *insha'Allah,* no matter what I'm heading for.

Although Sihem clearly acknowledged her own responsibility, she also insisted on the limits of her own agency and was adamant about the ultimate and supreme agency of a divine power. These two dimensions of agency do not sit in opposition but form a mutually related whole. Concretely, though she recognized and actively contested structural difficulties for Muslim practitioners in the German context, she nonetheless understood God to be the ultimate and omnipotent agent; it is God who will have the final say on all matters, including whether or not she can pursue a professional career while wearing her headscarf. I frequently witnessed participants in the revival circles emphasizing choice, reflexivity, and resistance while at the same time locating ultimate agency in the divine.[42] This explains why my interlocutors' decisions regarding whether or not to don the veil, whether or not to take the veil off at the work-place or even full-time were commonly preceded by *istikhara,* the prayer in which the believer asks for guidance in making difficult choices.

This understanding of the nexus between individual agency and an omnipo-tent divine agency also impacted my interlocutors' reflections on their activism for Muslims' right to practice their religion in public. Numerous women I talked to claimed that the quest for recognition in mainstream society (through activist groups and so on) was not enough and insisted instead on bringing their de-mands first and foremost to God. Hence, a difficult situation becomes an oppor-tunity to cultivate certain virtues and develop one's relationship with God. Many of my interlocutors were quite ambivalent toward activist groups that defended Muslims' rights, which emerged especially in the years before and after the 2004 ban on conspicuous religious signs in French public secondary schools, and also ambivalent about court appeals instigated by individual Muslims in Germany.[43] Olfa addressed this dilemma quite often in her classes, as well as during the Sat-urday brunches. She herself worked for several years with groups like Le Collec-tif des Féministes pour l'égalité *(Feminists for Equality Collective)* and Une École pour tous et toutes *(One School for All Collective).* While she valorized their work, she was at the same time skeptical about that kind of activism, which she called "too restricted." She elaborated on this point in one of our conversations:

> If I claim my rights but do not also ask for Allah's help, my approach is wrong—you see what I'm saying? My approach is to say that Allah can do everything. The problem is that if I put my hope in human beings, in my claim for rights, I don't put my hope in Allah; then my approach is biased. Of course you have to claim your rights, although this is pretty hopeless these days, but I do not lose faith in Allah's help in this situation. And so, if I do have this lucidity in regard to this situation, then I can take the approach, as I mentioned earlier, which tries to satisfy Allah in spite of all these constraints.

As Olfa spelled out, restricting oneself to "claiming rights" could even be counterproductive relative to the ultimate goal of leading a pious life. Hence, next to claiming rights, Muslims must appeal to God, in whom one should place all of one's confidence (*tawakkul*), trusting in his ability to intervene in the situation. Several women who had been engaged in a similar political activism felt that in these contexts "God was absent," and introducing that dimension into the debate was not highly appreciated. Over time, they felt that practices like wearing the *hijab* might even lose their original meaning because they had to be submitted exclusively to the discursive regimes of rights and freedom.[44] As Saliha, who had been active for several years in these associations, put it, "At one point I didn't even remember why I wore it [the hijab] in the first place."

Perceiving the difficulties they encountered as divine trials, the other virtue often invoked by my interlocutors, which was closely linked to *tawakkul,* was *sabr* (patience, endurance). These two virtues enabled my interlocutors to deal with suffering related to their experiences of exclusion. A fundamental virtue in the Qur'an, *sabr* was elaborated by Islamic theologians as a central pillar of piety.[45] Of course, as with other Islamic virtues, *sabr* does not come naturally with faith but must be cultivated. Linked to *tawakkul* and to the dogma of predestination (*qadr*), the concept of *sabr* is often analyzed by non-Muslims as proof of the passive or even fatalist attitudes that the Islamic religion supposedly promoted (Starrett 1995: 956). *Tawakkul, sabr,* and *'amal* (hope), which are founded on a metaphysical hope, seem to contradict the idealistic conception of the subject and its capacity for agency. However, for the practitioners I encountered, such an interpretation would betray the specific agency that this mode of being triggered. This is what Olfa succinctly explained during a class devoted to *sabr.* In her lecture, she connected the cultivation of that virtue to the acknowledgement of the dogma of predestination: "If God wants me to experience hardship, I need to know that I have the capacity to endure it and to react accordingly. In the resignation to God, you put Allah's will next to the human will."

It is on the basis of a similar logic that scholars have argued for quite some time now that hope and endurance gesture toward the possibility of encountering specific historical conditions differently, and toward different modalities of engagement with the world, often through modes of temporal apprehension that are distinct from "chrononormative" time. Talal Asad (2003: 91), for instance, shows that notions like suffering and endurance are not synonymous with "passivity" but may "create a space for moral action."[46] Pierre Bourdieu (2000) captures parts of this dimension quite well when he defines hope as an emotional expression of *protension,* defined as a *practical* sense of the forthcoming. But because he too closely connects the capacity for hope with power and objective opportunity related to social location, and because he situates it purely within the immanent world, he cannot quite grasp the kind of metaphysical hope I am concerned with here.

Phronetic reasoning in the tradition discussed by Salvatore and Lambek can better account for the multiple layers of moral reasoning, for intentionality and proactive reflexivity, for bearing and enduring, for suffering and being acted

upon, and for being passionate and affective. Rather than opposing these different facets in a way that is often associated with Kantian reasoning, the modes of
ethical reasoning enacted by these devout women integrate "rational," contemplative, and observational reasoning with deep emotions (fear, doubt, compassion, love, ambition, and hope); activist positions and confrontational stances
can occur in conjunction with the appeal to divine help and with inspirations
acquired through *istikhara* prayers or dreams. I do not want to overemphasize
the notion of an "altered state of mind" (Lambek 2010; Mittermaier 2012) in
order criticize the ideal of the "unaltered state of mind." Rather, I think of both
dimensions as situated along a continuum, neither clearly distinct nor mutually exclusive, but more connected or interdependent than is at times suggested.
Furthermore, these modes of ethical reasoning do not stand in opposition to
practices of self-cultivation, but they require prior learning and habituation of
virtuous action, and they provide further occasion for ethical self-practice.

Although all of my interlocutors shared the same *telos,* that is, the ideal of a
good life defined as leading a life pleasing to God within an eschatological vision, the means these women chose to realize that supreme goal were diverse,
divergent, and contested. They depended, on the one hand, on their individual
perceptions of their place as members of a stigmatized minority in a democratic
society in which they could also contemplate the possibilities that this society
could potentially offer. On the other hand, the means they chose were linked
to personal hierarchizations of their duties toward God: the individual's duty
toward a particular religious practice; the duty of doing *da'wa* (in the sense of
representing Islam well to a hostile outside world); and the duty to respond to
difficult situations (considered to be divine trials) with specific Islamic virtues
(such as *sabr* and *tawakkul*) while acknowledging God's supreme agency in
this world. These women's diverse and divergent negotiations in pursuit of the
higher good conveyed that different (and antagonistic) discursive formations
informed the individual subject, instilling very different emotional dispositions
and capacities within her. But all of these diverse and antagonistic arguments,
desires, and perceptions still reflected a similar concern for doing the *right
thing*—not only for oneself but in harmony with one's broader social obligations. These women's specific (phronetic) reasoning allowed them to create,
inhabit, and navigate their own complex moral spaces within post-Christian
secular society. In spite of considerable internal conflict, fragmentation, and
even revision of some former opinions, this reasoning could impart a sense of
moral unity in their lives.

7 PIOUS CITIZENS

"A political being is not to be defined as the citizen has been, as an abstract, disconnected bearer of rights, privileges and immunities, but as a person whose existence is located in a particular place and draws its sustenance from circumscribed relations: family, friends, church, neighborhood, workplace, community, town, city. These relationships are the sources from which political beings draw power—symbolic, material and psychological—and that enable them to act together. For true political power involves not only acting so as to effect decisive changes; it also means the capacity to receive power, to be acted upon, to change and be changed. From a democratic perspective, power is not simply force that is generated; it is experience, sensibility, wisdom, even melancholy distilled from the diverse relations and circles we move within."

—Sheldon Wolin 1985, p. 256

IN THE PREVIOUS CHAPTERS, I have attended to my interlocutors' various ethical struggles, caused not only by the difficulties of accepting and enacting the orthodox Islamic virtues promoted by the revival movement, but also by the intricacies involved in implementing them in an everyday life rooted within a secular society. One of the biggest handicaps the women faced was that many aspects of their orthodox piety could not easily be rendered intelligible through a mainstream (liberal-secular) discourse. This disability not only rendered their religious practices suspicious in the eyes of observers in their non-Muslim (and nonrevival Muslim) environment, but it also made it hard for the women themselves to interiorize many of these practices, given the impact of these very discourses on their own sense of self.

Especially in Chapters 2, 3, and 4, I chronicled the complications and struggles implied in adopting orthodox Islamic practices of self-cultivation, which at the same time revealed how these women—and young, European-born revival participants in general—engaged the Islamic traditions in ways that made sense to them, thereby retaining the tradition's "plausibility." In the process, the tradition itself did not remain unchanged; tradition, as well as the various practices it commands, was rethought. Practices gained new meanings that corresponded to the contours of a self that had also been impacted by and was engaging with the subject-fashioning project of modern secular discourses that circulate in European public spheres. Thus, the tradition was fine-tuned to the women's "modern" sensibilities while the self was worked upon to align it with tradition.

This double movement was necessary because the practitioners did not intend to "reform" Islam so as to adapt it to liberal sensibilities. Rather, they persistently emphasized the obligation to be in accordance with orthodoxy, referring to discourses of authenticity and legitimacy that were certified by orthodox scholars considered trustworthy. Throughout the book I have documented these various discourses and modes of reasoning, which reconfigured in subtle but important ways the orthodox Islamic tradition, albeit in a way that did not pose any direct challenge to the orthodoxy.

Another constant feature was the heightened awareness of their status, not only as a religious and racialized minority, but also as practitioners of an orthodox Islam (with its potential for visibility given its emphasis on codes of public conduct), which put them in a particularly vulnerable and isolated position within mainstream society. Conscious of this exposedness, they relentlessly thought about questions of representation. One effect of this awareness was that they had to take into account the signifying effect of practice, initially conceived in terms of self-cultivation but open to being (negatively) deciphered by the non-Muslims (and nonorthodox Muslims) around them. In such a context, the women tried to gain control over the signifying aspect of their embodied practices (and even of their bodies themselves), whether by reducing or increasing their visibility and public presence, or by resignifying the practice in question. They thereby hoped to communicate their difference in a more positive light to the ever-present suspicious gaze of the broader society, and to translate their unintelligible strangeness into an intelligible and "tolerable" difference. In the light of increased hostility to Muslims, and to Muslim women in particular, across Europe, including in France and Germany, one must concede that this communication project, quite optimistically undertaken by the pious practitioners I engaged with during the years of my research, has failed to a great extent. This failure, I would argue, must be read at least partially as the result of the extreme rigidity of discursive structures in contemporary European public spheres, and of the unwillingness of the actors in the public sphere to critically engage their own discursive foreclosures.

Talal Asad (2003: 184) has rightly stated that public spheres are "*necessarily* (not just contingently) articulated by power," and that this power not only shapes the space given over to free speech within the public sphere, but more so, it constitutes "sensibilities—memories and aspirations, fears and hopes—of speakers and listeners," "the manner in which they exist," and it shapes "their propensity to act or react in distinct ways" (2003: 185). Thus, to understand the visceral discomfort elicited in certain "secular" subjects when they perceive visibly practicing Muslim bodies like those of my interlocutors within a secularly defined public sphere, one needs to acknowledge that these acts might constitute the "dislocation of [a] moral world" (2003: 185). It is this affect-shaping dimension that explains the capacity of the public sphere to render other ways of being not only unintelligible, but also unthinkable and undesirable.

Pious Virtues and Social Ethics

In the contemporary post-9/11 political climate that has given license in Europe and beyond to an unprecedented Islamophobic discourse and mode of governance, a project like this book necessarily seeks to shed a sympathetic light on the current victims of this climate. Violence against Muslim individuals, especially women, and toward Islamic buildings all over Europe has increased in recent years to an alarming extent. In France and Germany more particularly, the series of attacks against Muslim houses of worship has continued apace; the murder of Marwa El-Sherbini in Germany in 2009 (and especially the lack of attention accorded to it), as well as numerous violent attacks on veiled Muslim women in France especially since 2010, which left several of them seriously injured, confirm this trend. The success of the German organization PEGIDA (Patriotic Europeans Against the Islamization of Europe) founded in October 2014, which succeeded within six months to mobilize up to 25,000 people for its demonstrations in various German cities and the murderous attacks on the French satire magazine Charlie Hebdo in January 2015 committed by three young French Muslim men followed by a new wave of violence against Muslim individuals and houses of worship have exacerbated this hostile and violent climate. In such an atmosphere, writing a book on orthodox Muslim women in Europe is not without its challenges. One consequence is that this book also becomes an attempt to promote a better understanding of my interlocutors' "unintelligible" lifestyle and practices, and to evoke nuances where nuances are often made unavailable. Furthermore, even while acknowledging the at times patriarchal assumptions of my interlocutors, I did not make the critique of these positions a priority but instead situated them within the larger space of an evolving and internally contested debate.[1] In pursuing this approach, I have also been mindful of the possibility that some of my interlocutors' statements—which can seem rather problematic according to liberal or progressive standards—would be taken out of context and used to bolster political messages that I would not endorse.[2]

I have instead emphasized the different modes of agency, reflexivity, and subjectivity of these women, even if they did not always map onto liberal definitions of these terms. Following the lead of authors such as Talal Asad, Saba Mahmood, and Charles Hirschkind, I have equally highlighted the differences between secular and nonsecular modes of perception and modes of reasoning. As Mahmood writes in the conclusion to her book *Politics of Piety* (2005: 191): "the juxtapositions of the practices of the pietists against secular-liberal understandings of agency, body, and authority . . . take on a necessary quality" because "the horizon of secular-liberal presuppositions about the proper role that religiosity should play in the constitution of a modern subjectivity, community, and polity will inevitably structure my audience's reading of this book." At the same time, my material obliged me to place a much stronger emphasis on the imbricatedness of these different regimes, which made it difficult to depict them in binary ways, even for analytical purposes. Ironically, however, in spite of this entangledness, the pious life-worlds that I document always run the risk of being (mis)read through the lens of concepts and theories built on this same set of binary constructions.[3]

In addition to its strategy of unsettling and displacing these binaries, which continues to be an obligation for everyone working on orthodox Islamic life-worlds, this book has another objective. In current debates on Islam's supposed challenge to liberal Europe, much thought is invested in defining the civic virtues necessary for enabling a pluralist society in which members of divergent religions, ethnic and racial groups, and sexual orientations can live together harmoniously—virtures that (especially orthodox) Muslims supposedly lack. Throughout the book I have provided ample material that identifies a specific modality of social ethics that these pious practitioners sought to embody. In the remaining pages, I probe this finding of my research for its potential to contribute productively to current discussions of civic virtues in a context of pluralism.

Let me remind the reader here of my interlocutors' strong concern for the broader social consequences of their various pious duties, not only for the Muslim community but also for the wider society. I began in Chapters 2 and 3 by discussing different practices of ethical self-cultivation, which the practitioners also defended in terms of their broad social benefits. On the one hand, the women valorized these practices for improving their conduct in public, for increasing their civility, politeness, restraint, and respect in regard to other persons. On the other hand, they connected the ethical lifestyle enabled by these practices to the core aspiration of improving the general condition of the

Muslim *umma,* particularly in the immediate French or German context. Thus, the knowledge transmitted within the revival circles regarding what was considered authentic Islamic conduct, in public and in private, was considered to counteract precisely those problematic social practices (such as "forced" marriages and violence against women) carried out by certain individuals of Muslim faith that the mainstream society generally perceived to be characteristic features of the Muslim community and serious impediments to its successful integration. In Chapter 4, I discussed how my interlocutors' cultivation of certain gendered pious virtues stood nonetheless in an interesting relation to a broader consideration of what constituted the just society and of the personal ethic essential to realize that ideal. They all insisted relentlessly that any rights claim within human relationships had to be accompanied by considerations of duties, obligations, and responsibilities. By doing so, they defined social relations—in the private sphere but also in the public domain—by mutuality and dependency rather than by any priority of individual rights. Finally, in Chapters 5 and 6, I investigated how my interlocutors dealt with moral conflicts caused by the contradictory ethical demands to which they felt committed. These conflicts arose because their desire to embody certain Islamic values and to exercise specific religious practices often risked impeding their participation as full members of society (partly because of the restrictive nature of the secular society in which they lived), which would then jeopardize their aspiration to make a positive contribution to society.

It is in this context that I extended my theoretical framework from self-cultivation to the Aristotelian concept of *phronesis,* a notion that has also been elaborated in different ways within Islamic ethical and legal traditions. Using this term, I demonstrated that the negotiations enacted by my correspondents were informed by a reasoning that went beyond sheer self-interest and reflected a deep obligation to a larger common good. This commitment provided the shared ethical ground for a variety of distinct individual decisions with very divergent outcomes and social consequences.

I am not arguing that my pious interlocutors' social ethics were uniquely informed by Islamic traditions. As I have shown throughout the book, their opinions, discourses, and subjectivities were clearly shaped by a variety of modes of reasoning, principles, and concepts stemming from different discursive traditions and multiple concrete life experiences. Among these were the impacts of liberal political concepts such as democracy, rights, and equality, which also affected their engagement with the Islamic sources. The respective national interpretations of these concepts were influential for women in both countries in their reading of these terms and for the ways in which they situated themselves in regard to these categories. In this sense, observing how my interlocutors sought to inhabit their social environment in ethical ways not only challenges us to think about the different moral sources for citizenship, but also demands that we acknowledge that a person's civic ethic can be fashioned out of a variety of sources that interact in various configurations.

When it came to the specific modes of reasoning employed to solve moral dilemmas, however, something was at work that was substantially rooted in those Islamic ethical traditions that reflect phronetic modes of reasoning. This type of moral reasoning, which is intrinsically and not contingently committed to the implementation of a common good, that I argue can challenge some of the dominant secular assumptions about citizenship ethics. In elaborating this claim, I also bring into the debate alternative approaches that have not been given much voice so far but that carry within themselves the potential to provide a more robustly pluralist account of citizenship ethics.

Ethics of Citizenship

Much ink has been spilled by political theorists about the qualities or dispositions required of citizens in liberal pluralist democracies. The dominant narrative depicts the juridical citizen as a universally stable category, emancipated from religion—one who stands at a self-reflexive distance from, or takes a critical attitude toward, her inherited (local or parental) traditions. This attitude is often considered not only to promote personal autonomy directly, but also to foster the capacity "to put [oneself] in other people's shoes," which in turn becomes a necessary condition for "public reasonableness" (Kymlicka 2001: 307–310).

Although not identical to these political theories, contemporary cosmopolitan writings have formulated a similar stance. Most cosmopolitan thinkers, whatever their specific political leanings, consider the attitude of critical distance from one's own personal identity and modes of life to be the central virtue that enables an individual to commit to such a cosmopolitan mind-set. It is in this regard that Martha Nussbaum (1997: 57–58), for instance, encourages us, in her neo-Stoic cosmopolitanism,

> to become, to a certain extent, philosophical exiles from our own ways of life, seeing them from the vantage point of the outsider and asking the questions an outsider is likely to ask about their meaning and function. . . . In other words,

a stance of detachment from uncritical loyalty to one's own ways promotes the kind of evaluation that is truly reason based."

This path involves a lonely and almost heroic condition, according to Nussbaum, because one is equally exiled from "the comfort of assured truths, from the warm nestling feeling of being surrounded by people who share one's convictions and passions" (1997: 83).[4]

Since 9/11 and the July 7, 2005, bombings in London, cosmopolitanism has enjoyed a new wave of success in Europe (and beyond) as an alternative to multiculturalism, which is attacked for not sufficiently addressing integration or social cohesion, and thereby for implicitly contributing to the growth of Islamic extremism.[5] Recent European cosmopolitan theorizing, which has to be understood as part of this wider critique of multiculturalism, has sought to reintroduce some notions of shared values into conceptualizations of democratic pluralist societies. In this line of thought, Ulrich Beck (2004: 449), for instance, urges the acknowledgment of a "universalist minimum" that consists of a certain number of inviolable norms and is accompanied by a new cosmopolitan awareness defined by "reflexivity" and that valorizes "experiences of being foreign or living between, of social isolations, ambivalence and rootlessness." This attitude, which Beck calls "both/and consciousness," should be emerging in the self-understanding of individuals, groups, movements, and, Beck contends, "ultimately even religions." In similar fashion, Paul Gilroy, one of the eminent thinkers of postcolonial Britain, proposes a minimal condition for any form of "cosmopolitan commitment," which he defines as "the principled and methodical cultivation of a degree of estrangement from one's own culture and history" (Gilroy 2005: 67).

Another proposal for an "ethics of citizenship," one that looks more specifically at religious pluralism in liberal democracies at a moment in time that has revealed that the "secular age" has not in fact done away with religion, is proposed by Jürgen Habermas (2005, 2006, 2008). Rather than exclude religion from the secular public domain—two arenas that Habermas continues to define as separate from each other—he recognizes the potential of religions to have a positive impact as they "articulate moral intuitions" that can be conducive to the democratic state. But this potential can be realized only through a significant change of mentality in both secular and religious citizens: they must self-critically reassess their respective traditions and modalities of reason (whether religion or Enlightenment derived). Only such a self-critical reassessment will make it possible, according to Habermas, for the two groups to enter into a dialogue, and for each to "translate" its particular language into a "publicly accessible language"

(Habermas 2005: 28). Although he requires this self-reflexive work from both religious and nonreligious citizens, Habermas nonetheless places a significantly higher burden on religious citizens, asking them to accept the priority of secular reason in the formal political domain and to differentiate their own religious community from the wider political one (Habermas 2003: 6). And though he acknowledges post-Enlightenment/post-Reformation (Judeo-Christian) religiosity as particularly apt to perform such a reflexive labor, Habermas is convinced that Muslims still need to go through the same process if they want to develop the qualities indispensible for citizens in a liberal democracy (Habermas 2008).

In all of these writings—which reflect a wide range of political and philosophical sensibilities and projects—there seems to be the conviction that in order to be a citizen in a pluralist society or pluralist world, one has to adopt a self-critical and therefore a somehow distanced stance toward one's own identities and belongings, traditions, histories, and intimate convictions. Only this peculiarly reflexive, detached, and allegedly dispassionate viewpoint is seen as capable of preventing not only exclusivist nationalisms, ethnocentrisms, and racisms, but also religious fundamentalisms, from taking root, so that a shared life and commitment to a broad sense of justice and the common good becomes possible. And as Habermas makes explicitly clear, this reflexive capacity is the result of the achievements of modern Western rationalism (Habermas, quoted in Euben 2001: 275). Such an understanding of the requirements of modern democratic citizenship makes religious subjects like my interlocutors seem less likely to fit the category of modern citizens, given their continued "strong attachment" to the Islamic tradition and the Muslim *umma*.

The requirement of detachment that is defended by liberals, cosmopolitans, and a number of postcolonial critiques alike as a central value for modern democratic citizenship resonates strongly with what Webb Keane (2007; discussed in Chapter 2) calls the "moral narrative of modernity," defined as a story of "estrangement." The reflexive individual who is capable of distancing herself from the world and from social relations and who can properly distinguish between nature and culture, subject and object, is understood to be a more autonomous subject, more capable of agency and, above all, of being critical. All variations of estrangement require an understanding of "a certain notion of modern disenchantment and alienation—and thus, by back-projection, of nonmodern enchantment and unities, of which we must be wary" (Keane 2007:12).[6]

As is apparent throughout this book, I did not formulate my critique of these assumptions by positing, through my ethnographic material, a wholly oppositional—that is nondetached—mode of being in the world. Rather (and in line with Keane's argumentative strand), I questioned the moral implications of this epistemological claim by highlighting that modalities of reflexive distanciation, far from being peculiarly modern, not only are part of the fabric of many different traditions, including the Islamic tradition, but also result from the experiences of social life itself, and these diverse modalities of reflexivity interact in various ways with more markedly "modern" ones.

I have shown throughout the book a range of modalities of detachment that are persistent within the discourses, modes of reasoning, and practices enacted by my interlocutors. One such mode, observable in conduct and discourse, was the women's constant awareness of their minority positionality relative to the dominant society. Neither a specificly modern phenomenon nor connected to the Islamic tradition, it is simply part and parcel of the existential condition of any stigmatized minority to view itself through the gaze of the dominant Other, to always take into consideration the majority's vantage point, ways of thinking and possible reactions. The women I studied showed a constant awareness that every visible action they undertook could be unfavorably observed by the majority society and prone to use it against them, individually or collectively.

Another mode of detachment, or objectification, that I discussed is more closely in line with certain assumptions of the "moral narrative of modernity." As discussed especially in Chapters 2, 3, and 4, my interlocutors conveyed a certain objectified relation to the Islamic religion as being the more "authentic" and "authenticated" approach to Islam. They considered a critical reflexive awareness to be indispensible to distinguishing inherited cultural traditions (which, according to the women, were often falsely believed to be rooted in religion) from "true" Islam. In this distinction, the older generations figured as traditional counterparts from which one had to set oneself apart. In their discussions about the distinction between reflexivity and unreflexivity, notions such as sincerity, conviction, and deep understanding were also discussed and promoted.

Finally, a third form of distanciation was inherent in the phronetic reasoning that my interlocutors commonly enacted in the context of difficult decisions and moral dilemmas, as elaborated in Chapters 5 and 6. This detachment involved relativizing one's personal desires to a certain extent because the ethical command "to do the right thing" required a regard for a "common good" that had to go beyond (though not necessarily against) the limited interests and aspirations of the individual self. This modality of detachment was not based on the peculiar modern reflexivity evoked earlier but was instead connected to certain Islamic traditions of ethical reasoning. It offers an interesting and strong example of a mode of reflexive distancing that is neither secular nor modern nor dispassionate. While my correspondents sought (with varying degrees of success) through practices of self-cultivation to work precisely against any kind of "ambivalence" or emotional "detachment" from their religious tradition, these very practices simultaneously enabled an ethical reasoning that involved a critical distancing from their immediate personal interests in order to take into account an enlarged understanding of the common good. And whereas this understanding of the common good often focused on the diasporic Muslim community, it was not limited to it.

Various political theorists have recovered the notion of *phronesis,* which Aristotle defined as the essential quality for political leadership and considered to be a core faculty for public and political action (see, for example, Barber 1988; Beiner 1984; Beiner and Nedelsky 2001; Arendt 1982).[7] Most of these approaches have been strictly limited to discussion of Western political theory and democratic thought. It is to the merit of Armando Salvatore (2007), whose work is discussed in the previous chapters, that he pluralized (or deprovincialized) his theoretical framework in order to think about the foundation of publicness, and ultimately of potential democratic action, from within different (not exclusively secular or Western) traditions.[8] For Salvatore, *phronesis* too is "the stepping stone for assessing the genesis of public reasoning" (2007: 11). But he traces how this classical Greek concept is transformed by and within different traditions, including the Islamic one such that it came to have a central impact on Muslim practices of public reasoning. Salvatore does not reject articulations of *phronesis* that are grounded in transcendence—built here on the "triadic model between ego, alter, and Alter/God" (245) and connected to a *telos*—because for him such grounding is not equivalent to unreflexivity or to an inability to take into account a larger general good beyond one's own *telos.* Rather, he argues, such a perspective also involves "reflexivity, change, and constant revision" (2007: 74). Similarly, Salvatore contends that "a full-fledged *telos* does not configure a 'substantive' anchoring of specific conceptions and hierarchies of the goods pursued but is the given, yet *contestable and revisable* form of argumentation and reasoning" (Salvatore 2007: 77, my emphasis).[9]

Salvatore's reflections are central for expanding dominant secular theorizations of citizenship, which are usually fraught with anxiety toward notions such as transcendence and *telos*. It is probably the work of Muslim thinker Tariq Ramadan who was influential among my interlocutors—that best exemplifies how this tradition of thought has been revitalized within the European context and made fruitful for developing an Islamic ethics of citizenship. At the core of Ramadan's preaching and writing is the goal of promoting among European Muslims an ethic of citizenship that is faithful to the principles of the "social" message of Islam, an objective that is spelled out, for instance, in his *Western Muslims and the Future of Islam* (2003). In this book, as in his many other writings, he insists on "social commitment" and "social action" as central "moral commitments" for Muslims (2003: 147). In his elaboration of the duties of Muslim citizens in Europe, Islamic traditions of phronetic reasoning, as invoked, for instance, in Salvatore's work, clearly resonate. They are especially salient in Ramadan's reflections on the possibility of action within the larger framework defined by the Islamic ethical and legal tradition. Here Ramadan distinguishes, interestingly, between the search for new rulings, which can be accomplished only by religious scholars, and the possibilities for choice in conflicting situations that present themselves in everyday life.[10] And whereas these choices have to reflect the Islamic principles and directions laid out by religious scholars, they are not completely prescribed by them:

> Bearing in mind the general message and its ethic, which directs their conscience, wherever they are, to defend justice, promote the good, and reform their society, Muslims have a duty to make an appropriate study of their society in order to determine the features of the common good (*maslaha*), the main achievements to be preserved, the injustices to be fought as a priority, and the means at their disposal and, at the same time, to identify the actors and the key points in the social and political dynamics of their society. It is then a matter of applying concretely the body of directions put forward by scholars: to work for justice and against every form of injustice, *to choose the best possible of the good things available and the least evil, and never to forget ethics when evaluating the causes, consequences, and means of carrying out an action and in all circumstances to evaluate the ultimate purpose of one's deeds. . . .*
>
> "The way of faithfulness" is a way that leads toward more justice, and civic and political involvement in a society of whatever kind must move in the same direction. So, *individuals should in their own hearts and consciences, according to their own understanding of the world and their own opinions, weigh their involvement according to this criterion and note the scope for maneuver* that their society allows them." (Ramadan 2003: 162–164, emphasis added)[11]

For Tariq Ramadan, then, citizenship is deeply inspired and enabled by spirituality. It is up to the central principles of Islam to lay out the contours of a civic ethic capable of transcending narrowly "communitarian" perspectives (*communautarisme*):

> "Promoting an ethic to be applied to the citizenry demands first of all that one feel entrusted with a mission that consists in reminding one's fellow citizens of the demanding responsibility they have, on both the individual and collective levels, to respect their fellows and the creation as a whole. . . . The principles that undergird the "community of faith" require that we act against communitarianism and the thinking of the ghetto and sectarianism. . . . [A] commitment, if it is inspired and fed by the principles and ethical message of Islam, must be put at the service of all, for the good of all." (2003: 168).[12]

In Ramadan's thought, then, the commitment to live according to Islamic principles—rather than ambiguity, rootlessness, or the methodical cultivation of estrangement from one's culture—can afford a mode of detachment from personal and immediate community-related interests, imposing the obligation to acquire a larger understanding of justice for society as a whole.

It is clearly these types of teachings that also inspired my interlocutors' pronounced commitment to being socially active in their society. They understood it as part of their Islamic duties, and it channeled their reasoning when they faced conflicting demands in regard to this overall objective. Of course it does not follow that all these women embodied Ramadan's encouragements in an ideal-typical way; many of them did so in less activist and methodical terms than Ramadan may have had in mind. Nor does it follow from this commitment to a common good beyond the limits of the community that all the women became equally willing to build extra-community alliances in the struggle for broader justice. Just as they derived very different decisions from the mode of moral reasoning I discussed in the last two chapters, this overall commitment could implicate various stances, some of which we might find more suitable than others for progressive democratic action and intercommunity world-making. Evidently, this variability is not peculiar to revival Muslims but generally illustrates the wide range of investments and priorities that one can find among any group of people. Although the ethical reasoning I have been concerned with enables, as a potentiality, the development of certain political sensibilities and virtues that allow active engagement in larger societal and political debates, my interlocutors activate and nourish them in very different ways. This is also why we find among revival Muslims in Europe—in this case, in Germany and France—ongoing and lively debates over how to practically define or delineate the required mode of civic engagement.

What I find important to emphasize again, however, is that, for my interlocutors, it is a specific understanding of Islamic ethics, which they read in the light of their particular historical and social contexts, that produces a certain "care for the world" (Arendt 1982: 52). This "care for the world" is not set against the "care for the self," as Hannah Arendt would have it, but is intimately attached to it. The latter provides the necessary virtues, dispositions, affective attachments, and sensibilities that enable the former. A similar reflection causes political theorist Fred Dallmayr (2001: 72) to acknowledge that one of the contributions that ethical teachings (including religions) might provide for the discussion of democratic politics is the "reconnection of ethics and politics." Here, in contrast to the more modern understanding of a disembodied mindset, *ethics* refers to the "sustained labor of formative maturation or paideia," that is, it is "the rechanneling of human energies in the direction of the public good, requiring the cultivation of moral dispositions" (2001: 72). In his work, Dallmayr joins a range of thinkers who seek to destabilize the dominant framing of the citizen as a universal constant, necessarily emancipated from religion, sustained through an independent political ethic that is accessible to all. They wish to imagine instead a space of political possibility composed of a variety of ways of being-in-common, in which different "strong identities," different temporalities beyond the secular-linear template, can be co-present; a space where religion could be one of the possible foundations for ethical citizenship.

My ethnographic material has provided one such possibility of (future) citizens being informed by particular religious ethics in their understanding of the prime importance of the common good and social justice. Such a deeply relational and intersubjective political-ethical engagement counters other contemporary neoliberal transformations of Islamic religiosity that have been increasingly noticed in various contexts, impacted by stronger individualist notions of the self. Precisely how my interlocutors' ethical dispositions will materialize in a political self depends not only on their own ongoing and evolving engagement with the Islamic sources, as European-born Muslims shaped by and grappling with powerful (neo)liberal paradigms, but also on their positionality within European discursive regimes, and especially on the willingness of those in the European public spheres to listen to them.

NOTES

Chapter 1

1. Anthropologists' preoccupation with ethics has been significantly instigated by the so-called ethical turn in the field of philosophy, to which a divergent group of thinkers stemming from a variety of intellectual currents have contributed. The contemporary ethical inquiry can be roughly split into two larger streams: a more narrative, neo-Aristotelian current and a more "deconstructive" one. In spite of their significant differences and distinct intellectual projects, Alastair MacIntyre ([1981] 2007), Hans-Georg Gadamer ([1975] 2004), and Martha Nussbaum (1986) articulate the first current. The second is associated mostly with Emmanuel Levinas (1998) and the more recent work of Jacques Derrida (1995, 1997). Without abandoning the insights of anti-foundationalism and poststructuralism, these thinkers want to find, nonetheless, an ethical framework for an increasingly pluralist world. On this second strand of postcritique ethics, see, for instance, Hoy (2004).

2. See, for instance, Barker (2007), Evens (2008), Faubion (2001, 2011), Hirschkind (2006), Howell (1997), Laidlaw (1995, 2002), Lambek (1993, 2000, 2002a), Mahmood (2005), Mittermaier (2010), Robbins (2004, 2007), and Zigon (2008). The emergence of this field as a subdiscipline is furthermore signaled by two recent volumes edited by Michael Lambek (2010) and Didier Fassin (2012).

3. In the French literature, the Islamic revival movement is frequently referred to as *renouveau islamique,* and in the German literature as *Neo-Islam.*

4. This development is discussed in a large body of European scholarship. See, for instance, Amiraux (2001), Césari (1994), Dassetto (1996), Doomernik (1995), and Kepel (1987, 1994).

5. See, for instance, Heckmann and Schnapper (2003), Kastoryano (1996), Todd (1994), and Fetzer and Soper (2005).

6. For a critique of the problematic underlying assumptions that govern the universalism—particularism binary, see, for instance, Silverstein 2004 or Joan W. Scott 2007.

7. See especially John Bowen's (2010) work on the struggles by Muslims and state actors to institutionalize Islam in France.

8. The question about the impact of the French model of *laïcité* and the affective modes of identification it produces not only on the integration of Islam but also on how the French political establishment and media respond to religious Muslims (especially

those engaged in Islamic revival movements) has given rise to a plethora of English-language literature. See, for instance, Bowen (2007, 2010), Killian (2006), Keaton (2006), Joan W. Scott (2010), Selby (2012), and Winter (2008).

9. Given the historical embeddedness of these representations of Islam, it is hardly surprising to observe the perpetuation of such binaries within academic literature. Dassetto (1996: 128–129), for example, formulates his hesitations regarding a probable secularization of the Muslim population in France in the following terms: "[An] incertitude could arise as to the privatization of the religious and a secularization similar to the one observable in Europe. . . . The whole question is to know to what extent a type of reformulation of Islam can be maintained that defines itself only as *din* and dissociates itself from other components (*umma, dawla, jama'a*)."

10. On the state's problematic manner of selecting the members to the *Islamkonferenz* and its ambitions to shape a certain kind of Muslim subject, see especially Amir-Moazami (2011), Peter (2010a), and Tezcan (2012).

11. The term *public sphere* has been widely and controversially discussed in the literature ever since Habermas's (1991) influential work. In the present work, *public sphere* is understood as the particular space in which discourse circulates, always connected to a project of "world-making," that is, to the production of norms. This circulation of discourse happens not only in a rational, abstract, and disembodied way, but also through direct encounters, confrontations, and so on that are impacted by the affective dispositions, anxieties, fears, and passions of the various participants (Warner 2002). Because the public sphere is not a neutral, power-free space, it tends to exclude those who are seen as a threat to the world-making project of the majority. The contemporary public controversies over Islam in Europe have to be understood in this context (see Göle 2013b).

12. After a yearlong series of public debates, in September 2010 France enacted a law that banned women from wearing the face veil in public beginning in Spring 2011. See, for instance, Davis (2011) and Ismail (2010). For a thoughtful study on women in France who wear the face veil, see Parvez (2011).

13. Thilo Sarrazin, a Social Democratic politician and former member of the executive board of Germany's Central Bank (Deutsche Bundesbank), published a book in 2010 entitled *Deutschland schafft sich ab* (Germany Abolishes Itself), which became a bestseller. It claimed that Muslim immigrants of Turkish and Arab origin and their descendents were "destroying" Germany because of their inability and unwillingness to integrate. Although it broke sale records, it has also been widely criticized. See, for instance, Dornhof (2012).

14. Other debates have turned on certain Muslim students' refusal to participate in co-ed physical education lessons, on claims for gender-segregated swimming pools, on female genital cutting and male circumcision, or on arranged or forced marriages. Still others were concerned with *halal* (permissible) meat, mosque constructions, and blasphemy. These issues have been documented extensively in the literature. See Amir-Moazami (2007), Bowen (2007), Caeiro and Peter (2007), Ewing (2008), Göle (2013a), Guiné and Fuentes (2007), Mahmood (2013), and Joan W. Scott (2010).

15. The colorblindness of European self-descriptions that imagine Europe (in op-

position to North America) as unaffected by issues of race and, by implication, of racism, of course, has been exposed by several scholars. See, for instance, El-Tayeb (2011), Goldberg (2006), Lentin (2008), and Silverstein (2005). For how this incapacity to think about issues of race and racism has played out, particularly in the German debates about headscarves, see Rottmann and Marx Ferree (2008).

16. Although Merkel and Sarkozy echo UK Prime Minister David Cameron's statement made in 2011, their claims are contextually different in that France and Germany, unlike the United Kingdom, never explicitly committed to a politics of multiculturalism.

17. Observers who have noted the convergences in these distinct national strategies are, for instance, Galembert (2005) and Koenig (2005, 2007).

18. Since that time, voices throughout Europe have increasingly criticized "multiculturalism" (see, for instance, Amir-Moazami 2005; Gilroy 2005; Lentin and Titley 2011; Werbner 2009). In that sense, the declarations of Nicolas Sarkozy and Angela Merkel in 2010 and 2011, respectively, merely constitute official confirmation of mounting public skepticism.

19. The expression "culturalization of citizenship," made especially in reference to the Netherlands (see, for example, Geschiere 2009; Moors 2009; Verkaaik 2010), has also been used in regard to other European contexts (Bracke 2013; Fortier 2006; Lithman 2010). This specific redefinition of citizenship is not disconnected from the culturalization of racism, "a kind of moral racism in which the terms of racism have shifted into a new arrangement—emphasis on values and its impact on different degrees of differences attributed to different groups—while the focus remains the same—ethnic differences and the maintenance of white hegemony" (Fortier 2006: 322).

20. See, for instance, Allen (2010), Bunzl (2005), Geisser (2003), Morey and Yaqin (2011), and Werbner (2005). Scholars such as Silverstein (2004, 2005), El-Tayeb (2011), and Masuzawa (2005) furthermore emphasize the need to think of contemporary forms of anti-Muslim racism, or Islamophobia, in connection with earlier forms of racialization whose origins lie in European colonial rule, if not even earlier.

21. Philosphers commonly associated with theories that articulate a politics of recognition are Charles Taylor (1989, 1994) and Axel Honneth (1995). Critiques (Connolly 2002; Brown 1993; McNay 2008; Fraser 1997) especially voice concern over the political consequences of these struggles—that they lead to the essentialization of these identities and that they end up affirming an inclusive and humanist liberalism and abandoning more radical materialist critiques of issues around structural inequality. A broader philosophical critique made by Lois McNay (2008) pertains to how these theories tie social action too tightly to identity, by proclaiming the individual's primordial desire for recognition. She argues, correctly in my opinion, that in spite of positing a definition of the subject that is dialogical, situated, and generated, these thinkers come close to the individualist and voluntarist accounts of subjectivity that they originally sought to dislodge.

22. One might argue here, however, that the emergence of the Islamic revival movement is already a response to an initial injury sustained through the experience of colonization and its concomitant discourses. This response has itself transformed older Islamic traditions.

23. Although diaspora models were traditionally and conservatively applied to communities with nonindigenous ancestry that maintained practical or imaginary ties to a center of origin (see, for example, Safran 1990; Sheffer 2003), most recent interpretations focus on the *shared experience* of diaspora, on notions of discontinuity, precarity, and marginalization, on the sense of resistance to continuing a certain marginalized and despised social existence, and on cultural means of maintaining a multinational institutional network (Helly 2006; El-Tayeb 2011). Fatima El-Tayeb (2011: xxxv) spells out—correctly, in my estimation—the analytical benefit of employing such an enlarged understanding of the term *diaspora,* rather than such notions as *migration* and *minority,* when writing about European racialized minorities: "While 'migration' does not grasp the experience of a population that is born into one nation, but never is fully part of it, and 'minority' does not quite encompass the transnational ties of that same population, 'diaspora' can bring both aspects together." El-Tayeb further highlights not only the transnational but also the "transethnic" (60) potential of that term, allowing for new kinds of solidarities. It is this potential that I find useful when thinking about the "Muslim diaspora" in Western Europe, because it allows the integration not only of Muslims of various ethnic backgrounds but also of white converts to that transnational and transethnic space.

24. We now see such redeployment surfacing in the diaspora in the form of slogans like "hijab is beautiful" and "Muslim pride."

25. According to Kant (1998), morality proper is the product of an abstract and universally valid human reason that operates independently from embodied conduct, that is, from the subject's habits and dispositions. Moral philosophers such as MacIntyre ([1981] 2007) and Taylor (1989) criticized this account of ethics and morality.

26. Foucault's lack of attention to these kinds of complications is also connected to his understanding of ethics as potentially expanding a subject's capacity for freedom beyond modern disciplinary power, a view inspired by an almost Kantian ideal of freedom. This approach is especially palpable in his most recent writings, where he reconceptualizes late Hellenic and Roman (especially Stoic) ethics in order to articulate a contemporary model for ethics, which he defines as an aesthetic mode of existence. He specifically contrasts his understanding of ethics to religious morality, that is, to transcendental and metaphysical certainties. Ethics appears here as a "practice of freedom" that excludes any appeals from foundational perspectives (Foucault 1997a). Foucault likens ethical self-fashioning to "a work of art" and develops a personalized maxim of aestheticism that reflects Nietzsche's idea of "giving style" to one's character (Foucault 1997b: 262). Without the very Foucauldian vigilance of power (which Mahmood, for instance, enacts more carefully than Foucault himself did in his last writings on ethics), such an approach can also lead to a very postmodern conception of ethics, one reduced to a Baudelairean aesthetic reflexivity. See, for instance, Scott Lash (1990) and Mike Featherstone (1990). For a convincing critique of such postmodern identity constructions, see, for instance, Lois McNay (1999, 2003).

27. In his later work, Bourdieu (2000; see also Bourdieu and Wacquant 1992) became more attentive to the possibility of altering habitus by rendering it conscious and mastering it.

28. A number of anthropologists have, for various reasons, formulated a critique of the limits of an approach to ethics in terms of self-cultivation. See, for instance, Mattingly (2012), Mittermaier (2012), Schielke (2010), and Bangstad (2011). My concern here is slightly different in that I do consider practices of self-cultivation to be one important domain, among others, for ethical interventions. Furthermore, I do not understand discipline and the moral codes in which these practices are embedded to pose a limit to other fields of ethical work.

29. It is not a coincidence that Aristotle defined *phronesis* in his *Politics* as the paradigm virtue of the ruler ([1941] 2001: 1182).

30. Here Foucault articulates a Stoic version of the care of the self (as opposed to the earlier Hellenic version): not only is it a lifelong practice (rather than a practice related only to the education of character within young men) but it is also disconnected from concern for the care of the polis. Taking care of oneself "for its own sake" (Foucault 1997b: 260) is a central maxim in Stoic thought, and it is the recuperation of this emphasis that Foucault finds promising for contemporary ethics. Foucault's seeming preference for the Stoics in this instance is rather surprising given that so many aspects of their thought seem to be precisely opposed to many of his other central ideas (see, for instance, Euben 2001).

31. A similar argument has been made by Salvatore (2007). I engage further with his work in Chapters 6 and 7.

32. This anxiety about true agency and originality is also reflected in the distinction often established between ethics and morality as, for instance, articulated by Foucault. See note 26.

33. This approach is in line with Islamic ethical reasoning that can be considered to have contributed significantly to the "vulgarization" or democratization of Greek ethics (Peter Brown 1984). By claiming everydayness for my pious interlocutors, I oppose a critique recently formulated by scholars who have taken issue with the growing body of anthropological work that is preoccupied with Islamic piety or revival movements, claiming that this literature has marginalized the experiences of "ordinary" or "everyday" Muslims. Using this argument, they have clearly distinguished between these two supposedly stable groups and excluded revival Muslims from experiences of everydayness. Such a binary approach, which has been powerfully criticized by Nadia Fadil (2011b), is based on normative assumptions about what constitutes the "authentic" realm of "real" life that is grounded in particular liberal and secular imaginaries.

34. For more profound investigations of the mosque's activities, see Amiraux (2011) and Bowen (2010).

35. Frank Peter (2006b, 2010b) and John Bowen (2010) have both provided rich accounts of the French Islamic institutional landscape, of the role played by the UOIF but also of the important place of centers of Islamic learning such as the IESH and the CERSI. Bowen also points to the role of Tunisian exiles in the establishment of these institutions.

36. On CERSI's pedagogy and institutional structure, see Bowen (2010), especially pp. 66–84.

37. DITIP, the Turkish-Islamic Union for Religious Affairs (Türkisch Islamische Union der Anstalt für Religion), is run by the Turkish state. Milli Görüş or the Islamic Community Milli Görüş (Islamische Gemeinschaft Milli Görüş), was established in Europe as a diasporic association connected to Milli Selamat Partisi and Refah Partisi, the banned Turkish Islamic parties of former Prime Minister Necmettin Erbakan. Süleymanli is the Union of Islamic Culture Centers (Verband der Islamischen Kulturzentren), an Islamic organization with roots in the Naqshbandi Sufi order. Nurcu is the Nur Movement, named after founder Said Nurci. A useful study of the different Turkish associations in Germany is provided by Yükleyen (2011). Excellent German-language ethnographies of the Milli Görüş and the Süleymanli are provided, respectively, by Schiffauer (2010) and Jonker (2002).

38. Several of the women of Middle Eastern background (from Syria, Jordan, and Palestine) were connected through their families to the Islamic Center Aachen, loosely affiliated with the Syrian Muslim Brotherhood.

Chapter 2

1. Studies that articulate the image of a migrant locked up in his or her tradition as a trope to accentuate the struggles of the "second generation" against their more traditional parents abounded throughout the 1990s in France and Germany. See, for instance, Hassini (1997), König (1989), Lacoste-Dujardin (1992), Riesner (1990). For a critical review of these representations of Turkish immigrant men and women in Germany, see Ewing (2008). For a critical analysis of this representation in the French context, see Bigley (2011) and Silverstein (2004).

2. Keane (2007) argues that even though this specific self-awareness stems from a post-Reformation, post-Enlightenment genealogy, it has become globalized (beyond the West) and heavily impacts contemporary forms of religious life.

3. The literature that treats this phenomenon is abundant. See Amir-Moazami (2007), Ewing (2008), Fadil (2008), Jacobsen (2011), Nökel (2002), Tietze (2002). This is, of course, not a phenomenon restricted to Europe but is characteristic of Islamic revival circles worldwide. See, for instance, Lara Deeb's (2006) study on Lebanese Shi'a Muslims.

4. These experiences have been discussed in several studies. See, for instance, Amir-Moazami (2007), Nökel (2002), Klinkhammer (2000).

5. The Islamic education received in local mosque organizations provided children with the basics of Islamic worship and norms, such as the ability to read the Arabic alphabet, Qur'anic recitation (*tajwid*), and the fundamental aspects of doctrine (*'aqida*). This early mosque education was especially common for my interlocutors of Turkish background in Germany; only about a third of those of Arab Middle Eastern and North African background in France and Germany had received a similar kind of early religious education.

6. The highlighting of the Islamic difference in German schools does not mean that this difference was therefore specifically valorized or promoted. To the contrary, several of my interlocutors who had worn hijab in school described how the classroom envi-

ronment as well as the teacher generally discouraged this practice. Similar experiences are also documented in Ewing (2008) and Partridge (2012).

7. Tricia Keaton (2006) provides an insightful and sensitive ethnographic study on educational inequality in France and the impact it has on young French Muslims.

8. When my interlocutors in France were still in school (pre-2004), it was not yet legally forbidden to wear the headscarf. Whereas some encountered problems in covering their heads at school, others had more lenient school directors and were therefore able to attend classes wearing hijab.

9. Keane (2007: 213) engages here with Talal Asad's argument that ideologies of modernity have produced a universalizing definition of religion. Keane elaborates on Asad's thought, explaining that this universalizing definition involves "belief statements" that need to be embodied in a "concrete semiotic . . . form."

10. Throughout this book we see how Muslim practitioners felt themselves to be in constant need of justification, which is, even if not exclusively, a discursive undertaking. This obligation for Muslims in Europe—most notably women—to provide discursive justifications has been discussed aptly by Sarah Bracke (2011) through the concept of "talking back."

11. *Ilmihal* literature compiles the central Islamic doctrines and norms of conduct. In the Ottoman context, *ilmihals* were widely disseminated among the population in an effort to regulate popular practices (Henkel 2005: 504).

12. The Islamic novel, written in the tradition of a *Bildungsroman* (novel of education), is a genre of literature specific to the Turkish context. Numerous women of Turkish background mentioned reading Islamic novels, especially those written by female writers. For an analysis of the development of the Turkish Islamic novel, see Cayir (2004).

13. These studies do not merely postulate the thesis of individualization as a heuristic concept, but rather endorse it as a normative understanding of individualization that, along with its co-phenomenon secularization, is the desirable mode of religious belonging in the modern age. See, for example, Babès (1997), Karakaşoğlu-Aydin (2000), Klinkhammer (2000), Césari (2003). A useful overview and critical discussion of this trend is provided by Peter (2006a). For a very different (and non-normative) approach to the question of individualization and secularization among second-generation Muslims in Europe, see Fadil (2008, 2011a) and Mas (2006).

14. The idea that authentic knowledge is safeguarded by an orthodox establishment entails distinguishing between those scholars who are in the realm of orthodoxy and those who are not. Talal Asad (1986: 15) defines religious orthodoxy as the power to "regulate, uphold, require, or adjust *correct* practices, and to condemn, exclude, undermine, or replace *incorrect* ones." (emphasis in original). This definition implies that argument and conflict are always part of the process of establishing a position of orthodoxy within a discursive tradition (1986: 16). On the basis, therefore, of the concern for orthodoxy that is expressed within revival circles, it does not follow that only one opinion is acceptable. As Bowen (2010) demonstrates in his in-depth ethnography of Islamic institutions in France, the concern is to establish a framework of "consensus," within which different opinions can coexist and enjoy mutual recognition.

15. "Too extremist" generally referred to various Salafi-Wahhabi trends and "too soft" generally referred to the diverse trends of liberal Islam (often scoffed at as "Islam light") and their corresponding interpretations. (Similar observations are made by Bowen 2010 and Peter 2006b.) In France, in addition to rejecting certain "liberal" Sufi activists, revivalists would also mark their distance from figures such as Malek Chebel, who enjoys considerable media attention. (On the work and reception of Chebel, see Mas 2011.) In Germany, women of Turkish origin would mention the Turkish liberal Muslim preacher Yasar Nuri Öztürk disapprovingly (on Öztürk, see, for instance, Öncü 2006), as well as local Islamic feminists (see Chapter 4 of this book).

16. Religious programmes broadcast on Satellite TV from the Middle East or Turkey, which were also viewed in their parents' homes, were likewise frequently mentioned by the women as important supplemental learning sources. Women from Arabic-speaking families frequently mentioned an *al-Jazeera* program that is highly popular among the Arabic-speaking diaspora worldwide: "Al-Shari'a wa-l-Hayat" regularly featured Yusuf al-Qaradawi as a guest. They also spoke of sermons and talks given by Amr Khaled, a popular Egyptian TV preacher, on *Iqra'* TV. Women of Turkish origin, for their part, had access to a range of TV programmes from Turkish broadcasting services such as Samanyolu or Kanal 7, two channels close to the Nurcu movement and to the major Islamic parties, including the former Refah-Partisi and the currently ruling Justice and Development Party, respectively (see note 37, Chapter 1). Among my Turkish-speaking interlocutors, a popular figure who appeared now and again at these broadcasting stations was Nihat Hatipoğlu, whose sermons and lectures were also available on CD, DVD, and in the past, VHS.

17. As Armando Salvatore (1998: 95) remarks correctly that, in that logic, buying a religious book already constitutes an "act of civilization." It translates the interest one takes in the destiny of the Islamic community, but also the will to improve oneself.

18. Christine Jacobsen (2011), in her study on second-generation Muslims in Norway, has succeeded in using the term *objectification* without falling into the trap of asserting a prescriptive modernization paradigm.

19. Keane uses the term *semiotic ideology* to elaborate on the concept of *language ideology* that is used in linguistic anthropology. In linguistic anthropology, Keane explains, *ideology* does not refer to "false consciousness" or other forms of "systemic deception," but to the "productive effects of reflexive awareness" (Keane 2007: 17).

20. The potential instability of faith is also tackled in the Islamic literature available to the women. Numerous books address this question and give advice on how to reinforce faith; see, for instance, Ismaïli (2005).

21. The European Institute for Human Sciences is affiliated with the Union des Organisations Islamiques de France and based at Château Chinon in Saint-Léger-de-Fougeret (in the Nièvre region).

22. Although the class took place in the facilities of the Mosquée de Paris, the teacher did not reflect the religious (and political) orientation of the mosque, which Naima assured me before I attended that class with her for the first time. Like most of my interlocutors in Paris, she was rather critical of the mosque's direction—even

while praying there regularly. On the political connections of the mosque, see Bowen (2010).

23. The Arabic term '*ilm* (plural '*ulum*), which is applied to both secular and presecular modes of knowledge production, is used in the Islamic centers more to talk about a faith-based approach to the study of Islam (Islamic sciences, '*ulum islamiyya)* than to speak of the secular academic study of Islam (Islamic studies). I return to this specific understanding of knowledge in Chapter 5.

24. Naima refers here to the annual gathering organized by the *Union des Organisations Islamiques de France* (UOIF) at the exhibition center in Le Bourget, a *banlieue* north of Paris.

25. In the Aristotelian model of ethical pedagogy, which is concerned as much with acts as with affects, virtues are understood as dispositions toward both acting and feeling. For Aristotle, feelings and emotions constitute what he calls *pathos*—experiences that affect a person. As Lois A. Kosman (1980: 105) explains, Aristotle understands action and passion as "reciprocal concepts"; that is, the way in which one is being acted upon corresponds to one's acting in a certain way. Thus, Aristotle's moral theory is a theory not only of "how to *act* well but also of how to *feel* well; for the moral virtues are states of character that enable a person to exhibit the right kinds of emotions as well as the right kinds of actions. The art of proper living, we should say, includes the art of feeling well as the correlative discipline to the art of acting well" (1980: 105). It is for this reason that Aristotle understands moral philosophy as the outcome of a sentimental education geared toward the proper cultivation of feelings.

26. This scholarship takes issue with an approach to education that has defined its ultimate goal (at least since Rousseau) as the development of reason. Especially under the influence of Piaget, formal education has focused on the training of abstract and mathematical reasoning. Such an approach dovetails with neoliberal thinking, which assumes that the ideal human is a self-sufficient, rational, economic actor (Noddings 1984). More recent studies in developmental psychology that have recognized the significance of emotional intelligence (for example, Gardner 1999; Cohen 2006) have not succeeded in unsettling this powerful paradigm.

27. Another philosopher, Spinoza, has equally emphasized the emotional base of virtues, arguing that "affect" constitutes ethics. Spinoza insists on the embodied aspects of cultivating emotions, and therefore on the link between body and affect. See, for instance, Connolly (2002) and Massumi (2002). It is Spinoza (more than Aristotle) who has inspired a great deal of contemporary theoretical thinking on affect, and it was especially after the publication of Deleuze and Guattari's (1987) discussion of Spinoza's work that a whole scholarship on affect and embodiment emerged.

28. See Berkey (1992), in particular Chapter 2.

29. This mistrust of Sufism, which I encountered especially in the French circles, evokes an attitude that was developed by the reform movements of the late nineteenth century and took a particularly virulent form in the Algerian reform movement (Merad 1967). In the German circles, with their Turkish Muslim majority, this skepticism was less frequent, which might be explained by the fact that the Turkish reform movement,

in contrast to those in North Africa, was not built on anti-Sufi polemics. In addition, Sufi and neo-Sufi groups played a significant role in Islamic life after the instauration of the Turkish Republic and in the Turkish Islamic revival. When classical Sufi literature was employed in some classes at the Islamic centers I attended in France and Germany, it was generally discussed in a way that highlighted shortcomings and "exaggerations" of Sufi practice, of which revival circles were generally wary. Teachers like Olfa or Salwa would notably criticize references in texts to the central role of Sufi *shuyukh* as intermediaries between the individual believer and the Divine.

30. When I speak here of a "thoroughly European" revivalist Islam, I do not imply a certain set of norms associated with "moderate" Islam, which is often debated when activists from various tendencies invoke the necessity of building a European Islam. I use the term here simply to account for the aspirations and needs of Muslims born in Europe, who find themselves at times a bit "stranded" in a diasporic context that often is not fully understood by their parents' generation or by Islamic authorities, for whom the point of reference is still the Muslim majority context.

31. Since the early days of Islam, *da'wa* has been viewed as a duty incumbent on believers to shepherd fellow Muslims in their struggle to lead a more devout and pious life (Canard 1965). See also Mendel (1995).

32. Reformist thinker Rashid Rida, who insists that *da'wa* should be an obligation for every individual believer and not for the community as a whole, is a particularly important source for modern perspectives on da'wa (Roest Crollius 1978: 276–277; see also Mahmood 2005: 57–64).

33. This sense of duty is also connected to the shifted and broadened understanding of *da'wa* as representing Islam in word and deed. I treat this topic in more detail in Chapter 6.

34. The pressure, especially but not only for Muslim women, to assimilate and abandon Islamic ways of life in order to obtain full freedom is reflected in many political discourses and social work policies and has found an outlet over and over in popular culture products, films, and media in both Germany and France. See, for instance, Ewing (2008), Bigley (2011), Silverstein (2004).

35. On this point, see also Amir-Moazami (2007) and Amir-Moazami and Salvatore (2003).

36. In a struggle against *taqlid* (the supposedly blind imitation of previous scholarship by successive Muslim scholars) as well as against the practices of popular Islam, the Islamic reform movement made "return to the sources" their leitmotif (see Merad 1973). This movement also had a strong presence in the Maghrebi countries. See, for instance, Merad (1967).

37. The search for authentic Islam as the basis for a new Islamic politics has occupied Islamic thinkers since the time of the reform movements. See, for instance, Lee (1997).

38. Similar observations have been made repeatedly in the literature, which interprets this female critique as an emancipatory trend (Karakaşoğlu-Aydin 2000; Nökel 2002; Venel 1999). I discuss some of these positions, as well as my interlocutors' specific ideas on the notion of "female emancipation," more thoroughly in Chapter 4.

39. The use of these nonbinding legal opinions to address practical religious problems in everyday situations reflects a shift away from the fatwa's traditional focus on legal subjects (cf. Messick 1996: 317–319; see also Mahmood 2005).

40. Al-Ghazali's popularity is not specific to the European revival context but is characteristic of contemporary Islamic revival movements worldwide, whether orthodox or Sufi inspired. Miriam Cooke accounts for this popularity by pointing to Al-Ghazali's capacity to transcend cleavages between various *madhabs* (schools of law), sects, and tendencies (cooke 2000: 509). Franck Frégosi (1998: 133) equally observes that this classic Islamic thinker, though Sufi, is not contested among orthodox Islamic groups in France, and thus is widely taught in Islamic institutes there. I made the same observation in the centers where I conducted fieldwork.

41. On the complicated and dialogical body-spirit relationship in Al-Ghazali's work, see Moosa (2005: 217–218).

42. Lapidus resumes this approach in the following words: "In al-Ghazali's psychology, thoughts and impressions in the mind engender desire, decision of the will, resolve, intention, and finally, action. This knowledge so impregnates the mind that all thinking runs by allusion from one passage of the Qur'an to another, totally controlling the will and the actions of the believer. Such knowledge is a 'disposition deeply rooted in the soul from which actions flow naturally and easily without need of reflection or judgement'" (Lapidus 1984: 50).

43. On this point, see also Fernando (2010).

44. This attitude is regarded with a rather skeptical eye by many European scholars, as reflected, for instance, in the following comment: "The most trivial of actions, since they are accomplished with the goal of non-transgression of Allah's law, is a tribute to the Creator. By ritualizing everyday life, this system renders null and void the principle of duality between the sacred and the profane" (Weibel 2000: 15).

Chapter 3

1. A variety of opinions exist among religious scholars regarding this question. In contrast to Al-Ghazali, the majority of '*ulama* (scholars) claim that the minimal amount of concentration required for prayer to be valid is for the believer's heart to be present during the *takbir,* the invocation of God (Monnot 1995: 965).

2. European skepticism toward Islamic religious (bodily) practices is of course not a recent development. Nineteenth-century British travelers to Egypt, for example, described *salat,* with its detailed choreography, not only as "sensual, primitive and irrational," but also, because of its ritualism and mechanical nature, as detrimental to "the religion of the heart" and to the "growth of internal piety" (Starrett 1995: 955–956). In line with modern understandings of religion, bodily movements were considered to inhibit reflection and interiority (ibid.). Similar ideas are still expressed in certain contemporary ethnographic studies. In her study on pious women in Germany, for example, Sigrid Nökel (2002: 85) claims that *salat's* supposed "fixed and repetitive" nature does not allow the practitioner to constitute herself as the subject of her acts.

3. It is interesting to notice here that the women's critique of an Islam of fear inter-

sects partly with earlier, nineteenth-century discourses articulated by European colonial observers and scholars on Islam, who described the relation of Muslims to their religion as one of fear and as lacking any feeling of love. This was, as scholars of religion argued back then, due to Islam's deeply semitic nature. See Masuzawa 2005.

4. See Chapter 2, n29.

5. Al-Ghazali (2004) has given much thought to the interaction between fear and hope (connected to love) in the constitution of piety and to the need to cultivate these feelings. This theme is also the subject of many small booklets available in Islamic bookshops; see, for instance, Khaled (2005) and Ismaïli (2005). Mahmood (2005: 140–148) provides an interesting discussion on how Egyptian revival participants conceptualize slightly differently than my own interlocutors the relation between these different emotions.

6. The superiority of love over fear is also developed in al-Ghazali (2004: 47).

7. Different studies show how reform movements in Islam have, from the nineteenth century onward, significantly strengthened the place of the individual. See, for instance, Goldberg (1991) and Mahmood (2005: 61–62).

8. Women of Turkish origin frequently invoked a specific Turkish proverb in this context—*alimin zikri neyse fikride odur* (The thoughts of the wise are like his prayers)—which connects *zikr* (arabic *dhikr*), the act of remembering God, with *fikr*, thoughts.

9. The proximity of Aristotelian concepts to those developed by al-Ghazali are not pure hazard. Ebrahim Moosa, who recognizes Aristotle's influence on al-Ghazali, notes that this influence is most evident in al-Ghazali's effort to construct a new ethical subjectivity (Moosa 2005: 30).

10. These claims have been widely acknowledged in the literature. For an account that shows the more complex nature behind these rather simplistic claims, see Fernando (2010).

11. In contrast to the debates in France, the German headscarf debates provoked much less public passion.

12. For some women, however, the decision to take the veil was spurred by this hostile climate, because they wished to show solidarity with this stigmatized group.

13. Similar observations have been made by Fernando (2010), Fadil (2008), Jacobsen (2011), and Deeb (2006).

14. *Bled* is a vernacular expression derived from the Arabic *balad* and means "country"—in this context, her country of origin.

15. It is undeniably not self-evident how veiling came to play such a central part in the current catalogue of reflexive Islamic self-disciplines. Rather, this has to be understood also as the outcome of a particular historical development that started with the Islamic reform at the end of the nineteenth century. At that time, female dress became the subject of vehement and controversial debate, notably in the face of the colonizer's assault on the practice of veiling (Ahmed 1992; Göle 1996; Mabro 1991; Yeğenoğlu 1998). Although veiling has always been theorized in Islamic theology in terms of modesty, the interrogation of its legitimacy in colonial discourses modified the debate: in their defense of the veil, Muslim scholars posited this practice as a symbol of authenticity and purity, and it is still portrayed as such in contemporary mainstream Islam. This debate, I would suggest set in

motion an "objectivation" of veiling, which subsequently turned this practice into one of the central techniques of self-cultivation for developing female Muslim piety.

16. Salwa refers here to the German headscarf debate instigated through the Ludin case. See Weber (2004).

17. The Qur'an (28:25) mentions only that she approached Moses in a chaste manner (*istihya'*) and asked him to return home with her so that her father could give him recompense for his help. The details of this story, as related by Salwa, are elaborated in the *hadith* literature.

18. A quite different reading of the same story is undertaken by the women interviewed by Mahmood (2005).

19. On this point, see also Nadine Weibel (2000: 43–45).

20. In classical Islamic theology, *akhlaq* plays a central role. For a discussion of *akhlaq*, its origins, and its development in Islamic theology, philosophy, and mysticism, see Walzer (1991).

21. In a similar fashion, Webb Keane urges scholars of religion to take seriously the study of material objects without reducing them to evidence for immaterial phenomena: "As material things, they are enmeshed in causality, registered in and induced by their forms. As forms, they remain objects of experience" (Keane 2008: 124).

22. A powerful example of the affective power that clothing can exert on the subject is given by Peter Stallybrass (1993), who discusses the materiality of clothes in connection with memory and mourning.

23. With such an approach, Warnier extends Talal Asad's (1993) critique of a tendency in anthropology to understand the body through what it signifies or represents. Not only the body, Warnier contends, but also objects have frequently been understood as "signs" and analyzed for their "sign-value" (Baudrillard 1998), that is, in relation to representations and systems of communication rather than in regard to their materiality and the facets through which they "mediatize motricity" (1999: 28). Although Warnier does not question that material objects linked to bodily conduct might also always signify something, he wishes to go beyond such a reading, because it fails to tell us how these embodied practices reflect processes of subjectivation and fashioning subjects, and ways in which subjects govern themselves.

24. Joan W. Scott (2005: 122) recognized this specific aspect when claiming that the veil makes explicit "the rules of public gendered interaction . . . which declare sexual exchanges out of bounds in public place."

25. Here, Naima employs the term *da'wa* (defined in Chapter 2 as "a type of moral guidance that seeks to encourage Muslims to follow Islamic prescriptions") differently, that is, in its representational sense, which broadens the meaning of the term for the diasporic context. I discuss some of the implications of this broadening in Chapters 5 and 6.

26. On this point, see also Schiffauer (2000: 102).

Chapter 4

1. See, for instance, Amir-Moazami (2011), Bracke (2011), Chin (2010), Guenif-Souilamas (2006), Ewing (2008), Joan W. Scott (2010).

2. This issue has been tackled in numerous studies. See Amir-Moazami (2007), Amiraux (2001), Cheruvallil-Contractor (2012), Göle (2005), Jacobsen (2011), Karakaşoğlu-Aydin (2000), Klinkhammer (2000), Nökel (2002), Venel (1999), Weibel (2000).

3. The struggle with mosques and prayer rooms that did not provide an appropriate space for women seemed to be more important in France than in Germany, where mosques (notably the Turkish ones) generally included well-equipped women's areas. On the availability of women's spaces in mosques in Germany, see, for instance, Spielhaus (2011). However, when it came to the political and institutional marginalization of women in Islamic (mosque) associations, German women formulated complaints similar to those expressed by their peers in France.

4. This position has been adopted by, for example, Benhabib (2006), in her analysis of veiled women's positionality in the context of the French *affaire du foulard*. For Dipesh Chakrabarty (2000), these types of analyses, which explain phenomena in non-Western contexts in terms of "not yet," reveal broader ideas about non-Western temporalities, seeing them as always late in comparison to the Western sense of historical time, which constitutes the normative time frame.

5. Butler (2008) investigates how this progressive temporality informs the new sexual politics in Europe. Although it appears to defend freedom and inclusiveness, it is in effect particularly exclusionary toward Muslim communities. Butler's critical consideration of the time of the "now" resonates with Asad's (1986: 17) attention to how modern social forces build on specific patterns of "forgetfulness."

6. The idea of Eve as the original sinner is not mentioned in the Qur'an but appears in several hadith, which have been disqualified by thinkers of the reform movement as Judeo-Christian legends, called *isra'iliyat* (Stowasser 1994: 27–28).

7. One of the verses of the Qur'an that evokes the creation of humanity is 4:1: "O mankind, fear your Lord, who created you from one soul and created from it its mate and dispersed from both of them many men and women." Building on the *hadith* literature, Muslim exegetes generally explain the genesis as Adam's creation from clay, followed by the creation of a woman, Eve (Hawwa), from Adam's bone. Reformist Muhammad 'Abduh has already questioned this interpretation, and today feminist Islamic thinkers in particular continue this critique (Barlas 2002; Wadud 1999). According to these thinkers, the Qur'an indicates that humanity was created "from a single substance" (*min nafsin wahida*) from which a partner (*zajw*, plural *azwaj*) was generated. Traditionally this term has been translated as "wife," but these feminist theologians insist that the term *zawj* is not gendered and that the Qur'an does not specify which gender was created first. For these thinkers, the claim of Adam's anteriority is part of the *isra'iliyat*.

8. Compare Lamia's critique, reiterated by many of my interlocutors, to the one formulated by Safinaz Kazim, an Islamist woman activist, who denounces as the "new jahiliyya," or new "age of ignorance," the "materialist, business mentality that has gone to extremes to exploit women's femininity to sell products, attract tourists, and incite desire, make the female public property that is circulated and presented as a course of pleasure to the master man" (quoted from McLarney 2015). On Kazim's work, see also Karam (1998).

9. This situation echoes the colonial context, in which the onslaught of colonial rule instigated corresponding debates among Muslim scholars, intellectuals, and the broader, emerging public in Muslim societies (Ahmed 1992).

10. Of course many feminists would disagree with Naima's slightly simplistic account of feminism. Rather than being concerned "only" with the cause of women, as Naima put it, many within this heterogeneous movement saw and continue to see their struggles as multidimensional and part of a broader emancipatory project in which gender injustices are thought about together and critiqued along with struggles against racism, imperialism, homophobia, and class domination.

11. One could point to Tariq Ramadan as the figure in Europe who best represents this kind of Islamically defined political commitment.

12. Interestingly, this specific political awareness seemed to be slightly more pronounced in France than in Germany. The Maghrebi women I worked with in France appeared more clearly embedded in anticolonial, Third World, and antiracist discourses. Although my (German-Turkish) interlocutors were equally aware of racism and social inequality, their often very strong identification with the Turkish nation-state, which was not colonized in the way North Africa was, seemed at times (but not always) less conducive to the formulation of a discourse of internationalist postcolonial solidarity. Solidarities were more often formulated through the experience of migration, class, and foreignness within the local context of Germany.

13. For a nuanced study that exposes the complexity of that relation and the various possible outcomes, see Bano and Kalmbach (2012).

14. There is by now a flourishing scholarship on Islamic feminism within both Muslim majority and diasporic contexts. See Badran (2001, 2005), Cooke (2000), Hammer (2008), Kynsilehto (2008), Moghadam (2002), Pepicelli (2008). On the concrete impact that this current has had in specific national contexts, see Archer (2007), Eddaouda (2008), Mir-Hosseini (2006), Salime (2011), Vatuk (2008).

15. See Amiraux (2001), Bouzar (2004), Jonker (2003), Venel (1999).

16. For a theological discussion of this event, see Hammer (2010, 2012) and Silvers and Elewa (2011). For a larger survey of the Islamic textual sources on women's prayer in mixed congregations, see Melchert (2004).

17. Amina Erbakan and Sabiha El-Zayat are personally connected with the Erbakan family, which is closely associated with the Turkish diasporic association *Milli Görüş*. Sabiha El-Zayat, furthermore, is the wife of Ibrahim El-Zayat, former chairman of the Islamische Gemeinschaft in Deutschland (Islamic community Germany), who was often accused by German politicians and the media of promoting Muslim Brotherhood ideology in Germany. See, for instance, Jouili and Tietze (2008) and Jouili and Kamp (2013).

18. ZIF has, for instance, published a booklet that employs an alternative hermeneutics to read the Qur'anic verse 4:34 (Zentrum Islamischer Frauenforschung 2005). See Jouili and Tietze (2008), Jouili and Kamp (2013).

19. As the members told me during a conversation, their main audience today consists of interfaith circles, especially other religious (Christian and Jewish) feminists.

20. As Asad (1993: 35) shows, orthodoxy always involves excluding, forbidding, and

denouncing certain principles and practices so as to make them "unthinkable." This is of course not an ahistorical phenomenon but a process shaped by social and historical conditions and by continually responding to new challenges and redefining legitimate positions.

21. This attitude is crucially connected to colonial history. Colonial administrators employed a feminist language in their moral justification of the imperialist project and were backed by the emerging feminist movement in Europe. Leila Ahmed (1992) argues that European feminists thereby became accomplices to the colonial regime. From that time forward, Western feminists have generally been perceived in Islamic discourses as imperial collaborators, and feminism has been conceived as anti-Islamic. The critique of Western feminism as part of Western hegemony has equally been made by feminists of color and Third World feminists (see Anthias and Yuval-Davies 1992; Mohanty 1991).

22. *Ijtihad*, which means personal interpretive effort, or independent reasoning, is a technical term used in Islamic law. Until the beginning of the tenth century, it was a tool commonly used by Muslim jurists to deduce Islamic rulings if other sources of law were not specific about a given problem. After that, the "door of *ijtihad*" was considered closed within the Sunni law schools, which imposed on future generations of Sunni Muslim scholars' unconditional acceptance of the doctrines of the established schools. *Ijtihad* survived, however, within the Shi'i law schools. Since the advent of reformism, voices have called for the door of *ijtihad* to be reopened; it does continue to be a prerogative of trained religious scholars. On the history of *ijtihad*, see Hallaq (1995).

23. For the rather vaguely defined notion of who the trustworthy scholars are, see Chapter 2, p. 34.

24. On *taqlid*, see Chapter 2, n36.

25. See, for instance, Bowen (2010), Caeiro (2004, 2010), Peter (2010b).

26. My interlocutors did not seem to engage so much in what has been called "fatwa shopping," in which an individual searches for a religious opinion that will most suit her personal aspirations.

27. This aspect is also discussed by Saba Mahmood (2005: ch. 3).

28. Nadia Fadil (2011a) makes a similar argument, albeit in the reverse sense, that is, she talks about "changing regimes of self-governance" from a religious to a secular lifestyle.

29. Wendy Brown (1995: 6) likewise cautions against treating freedom as outside of "existing configurations of power—economic, social psychological, political." She proposes understanding freedom as a "relational and contextual practice that takes shape in opposition to whatever is locally and ideologically conceived as unfreedom."

30. Individual autonomy as part of neoliberal governance has, beyond the restructuring of subjectivity, important political and social ramifications, most notably normalizing and depoliticizing effects. As Lois McNay (2009:64) puts it, "At the most fundamental level, neoliberal governance of the self erodes conceptions of the public domain which, in the words of Zygmunt Bauman, is being "stealthily but steadily colonized by private concerns, trimmed, peeled and cleaned of their public connections and ready for

private consumption but hardly for the production of social bonds" (2001: 190)." Many critiques of neoliberalism show cogently how such a conception of individual autonomy has depoliticizing effects, most drastically in the way it construes issues of social injustice as a problem of (ir)responsible self-management. In this sense, individuals are increasingly "compelled to responsibility" as they are obliged to take responsibility for a state of affairs beyond their scope (see, for instance, Brown 1995; McNay 2009; Hartman and Honneth 2006: 52).

31. There are numerous Islamic booklets on the market today that discuss these virtues and provide concrete guidance on how to achieve them. See, for example, Samb (2005).

32. According to the majority opinion in classical Islamic jurisprudence, the testimony of two women equals the testimony of one man. Although alternate opinions exist, they did not seem to be taught in the Islamic centers where I did my fieldwork. Interestingly, an alternative reading was published on a French Muslim website frequently consulted by my interlocutors. See Tahar Mahdi (n.d).

33. See, for instance, Hervieu-Léger (1999).

34. Although the social contract theorists of the sixteenth to eighteenth centuries—from Thomas Hobbes and John Locke to Jean-Jacques Rousseau—have significantly "shifted the social dimension of human existence to the notion of the private and autonomous individual" (Hodgson 2003: 13), these thinkers "continued to emphasize the importance of community even as they brought the individual to prominence, thus establishing the principle of individual duty within individual autonomy" (Morgan-Foster 2005: 77). John Stuart Mill made the fulfilment of duties to others synonymous with "social morality" (Morgan-Foster 2005: 78). One of the legal thinkers who contributed most radically to this shift to a highly individualistic account of rights is Ronald Dworkin, who defines individual rights as "trump cards" (Dworkin 1978).

35. The sense of obligation in this perspective is so strong that some Islamic scholars prefer the term *human necessities* to *human rights* (see Morgan-Foster 2005: 105).

36. I elaborate on this question in Chapter 5.

37. In the French and German context, see, for instance, Nökel (2002), Venel (1999), Weibel (2000).

38. Especially when codified into law in Muslim-majority contexts, this principle has often been used to legitimate the severe curtailment of women's rights (Mir-Hosseini 1999; Abu-Odeh 2004). However, such a codified application does not necessarily correspond to the ambivalent, diverging, evolving, and contextual ways in which my interlocutors reasoned through the principle of equity.

39. The scepticism that my interlocutors articulated about the unlimited use of rights discourses poses interesting questions regarding the relationship they maintained as citizens with the French or German nation-state, in particular regarding the ways in which they might formulate their demands or rights claims as a stigmatized and racialized religious minority that is struggling to make a place for itself in society. This question is addressed in Chapter 6.

40. Numerous critiques have challenged liberalism's pretension to neutrality in re-

gard to human goods, effectively showing that it is a doctrine that also imposes a particular conception of the good life. See, for instance, MacIntyre (1988).

41. Foucault, for instance, in his 1984 lecture on human rights, recognizes the insufficiency of a human rights discourse that is exclusively articulated using the concepts and language of human rights, thus suggesting the necessity of embedding individual rights into a vision of rights and duties that creates solidarity: "There exists an international citizenship that has its rights and its duties, and that obliges one to speak out against every abuse of power, whoever the authors, whoever its victims. After all, we are all members of the community of the governed, and thereby obliged to show mutual solidarity" (2000: 474). In opposition to the "conventional liberal fetishization of rights as the sine qua non of social justice" (McNay 2009:71), Foucault (1997d) recognizes a mere strategic and momentary utility for rights discourses, in a longer struggle for justice. See also Brown (1995), Mendus (1995), Waldron (1987), Glendon (1991).

42. See, for instance, Brown (1995: chapter 6); see also Lynch, Baker, and Lyons (2009: chapter 4).

43. Although these women's critiques of liberal individualism are the framework within which hierarchical and patriarchal gender conceptions could be articulated, I would of course not claim that such critiques are a necessary condition for articulating these gendered conceptions, nor do they inevitably lead to these conceptions.

Chapter 5

1. Many studies have noticed that Muslim women active in the global revival movement emphasize the value of education for women and, indeed, are often highly educated themselves. See, for instance, Adely (2012), Amir-Moazami (2007), Bouzar (2004), Göle (1996), Nökel (2002), Venel (1999).

2. From the Enlightenment onward, the notion of belief itself has alluded to a state of tension between doubt and faith. This state of tension was further translated into modes of interpretation proposed by anthropology, which for long time treated belief as the necessary result of an intrinsic lack of rationality and the manifestation of a specific type of mental activity (Lenclud 1990: 8–13; see also Asad 1993).

3. The argument, frequently advanced in these circles, that the Qur'an anticipated many modern scientific discoveries must also be placed in this context. Islamic books on this topic are abundant in Islamic libraries across Germany and France. This idea is closely connected to another project that circulates in the Islamic revival movement, namely, the Islamization of science. For more on that topic, see, for instance, Marfleet (2000) and Abaza (2000).

4. For a thoughtful response to the uproar caused by the Pope's statements, see Ramadan (2006).

5. As Schirin Amir-Moazami (2007) has shown, this argument was frequently formulated by opponents of the headscarf ban in public schools, who emphasized the pivotal role of the public school in emancipating these girls from their traditionalist family environments.

6. This argument vaguely invokes a symbolism developed in Islamic mystical thought,

according to which the ninety-nine divine names, which all allude to divine qualities, are divided into female and male qualities. *Rahma*, derived from the same root as "uterus" in Arabic, figures among the most important (female) qualities (see, for instance, Murata 1992). Interestingly, Emmanuel Levinas (1990), the French Jewish philosopher, refers in his ethics of compassion to the principle of maternity by using the Hebrew term *rahamim*, which, similarly to the Arabic term for "mercy," shares a root with the word for "womb" (*rehem* in Hebrew).

7. This legal concept is based on Qur'anic verse 4:34: *al-rijal qawwamuna 'ala al-nisa'*, which has often been translated as "men are in charge over women." Other Muslim translators prefer "men are protectors and maintainers for women." It is this rendering that my interlocutors too generally prefer. On the debate about this notion among contemporary Muslim scholars, especially in the West, see Roald (2001). Contemporary Muslim feminist theologians, such as Asma Barlas (2002) and Amina Wadud (1999), have invested much effort in reinterpreting the concept of *qiwama*.

8. In the legal texts of classical Islam, the duty of a wife was defined by two main functions: access to sex for her husband and participation in the reproductive process (Ali 2003; Najmabadi 1998).

9. On the impact of conceptions of the bourgeois (nuclear) family in modern Islamic thought, see, for instance, Abugideiri (2002), Shakry (1998), and Stowasser (1987).

10. Like their secular counterparts, Islamic reformers were influenced by European nationalist discourses of that time, which defined mothers as the guardians of the nation. Omnia Shakry (1998: 133) illuminates resemblances with the British nationalist discourse of the nineteenth century, which valorized motherhood in accordance with national and imperialist interests in a strongly racialized logic. See also Vinken (2001).

11. These concerns resonate with arguments put forth by feminists of color, who have claimed for quite some time now that for women of color the experience of mothering is connected to the sociocultural concerns of the racial or ethnic community. Beyond individual reproduction, mothering is here linked to group survival, empowerment, and identity. See, for instance, Collins (1990).

12. Although this discourse resembles neoliberal family ideologies (see, for instance, Grewal 2006), the different vantage point from which this discourse is articulated here is significant.

13. This position has been elucidated by Zeinab al-Ghazali, for instance, the eminent Egyptian Islamist female activist, who was close to the Muslim Brotherhood. Her work was read and admired by many of my respondents in both France and Germany, and she was often upheld as the model par excellence of the successful contemporary professional Muslim woman. She declares, "Islam does not forbid women to actively participate in public life. It does not prevent her from working, entering into politics, and expressing her opinion, or from being anything, as long as that does not interfere with her first duty as a mother, the one who first trains her children in the Islamic call. So her first, holy, and most important mission is to be a mother and wife. She cannot ignore this priority. If she then finds she has free time, she may participate in public activities" (Hoffman 1985: 236–237; see also Cooke 1994).

14. McLarney (2015) shows that even though most of the writings of the Islamic revival in Egypt in the 1970s, 1980s, and 1990s promoted women's child-care responsibilities and housework as their most "celestial mission," they rarely questioned the principle of the right to work. On this latter point, see also MacLeod (1991). This double acknowledgement of women's right to work and her maternal duties is similarly maintained in the Islamic literature on gender roles that is available in Europe.

15. Schirin Amir-Moazami (2007) has highlighted the differences in the national self-positionings of Muslim women in both countries. Whereas her French-Maghrebi interlocutors unambiguously situated themselves as French citizens, her German-Turkish interlocutors mainly insisted on their Turkish identity and their distance from German society. My own research, undertaken a few years after Amir-Moazami's, shows a slightly more complex picture for Germany. It seems that "being a part" of the German society, which often but not always involved becoming or being a German citizen, has been increasingly important for these young diasporic Muslims in the years since the 2000 citizenship reform.

16. Another important figure who promotes an intrinsic relation between faith and citizenship in Europe is, of course, Tariq Ramadan, who defines "social engagement as a proof of faith" (quoted in Bouzar 2004: 47). Ramadan epitomizes this tendency in Europe's contemporary Islamic discourse, in which "the definition of Muslim and that of the citizen converge" (Bouzar 2004: 46). Several authors have discussed the centrality of citizenship in the discourse of European Muslim preachers. See, for instance, Bouzar (2004), Frégosi (2004), March (2007, 2011), Mohsen-Finan (2002), Peter (2006a, 2006b).

17. The choice of this type of profession also corresponds to the idea that the community needs female professionals in its network of services so that it can accommodate the modesty and contextual gender segregation requirements of its clients.

18. Here again one finds a style of argument elaborated by the Muslim Brotherhood; see Mitchell ([1969] 1993: 256–257).

19. See also Dif (2002: 44).

20. According to Werbner, this approach has been articulated in many nascent feminist movements in Western as well as non-Western countries, in both colonial and postcolonial contexts. It aims to challenge the relegation of women to the private and domestic spheres, and it seeks to "feminize citizenship," as a response to (post-)Enlightenment thinkers who have defined the prime virtues required for participating in the democratic community—such as rationality, autonomy, and equality—as specifically masculine qualities (Werbner 1999: 224). In this way, "women translated their compassion into ideological agendas in the public sphere" (Werbner 1999: 240).

21. In spite of certain resemblances to earlier manifestations of feminist discourse, the "paradoxes of feminism" (Joan W. Scott 1996; see also Cott 1987) resulting from the simultaneous deployment of arguments about "equal rights" and "special contributions," or about "sameness" and "difference," are here substituted with a range of tensions and ambivalences, raising quite distinct ethical problems and conundrums (see last section of the chapter).

22. Their ambition to upward social mobility equals an effort of "de-proletariani-

zation" (White 2002: 208) of Europe's Muslim community. Jenny B. White, in her work on young pious Muslim women in Turkey, notes that, in the eyes of these women, education is the "most viable avenue for distancing oneself from one's working class background" (2002: 208).

23. The term *ethics of care* was coined by feminist scholars Carol Gilligan (1982) and Nel Noddings (1984). See also Tronto (1993), Kittay (1999), and Virginia Held (2006). And though this (in itself divergent) trend of feminist thought does not exactly map onto the ethical attitudes and motivations asserted by my Muslim interlocutors, there are some interesting convergences. Similar to the pious practitioners, feminist care ethicists (along with other feminist scholars) do embrace a conception of the person that is interdependent and relational. Even more important, feminist care ethicists count emotional and perceptual aptitudes, such as empathy and sensitivity (articulated by my interlocutors as *rahma*), as among the most important epistemic resources for ethical understanding and action. Equally relevant for my broader argument is care ethicists' critique of contemporary virtue ethics as too subject-centered (read primarily as care for the self). Moreover, care ethicists' ambition to develop a wider moral framework for thinking about morality that takes the interdependency and vulnerability of the human being seriously and postulates care as a fundamental element for human well-being and the good life converges with some of my own concerns here.

24. The contemporary German understanding of motherhood is also heir to National Socialism's deployment of motherhood for its racial-nationalist project (Vinken 2001; see also Koonz 1987). Given this emphasis on motherhood, working mothers of young children are at times referred to, in popular parlance, as *Rabenmütter* (raven mothers).

25. Olfa's arguments here closely follow polemical revival literature on the topic of working women in Muslim majority contexts. McLarney (2015), for instance, documents these debates in Egypt, which respond to various national and international developmental policies that seek to promote female waged labor in Egypt. McLarney calls attention to the fact that these debates are not unique to the Muslim world. In many Western countries, popular literature and media equally nourish continuous debate around issues of motherhood, waged labor, and the pros and cons of opting out of employment. Yet Adely (2009, 2012) contends that, when these debates occur in the Arab world, development reports and academic researchers often frame them with an isolated and culturalist perspective.

26. On this point, see also chapter 6 of Adely (2012).

27. There is a striking resemblance between Olfa's critique and the one formulated by Bint al-Shati, a popular Egyptian female Islamic scholar, in defense of an Islamic vision of motherhood. Al-Shati bemoans the "inferiority complex belonging to humble mothers . . . which cultural colonialism and intellectual invasion implanted firmly in the consciousness and mentality of the East" (quoted in McLarney 2015).

28. The importance of volunteer activism is also deeply ingrained in the global Islamic revival consciousness, the success of which is built mainly on the mobilization of volunteer activists. See, for instance, Bayat (2002b) and, for female volunteers more particularly, Deeb (2006).

29. Asad (1993: 210) writes, "It is too often forgotten that the process of determining orthodoxy in conditions of change and contest includes attempts at achieving discursive coherence, at representing the present within an authoritative narrative."

30. This style is quite similar to what Charles Hirschkind (2006: 110) has observed among pious Egyptian Muslims who listened to Islamic sermons on cassettes; significantly, they conversed in this way outside of any institutional structure: "The relationship between the speakers is not that of teacher to pupil nor of social superior to social subordinate, but rather of coparticipants in a common moral project, their speech structured around an orientation toward correct Islamic practice."

31. I agree here with Charles Hirschkind's response to a critique articulated by Samuli Schielke (2009) against scholars (including Hirschkind) who study Muslims of the revival movement and allegedly do not account for fragmentation and inconsistency in the lives of religious people. Hirschkind rightly replies that one should not posit these unavoidable elements of life as incompatible with the *desire* to conform to a religious ideal (2012: 20, fn.14).

32. The popularity of the profession of schoolteacher is not specific to Muslim women, but according to Vinken (2001: 48) it is observable among German women more broadly; it seems to constitute a compromise between professional ambitions and German norms regarding motherhood. Of course this professional aspiration has been heavily complicated by the headscarf bans for schoolteachers in several *Länder*, including North Rhine-Westphalia.

33. The BFmF offers so-called *Vätercoaching* (father coaching) seminars for fathers in the Turkish language.

34. As Salvatore (2007: 77) explains, the *telos* does not overdetermine practice, because "the given yet contestable and revisable form of argumentation and reasoning" offers direction without fixing specific conceptions and hierarchies of the good. Thus, the *telos* linked to a specific tradition does not provide a "formula for communitarian homogeneity," but is "the engine of the search for coherence" (2007: 92).

Chapter 6

1. Feminist geographers argue that paying attention to these spaces allows us to go beyond state-centric understandings of power relations and politics, and therefore enables a perspective that reveals how gendered subjects participate in and contest the production of politics. Cultural geographer Banu Gökariksel (2012) argues that it is precisely the state-centered perspective that has dominated much academic scholarship on the various European headscarf debates that have taken place all over Europe.

2. The complex theorization of modern temporality, together with its spatial dimension, has been central to scholarship investigating the exclusionary nature of modern time-space narratives, most notably for women and racialized subjects (see, for example, Butler 2008; Fabian 1983; Felski 2002). Writing about the modern temporal regime that underlies contemporary debates on Muslims in Europe, Butler (2008: 2) asserts that "certain notions of relevant geopolitical space—including the spatial boundedness of minority communities—are circumscribed by this story of a progressive modernity;

certain notions of what 'this time' can and must be are similarly construed on the basis of circumscribing the 'where' of its happening."

3. Heiko Henkel (2005: 497–498) observes the following in regard to *salat*: "At least five times a day practitioners become essentially Muslims while the secular and hetero-geneously constituted spaces of the life world are re-defined as Muslim spaces. Within these demarcations the *salat* is a space of Islamic practice, clearly defined, spatially and temporally bounded, and set apart from everyday activity. This separation calls to mind the break—the establishment of a radical duality between the profanity of everyday life and the domain of the sacred" (Durkheim 1995: 39)—that Durkheim saw as constitutive of ritual. In the case of the *salat*, however, the sacred-profane dualism is somewhat mis-leading. Neither is the time-space of the ritual prayer itself sacred (a destroyed *salat* is not seen as a sacrilege but simply as an invalid *salat* which thus has to be repeated) nor is the world outside of it necessarily profane. The *salat* introduces a break between the flow of everyday life (characterized by a variety of different kinds of social disciplines, Muslim and other) and a time-space ideally characterized by pure Islamic practice. In this sense the rigidly controlled boundary surrounding the ritual prayer demarcates a sphere—and thus a context—in which the practice of the *salat* is embedded." A similar argument is made by El-Guindi (1999: 77–78).

4. See Chapter 3, n2.

5. Michèle Tribalat (1995: 254) considers the diminishing practice of prayer to be a clear sign of desirable cultural integration. John Bowen (2004: 32) observes that, in France, whether a young man prays or not can have significant consequences when he is suspected of engaging in terrorist activities.

6. On the different experiences had in French and German public schools, see Chapter 2.

7. Butler's work pinpoints the gaps and flaws in performativities, conceived as "citational practices" by which sexed and gendered subjects are continuously fashioned, in order to identify the sites where regulatory norms are contested. According to her, it is through the "de-contextualization" of a performative practice—that is, through "the rehearsal of the conventional formulae in nonconventional ways"—that sites emerge for resignification, thereby "assuming meanings and functions for which [they were] never intended" (Butler 1997: 147).

8. One of the endeavors of the reformists was to prove the capacity of Islamic juris-prudence to adapt to the exigencies of modern times. It is in this spirit that Rashid Rida ([1928] 1984) wrote a book dedicated to the concept of facility: *Yusr al-Islam wa Usul al-Tashri' al-'Amm* (Facility of Islam and the sources of the general jurisprudence) (see, for instance, Johnston 2004: 260–261). The discourse on *taysir* is propagated in particu-lar by Egyptian Shaykh Yusuf al-Qaradawi, whose thought is very influential in both the French and the larger Western European context. See Caeiro (2010).

9. Certeau (1984: xix) defines a *tactic* as follows: "a calculus which cannot count on a 'proper' (a spatial or institutional localization), nor thus on a borderline distinguish-ing the other as a visible totality. The place of a tactic belongs to the other. A tactic in-

sinuates itself into the other's place, fragmentarily, without taking it over in its entirety, without being able to keep it at a distance."

10. Certeau (1984: xiv) strives "to bring to light the clandestine forms taken by the dispersed, tactical, and makeshift creativity of groups or individuals already caught in the nets of "discipline." By making this claim, he also engages critically with Foucault's account of power in *Discipline and Punish* (1977), which he reads as formulating an analysis of power that takes into account only its "subjecting" quality, thereby foreclosing on an understanding of possibilities of "resistance."

11. Talal Asad (2006b) rightly points to the fact that French public discourse regularly asks whether a veiled woman truly "desires" her veil, but the same question is never asked in regard to unveiled Muslim women and their condition of being uncovered. This is so, he continues, because it is naturally assumed that an unveiled Muslim woman does not wear the headscarf because she lacks the desire.

12. A large body of scholarship has examined the emergence of a specific discourse about and representations of Muslim women as part of the moral justification of European colonial projects (for example, Alloula 1986; Fanon 1965; El-Guindi 1999; Yeğenoğlu 1998).

13. Several women in this context referred me to a phrase pronounced by Tariq Ramadan during one of his conferences in which he is supposed to have encouraged women to overcome their fear of wearing the headscarf by saying, "Free yourself from humans and submit yourself to God" (*Libère-toi des Hommes et soumets-toi à Dieu*). In his books, he regularly uses the term *liberation* for the process that leads to the acknowledgment of and submission to one God (1995, 2004).

14. A 2012 Amnesty International report claims a general pattern of discrimination in employment for women in many European countries who wear the hijab (Amnesty International 2012).

15. The experience that Aziza evoked took place before the 2004 law banning religious symbols, when each public school had a different policy on how to handle veiled students.

16. More recently, similar efforts by Muslim students have become increasingly politicized. In April 2013, a teenage student was expelled from a middle school in the greater Paris region for wearing a hairband suspected to be a covert effort to introduce the headscarf into the school.

17. The book that Saliha referred to was *Al-hijab*, by Gamal Al-Banna, youngest brother of the founder of the Muslim Brotherhood, Hassan Al-Banna. Reading from the Islamic texts a strongly anti-authoritarian and egalitarian message, he is considered to be a reform Islamist. On the writings of this self-taught Islamic thinker, see, for instance, Lübben (2006).

18. Saliha is one of several women with whom I continue to have contact, even after the end of my fieldwork. In the meantime, she has completely abandoned the hijab but continues to practice and to pay attention to what she wears.

19. Many scholars writing on fashion have discussed its temporality as a condition for complying with the demands of modern industrial capitalism (Benjamin 2006; Simmel 1997; Vinken 2005). As Gilles Lipovetsky (1994: 47–48) puts it, "an unprecedented

social value was beginning to radiate, that of *novelty*. Fashion could not have existed without this reversal of the relation to historical evolution and to ephemera. In order for fashion to come into being, the "modern" had to be accepted and desired; the present had to be deemed more prestigious than the past; in an unprecedented move, what was novel had to be invested with dignity."

20. There were many discussions among my interlocutors about what makes Islamic dress pleasant or beautiful. Some women defended more traditional Islamic dress, such as the *jellaba* (a loose long robe) as beautiful and refused to "appease" or "please" the majority society by submitting to "their" fashion regime.

21. Here Keane shares concerns similar to those articulated in Mahmood's (2005) work.

22. With this question Keane also moves beyond Jean-Pierre Warnier's (1999, 2001) approach to material culture, discussed in Chapter 3.

23. "Signifying practices can be experienced in contrasting ways. On the one hand, as vehicles of meaning and inhabitable dispositions, signifying practices form an intimate component of subjective experience and its cognizability. On the other hand, as concrete, publicly accessible forms, they can present themselves to subjects as external objects of experience. . . . I insist on the distinction here, . . . because it is analytically important to keep in mind the ways in which things and words are *not* wholly products of human intentions, mastered by human actions, and that they are not saturated with meanings. They are potentially objects in both the conceptual and material meanings of the word. The challenge that words and things can pose to persons is therefore not just a problem for the observer and the theoretician but is often a recurrent instigation *within* action itself. In their modality as objective semiotic forms, signifying practices *can*, in some circumstances, offer themselves up to reflection. Given the right background assumptions about the world, the objective character of signifying practices can even become a source of moral or political anxiety, demanding active intervention. At that point, the very materiality of semiotic forms can become, in effect, an agent provocateur of historical change" (Keane 2008: 14, emphasis in original).

24. Sarah Bracke (2013) shows that *mixité* has become the paradigm for the ideal of a harmonious "social and ethnic intermingling," as well as for a more contemporary and "mature" version of gender relations. It is thereby also considered as the "opposite of (gender) segregation," which is now understood directly as a "threat to the public sphere."(2013: 262). See also Joan W. Scott (2010), Werbner (2007), and Guénif-Souilamas (2006).

25. In November 2004, for instance, a nationwide controversy erupted in the Netherlands after an *imam* refused to shake hands with the Dutch Minister of Integration, explaining that his religion did not allow him to shake hands with women (see Fadil 2009). In Denmark, Asmaa Abdol-Hamid, a Danish-Palestinian woman and practicing Muslim, made similar headlines when she became a national candidate for the Danish Socialist Party, because of her alleged refusal to shake hands with men (El-Tayeb 2011). In France, the topic of handshaking comes up regularly in public discussions about Muslims' refusal to endorse the French value *mixité*.

26. Much recent literature has pointed to the emergence of new consumption practices in Islamic movements, as well as to a Muslim-oriented culture industry. See, for in-

stance, Abaza (2001), Abu-Lughod (1995, 2005), Bayat (2002), Göle (2002), Jouili (2014), McLarney and Gökariksel (2010), Navaro-Yashin (2002), Saktanber 2002.

27. Fast-food restaurants have also become one of the main hangouts of *banlieue* youth in general.

28. This quote reflects how activities that had previously been performed without discomfort now, through the cultivation of modesty, evoked sentiments of unease and "embarrassment." See Chapter 3.

29. Certeau writes, "the 'consumer' knocks up with and in the dominant cultural economy [creating] innumerable . . . transformations of its law into one of their own interests and their own rules" (1984: xxxix).

30. Ilya Parkins (2010: 104) argues that this anxiety about modernity's temporality is connected to the dualism that inheres in modernity's understanding of time as "related to the recognition of the mutual imbrications of past and present—and therefore, in a progress-oriented temporal consciousness, of the future."

31. On that point, see also Butler (2008). She astutely shows that because the *now* is key for Europe's self-definition, it needs to project a premodern temporality onto an Other, in order to legitimize its own narrative of temporal progress, which is parochial and works in a structurally racist way.

32. Even though it emerges from similar conditions, this is a quite different way of responding to the structural constraints of secular public spheres than those enacted by "secular" Muslims, which are analyzed so sharply by Ruth Mas (2006).

33. This is of course a move that can also be contested. See, for instance, the challenging remarks made by Olfa on pages 144–146 in Chapter 5.

34. This reconfiguration does not happen, however, in an open-ended and free-floating way; rather, it takes place within the ethical and theological horizon provided by Islamic traditions, which, as we have seen in Chapter 2, always requires "authentification" (Deeb 2006) by accepted authorities.

35. See Chapter 1, n19.

36. Before taking her decision, Mariam also talked to several other Muslims, whom she considered more knowledgeable than her, who gave her very different advice.

37. Notable among the important contemporary Islamic scholars and thinkers who have written on *maslaha* and who were also important in the revival circles were Tariq Ramadan (2004) and Yusuf Al-Qaradawi (2000). *Maslaha* is often discussed in classes when an activist conception of citizenship and the Muslim duty to participate positively in society are being promoted.

38. On the use of *maslaha* in modern Islamic (legal) thought, see, for instance, Opwis (2005) and Zaman (2004).

39. Salvatore refers here to the definition of *ijtihad* advanced by fourteenth-century Andalusian jurist Al-Shatibi, who was one of the prime elaborators of this specific understanding of *maslaha*. He clearly alluded to a phronetic type of reasoning: "a process in which one exhausts one's efforts to one's full capacity in order to acquire exact or probable knowledge to reach judgment in a given case" (Masud [1977] 1995: 230, quoted in Salvatore 2007: 168).

40. It is the intention (*niyya*) of the agent that, in the end, defines whether or not *istislah* is involved in an action. As Al-Shatibi emphasizes, the individual always needs to support his pious intention with a view toward the consequences of his or her action (Salvatore 2007: 168).

41. Al-Shatibi's elaboration of *maslaha* was of course not uncontested, and other thinkers have developed a much more restrictive account of that term, limited to the expertise of the jurist (Salvatore 2007).

42. This confidence was also clearly exposed in Hawwa's account of her first day wearing hijab, discussed in Chapter 3.

43. In their demands for introducing religious conduct into the public sphere (such as the right to wear the headscarf at the workplace, or exemption from mixed sports lessons), Muslims in Germany tend to rely on the constitutional order. German political authorities increasingly criticize Muslims' reference to the law, perceived as purely instrumental, according to which they "pick and choose pragmatically what they deem adequate and necessary for their religious life conduct" (Amir-Moazami 2011: 23).

44. This concern is closely connected to their critique of liberal rights regimes, discussed in Chapter 4.

45. A virtue mentioned many times in the Qur'an, this notion has been extensively discussed by past and contemporary religious scholars. For instance, in a recent booklet, Youssuf al-Qaradawi (2002) discusses the importance of this virtue, which he considers a fundamental element of piety, as well as techniques that can help the believer to develop that quality.

46. In a similar vein, Saba Mahmood (2005) discusses the concept of *sabr*. For her, *sabr* is linked to a specific context of injustice encountered by women living in societies governed by a patriarchal logic.

Chapter 7

1. Many times when I have presented my work, I have been encouraged to be "more critical" of the women and their (gendered) practices.

2. Christian Joppke (2009: 110), for instance, has used Olfa's comment in which she talked about the significance of the ethical attitude of submission to God's will going along with a deep trust in the divine powers—which I quoted in an article I wrote with Schirin Amir-Moazami (2006), to confirm his very problematic argument that Islam is incompatible with Europe's liberalism and promotes women's subordination.

3. This is precisely what happened in the case mentioned in the previous footnote.

4. In a series of articles, Brian Turner (2000, 2001, 2002) develops a similar account. According to Turner, irony is the appropriate attitude for promoting a cosmopolitan relationship to the world. Building on arguments made by American philosopher Richard Rorty, irony is the condition for achieving distance from one's homeland and way of life, thereby adopting a skeptical stance toward "grand narratives" and "final vocabularies" (Turner 2002: 58–59). He writes, "the principal component of cosmopolitan virtue is irony, because the understanding of other cultures is assisted by an intellectual distance from one's own national or local culture . . . skepticism and distance from one's own tra-

dition are the basis of an obligation of care and stewardship for other cultures" (Turner 2002: 57; see also Smith 2007). For a good critique of this account, see Euben (2001).

5. In these debates, the figure of the Muslim fundamentalist appeared at times to be the antidote to the cosmopolitan figure (see, for instance, Appiah 2010; Held 2010), as Katherine Ewing (2010: 53) has correctly observed: "Could it be that, with the concept of cosmopolitanism, scholars are seeking to find a way to perpetuate this discursive structure, now that neither modernity nor modernism convincingly distinguishes "us" and "them"? . . . Within the past few years, and especially since 9/11, 'cosmopolitanism' has emerged as an analytic category that in some respects has supplanted the modern as a way of characterizing a progressive subjectivity."

6. Such an understanding also depends, of course, on certain strong affective attachments, which are, however, fully ignored by these different thinkers. For a critique of this omission, see Mahmood 2013.

7. Hannah Arendt, for instance, wrote that "this judging insight and speculative thought . . . what we usually call common sense . . . discloses to us the nature of the world insofar as it is a common world; we owe to it the fact that our strictly private and "subjective" five senses and their sensory data can adjust themselves to a nonsubjective and "objective" world which we have in common and share with others. Judging is one, if not the most, important activity in which this sharing-the-world-with-others comes to pass" (Arendt 1996: 221).

8. Salvatore thus pleads for the recognition of a "broad, transcultural dynamics of debating and defining the common good and the more discrete public goods" (2008: 250).

9. Salvatore (2007) integrates his genealogy of the public sphere into an "axial age" theory. This is the one aspect of his book that I find less convincing. Even if this theory provides a broader approach than one that looks merely at Western traditions, it still delineates a civilizational space with a linear time frame from which many other traditions remain excluded.

10. Ramadan's work has significantly evolved over the years, especially in regard to the role of law in Islamic ethics. On this point, see March (2007, 2010).

11. It is Ramadan's emphasis on a phronetic reasoning committed to social justice that makes him skeptical of a mode of reasoning that is present among some promoters of "minority fiqh," which he describes as confined to notions of "exception and necessity." As a consequence, he writes, "individuals are given the means to survive in the global system and thereby affirm it but not to participate in its reform. (Ramadan 2003: 160).

12. This is why Ramadan strongly criticizes Islamic organizations in Europe that limit their political activity to a defense of Muslims' interests: "so, in practice, they end up by forming the idea of a 'community,' whose members should think about political participation in the sense that they should get involved above all in order to protect the specific needs and interests of the community. . . . The universal message of Islam that should move Muslims' civic conscience to promote justice, right, and goodness everywhere is reduced to this: 'since we are a feeble minority'—a defensive, self-pitying discourse, narrowly concerned with the protection of self and 'the community'" (Ramadan 2003: 155).

REFERENCES

Abaza, Mona. 2000. The Islamization of Knowledge between Particularism and Globalization: Malaysia and Egypt. In *Situating Globalization: Views from Egypt,* ed. C. Nelson and S. Rouse, 53–95. Bielefeld: transcript Verlag.

Abu-Lughod, Lila. 1995. Movie Stars and Islamic Moralism in Egypt. *Social Text* 42: 53–67.

———. 2005. *Dramas of Nationhood: The Politics of Television in Egypt.* Chicago: University of Chicago Press.

Abu-Odeh, Lama. 2004. Modernizing Muslim Family Law: The Case of Egypt. *Vanderbilt Journal of Transnational Law* 37: 1043–1073.

Abugideiri, Hiba. 2002. Hagar: A Historical Model for "Gender Jihad." In *Daughters of Abraham: Feminist Thought in Judaism, Christianity and Islam,* ed. Y. Y. Haddad and J. Esposito, 81–107. Gainesville: University Press of Florida.

Adelson, Leslie A. 2005. *The Turkish Turn in Contemporary German Literature: Toward a New Critical Grammar of Migration.* New York: Palgrave Macmillan.

Adely, Fida. 2012. *Gendered Paradoxes: Educating Jordanian Women in Nation, Faith, Progress.* Chicago: University of Chicago Press.

———. 2009. Educating Women for Development: The Arab Human Development Report 2005 and the Problem with Women's Choices. *International Journal of Middle East Studies* 41 (1): 105–122.

Agrama, Hussein A. 2010. Secularism, Sovereignty, Indeterminacy: Is Egypt a Secular or a Religious State? *Comparative Studies in Society and History* 52 (3): 495–523.

Ahmed, Leila. 1992. *Women and Gender in Islam: Historical Roots of a Modern Debate.* New Haven, CT: Yale University Press.

Ahmed, Sara. 2004. *The Cultural Politics of Emotion.* Edinburgh: Edinburgh University Press.

Al-Banna, Gamal. 2002. *al-hijab* (The Headscarf). Cairo: dar al-fikr al-islami.

Al-Ghazali, Abu Hamid. 1997. *Al-Ghazali on Disciplining the Soul and Breaking the Two Desires: Kitab Riyadat al-Nafs and Kitab Kasr al-Shahwatayn, Books 22 and 23 of the Revival of the Religious Sciences—Ihya ulum al-din.* Trans. T. J. Winter. Cambridge, UK: Islamic Texts Society.

———. 2000. *Les Piliers du Musulman Sincère. Les Pratiques d'Adoration.* Beyrouth: Les Éditions Al-Bouraq.

——. 2001. *Les Secrets de la Prière en Islam. Revivification des sciences de la Religion (asrâr as-salât fî-l-islâm)*. Beyrouth: Les Éditions Al-Bouraq.

——. 2004. *Crainte et espoir*. Paris: Éditions Maison d'Ennour.

Al-Qardawi, Youssuf. 2002. *La notion de patience dans le Coran*. Lyon: Tawhid.

Al-Qaradawi, Yusuf, 2000. *Siyasa al-shari'a fi daw nusus shari'a wa maqasidiha*. Beirut: Mu'assassat al-Risala.

Ali, Kecia. 2003. Progressive Muslims and Islamic Jurisprudence: The Necessity for Critical Engagement with Marriage and Divorce Laws. In *Progressive Muslims: On Justice, Gender, and Pluralism*, ed. O. Safi, 163–189. Oxford, UK: Oneworld Publications.

Allen, Chris. 2010. *Islamophobia*. Surrey, UK: Ashgate.

Alloula, Malek. 1986. *The Colonial Harem*. Minneapolis: University of Minnesota Press.

Altwaijri, Abdulaziz O. 2001. *Human Rights in Islamic Teachings*. Rabat: ISESCO

Amir-Moazami, Schirin. 2005. Buried Alive: Multiculturalism in Germany. *ISIM Review* 16: 22-23.

——. 2007. *Politisierte Religion. Der Kopftuchstreit in Deutschland und Frankreich*. Bielefeld: Transcript Verlag.

——. 2011. Dialogue as a Governmental Technique: Managing Gendered Islam in Germany. *Feminist Review* 98: 9–27.

Amir-Moazami, Schirin, and Armando Salvatore. 2003. Gender, Generation, and the Reform of Tradition: From Muslim Majority Societies to Western Europe. In *Muslim Networks and Transnational Communities in and across Western Europe*, ed. J. N. Stefano Allievi, 52–77. Leiden: Brill.

Amir-Moazami, Schirin, and Jeanette Jouili. 2006. Knowledge, Empowerment and Religious Authority among Pious Muslim Women in France and Germany. *Muslim World* 96 (4): 617–642.

Amiraux, Valérie. 2001. *Acteurs de l'islam entre Allemagne et Turquie*. Paris: L'Harmattan.

——. 2011. Religious Authority, Social Action and Political Participation: A Case Study of the Mosquée de la Rue de Tanger in Paris. In *Producing Islamic Knowledge: Transmission and Dissemination in Western Europe*, ed. M. van Bruinessen and S. Allievi, 65–90. London: Routledge.

Amnesty International. 2012. Choice and Prejudice: Discrimination against Muslims in Europe. London: Amnesty International. http://www.amnesty.eu/content/assets/REPORT.pdf (accessed January 25, 2013).

Anawati, Georges. 1976. *Homo Islamicus, Images of Man in Ancient and Medieval Thought*. Louvain: Publications Universitaires.

Anderson, Jon W. 1982. Social Structure and the Veil: Comportment and the Composition of Interaction in Afghanistan. *Anthropos* 77: 397–420.

Anthias, Floya, and Nira Yuval-Davis. 1992. *Racialized Boundaries: Race, Nation, Gender, Colour and Class and the Anti-racist Struggle*. London: Routledge.

Appiah, Kwame Anthony. 2010. *Cosmopolitanism: Ethics in a World of Strangers*. New York: W. W. Norton.

Archer, Brad. 2007. Family Law Reform and the Feminist Debate: Actually-Existing

Islamic Feminism in the Maghreb and Malaysia. *Journal of International Women's Studies* 8 (4): 49–59.

Arendt, Hannah. (1958) 1998. *The Human Condition.* Chicago: University of Chicago Press.

———. 1982. *Lectures on Kant's Political Philosophy.* Chicago: University of Chicago Press.

———. 1996. *Between Past and Future.* Harmondsworth: Penguin.

Aristotle. (1941) 2001. *The Basic Works of Aristotle,* ed. R. McKeon. New York: Modern Library.

Asad, Talal. 1986. *The Idea of an Anthropology of Islam.* Occasional Papers Series. Washington, DC: Georgetown University Center for Contemporary Arab Studies.

———. 1993. *Genealogies of Religion: Discipline and Reasons of Power in Christianity and Islam.* Baltimore, MD: Johns Hopkins University Press.

———. 1999. Religion, Nation-State, Secularism. In Nation and Religion: Perspectives on Europe and Asia, ed. P. van der Veer and H. Lehmann, 178-196. Princeton, NJ: Princeton University Press.

———. 2003. *Formations of the Secular: Christianity, Islam, Modernity.* Stanford, CA: Stanford University Press.

———. 2006a. An Interview with Talal Asad by David Scott. In *Powers of the Secular Modern: Talal Asad and His Interlocutors,* ed. D. Scott and C. Hirschkind, 243–304. Stanford, CA: Stanford University Press.

———. 2006b. Trying to Understand French Secularism. In *Political Theologies,* ed. H. de Vries and L. E. Sullivan, 494–526. New York: Fordham University Press.

Babès, Leila. 1997. *L'Islam positif. La religion des jeunes musulmans de France.* Paris: Éditions de l'Atelier.

Badawi, Jamal. 1995. *Gender Equity in Islam: Basic Principles.* Oak Brook, IL: American Trust Publications.

Badran, Margot. 1995. *Feminists, Islam, and Nation. Gender and the Making of Modern Egypt.* Princeton, NJ: Princeton University Press.

———. 2001. Understanding Islam, Islamism, and Islamic Feminism. *Journal of Women's History* 13 (1): 47–52.

———. 2005. Between Secular and Islamic Feminism/s: Reflections on the Middle East and Beyond. *Journal of Middle East Women's Studies* 1 (1): 6–28.

Balasescu, Alexandru. 2003. Tehran Chic: Islamic Headscarves, Fashion Designers, and New Geographies of Modernity. *Fashion Theory: The Journal of Dress, Body and Culture* 7: 39–56.

Bangstad, Sindre. 2011. Saba Mahmood and Anthropological Feminism After Virtue. *Theory, Culture & Society* 28 (3): 28–54.

Bano, Masooda, and Hilary Kalmbach, eds. 2012. *Women, Leadership, and Mosques: Changes in Contemporary Islamic Authority.* Leiden: Brill.

Barber, Benjamin. 1988. *The Conquest of Politics: Liberal Philosophy in Democratic Times.* Princeton, NJ: Princeton University Press.

Barker, John, ed. 2007. *The Anthropology of Morality in Melanesia and Beyond*. Surrey, UK: Ashgate.

Barlas, Asma. 2002. *"Believing Women" in Islam: Unreading Patriarchal Interpretations of the Qur'an*. Austin: University of Texas Press.

Baron, Beth. 1994. *The Women's Awakening in Egypt: Culture, Society, and the Press*. New Haven, CT: Yale University Press.

Baubérot, Jean. 1990. *Vers un nouveau pacte laïque?* Paris: Seuil.

Baudrillard, Jean. 1998. *The Consumer Society: Myths and Structures*. London: Sage.

Bauman, Zygmunt. 2001. *The Individualized Society*. Hoboken, NJ: Wiley.

Bayat, Asef. 2002a. Piety, Privilege and Egyptian Youth. *ISIM Review* 1 (10): 23.

———. 2002b. Activism and Social Development in the Middle East. *International Journal of Middle East Studies* 34 (1): 1–28.

Beck, Ulrich. 2004. The Truth of Others: A Cosmopolitan Approach. *Common Knowledge* 10 (3): 430–449.

Beiner, Ronald. 1984. *Political Judgment*. Chicago: University of Chicago Press.

Beiner, Ronald Steven, and Jennifer Nedelsky, eds. 2001. *Judgment, Imagination, and Politics: Themes from Kant and Arendt*. Lanham, MD: Rowman & Littlefield.

Benhabib, Seyla. 2006. *Another Cosmopolitanism*. Oxford, UK: Oxford University Press.

Benjamin, Andrew. 2006. *Style and Time: Essays on the Politics of Appearance*. Chicago: Northwestern University Press.

Berkey, Jonathan Porter. 1992. *The Transmission of Knowledge in Medieval Cairo: A Social History of Islamic Education*. Princeton, NJ: Princeton University Press.

Bigley, Heather. 2011. Muslim Mothers and French Daughters: Women Caught between Religion and Secularity in a Post-Beur Film Culture. *Transitions: Journal of Franco-Iberian Studies* 11: 114–130.

Bourdieu, Pierre. 1977. *Outline of a Theory of Practice,* trans. R. Nice. Cambridge, UK: Cambridge University Press.

———. 2000. *Pascalian Meditations* Stanford, CA: Stanford University Press.

Bourdieu, Pierre, and Loïc J. D. Wacquant. 1992. *An Invitation to Reflexive Sociology*. Chicago: University of Chicago Press.

Bouzar, Dounia, and Saïda Kada. 2004. *L'une voilée, l'autre pas*. Paris: Albin Michel.

Bowen, John. 1989. The Social Meaning of an Islamic Ritual. *Man* 24: 600–619.

———. 2004. Muslims and Citizens: France's Headscarf Controversy. *Boston Review*, February 1, 31–35.

———. 2007. *Why the French Don't Like Headscarves: Islam, the State, and Public Space*. Princeton, NJ: Princeton University Press.

———. 2010. *Can Islam Be French? Pluralism and Pragmatism in a Secularist State*. Princeton, NJ: Princeton University Press.

Bracke, Sarah. 2008. Conjugating the Modern/Religious, Conceptualizing Female Religious Agency: Contours of a "Post-secular" Conjuncture. *Theory, Culture & Society* 25 (6): 51–67.

———. 2011. Subjects of Debate: Secular and Sexual Exceptionalism, and Muslim Women in the Netherlands. *Feminist Review* 98: 28–46.

———. 2013. From Fraternité to Mixité: Notes on How Gender Matters to the Secular. In *Religion, Gender and the Public Sphere,* ed. N. Reilly and S. Scriver, 257–267. London: Routledge.

Brennan, Samantha. 1999. Recent Work in Feminist Ethics. *Ethics* 109 (4): 858–893.

Brown, Peter. 1984. Late Antiquity and Islam: Parallels and Contrasts. In *The Place of Adab in South Asian Islam,* ed. B. D. Metcalf, 23–37. Berkeley: University of California Press.

Brown, Wendy. 1993. Wounded Attachments. *Political Theory* 21 (3): 390–410.

———. 1995. *States of Injury: Power and Freedom in Late Modernity.* Princeton, NJ: Princeton University Press.

Brubaker, Rogers. 1997. *Citoyenneté et nationalité en France et en Allemagne.* Paris: Belin.

Bunzl, Matti. 2005. Between Anti-Semitism and Islamophobia: Some Thoughts on the New Europe. *American Ethnologist* 32 (4): 199–208.

Butler, Judith. 1990. *Gender Trouble and the Subversion of Identity.* London: Routledge

———. 1993. *Bodies That Matter.* New York: Routledge.

———. 1997. *Excitable Speech.* New York: Routledge.

———. 2008. Sexual Politics, Torture, and Secular Time. *British Journal of Sociology* 59 (1): 1–23.

Caeiro, Alexandre. 2004. The Social Construction of Shari'a: Bank Interest, Home Purchase, and Islamic Norms in the West. *Die Welt des Islams* 44 (3): 351–375.

———. 2006. Religious Authorities or Political Actors? The Muslim Leaders of the French Representative Body of Islam. In *European Muslims and the Secular State,* ed. J. Cesari and S. McLoughlin, 71–84. Surrey, UK: Ashgate.

———. 2010. The Power of European Fatwas: The Minority Fiqh Project and the Making of an Islamic Counterpublic. *International Journal of Middle East Studies* 42 (3): 435–449.

———. 2011. The Making of the Fatwa: The Production of Islamic Legal Expertise in Europe. *Archives de sciences sociales des religions* 155: 81–100.

Caeiro, Alexandre and Frank Peter. 2007. Ham, Mozart, and Limits to Freedom of Expression. *ISIM Review* 19: 26–27.

Canard, Marius. 1965. Da'wa. In *Encyclopedia of Islam.* New Edition. Vol. 2. Leiden: Brill, 168–170.

Carré, Olivier. 1990. Statut de la science et modernisation dans l'islam contemporain. In *Le grand atlas des religions.* Paris: Encyclopaedia Universalis, 338–339.

Cayir, Kenan. 2004. Die Individualisierung des islamistischen Subjekts: türkisch–islamische Romane. In *Islam in Sicht. Der Auftritt von Muslimen im öffentlichen Raum,* ed. L. Ammann and N. Göle, 178–185. Bielefeld: transcript Verlag.

Certeau, Michel de. 1984. *The Practice of Everyday Life,* trans. S. F. Rendall. Berkeley: University of California Press.

Césari, Jocelyne. 1994. *Être musulman en France. Associations, militants et mosquées.* Paris/Aix-en-Provence: Karthala/IREMAM.

———. 2003. Muslim Minorities in Europe: The Silent Revolution. In *Modernising Islam: Religion in the Public Sphere in the Middle East and in Europe,* ed. F. Burgat and J. Esposito, 251–269. London: Hurst.

———. 2005. Mosque Conflicts in European Cities: Introduction. *Journal of Ethnic and Migration Studies* 31 (6): 1015–1024.

Chakrabarty, Dipesh. 2000. *Provincializing Europe. Postcolonial Thought and Historical Difference.* Princeton, NJ: Princeton University Press.

Cheruvallil-Contractor, Sariya. 2012. *Muslim Women in Britain: De-Mystifying the Muslimah.* London: Routledge.

Chin, Rita. 2007. *The Guest Worker Question in Postwar Germany.* Cambridge, UK: Cambridge University Press.

———. 2010. Turkish Women, West German Feminists, and the Gendered Discourse on Muslim Cultural Difference. *Public Culture* 22 (3): 557–581.

Cohen, Jonathan. 2006. Social, Emotional, Ethical, and Academic Education: Creating a Climate for Learning, Participation in Democracy, and Well-Being. *Harvard Educational Review* 76 (2): 201–237.

Collins, Patricia Hill. 1990. *Black Feminist Thought: Knowledge, Consciousness, and the Politics of Empowerment.* Boston: Unwin Hyman.

Connolly, William E. 2002. *Identity, Difference: Democratic Negotiations of Political Paradox.* Minneapolis: University of Minnesota Press.

———. 2002. Neuropolitics: Thinking, Culture, Speed. Minneapolis: University of Minnesota Press.

Cook, Michael A. 2000. *Commanding Right and Forbidding Wrong in Islamic Thought.* Cambridge, UK: Cambridge University Press.

Cooke, Miriam. 1994. Zaynab al-Ghazali: Saint or Subversive? *Die Welt des Islams* 34 (1): 1–20.

———. 2000. *Women Claim Islam: Creating Islamic Feminism Through Literature.* London: Routledge.

Cott, Nancy. 1987. *The Grounding of Modern Feminism.* New Haven, CT: Yale University Press.

Dallmayr, Fred. 2001. Beyond Fugitive Democracy: Some Modern and Postmodern Reflections. In *Democracy and Vision: Sheldon Wolin and the Vicissitudes of the Political,* ed. A. Botwinick and W. E. Connolly, 58–78. Princeton, NJ: Princeton University Press.

Das, Veena. 2010. Engaging the Life of the Other: Love and Everyday Life. In *Ordinary Ethics: Anthropology, Language, and Action,* ed. M. Lambek, 376–399. New York: Fordham University Press.

Dassetto, Felice. 1996. La construction de l'islam européen. Approche socio-anthropologique. Paris: L'Harmattan.

Davis, Britton D. 2011. Lifting the Veil: France's New Crusade. *Boston College International & Comparative Law Revue* 34 (1): 117–145.

Deeb, Lara. 2006. *An Enchanted Modern: Gender and Public Piety in Shi'i Lebanon.* Princeton, NJ: Princeton University Press.

Deleuze, Gilles, and Felix Guattari. 1987. *A Thousand Plateaus,* trans. B. Massumi. Minneapolis: University of Minnesota Press. Original edition, 1980.

Derrida, Jacques. 1995. *The Gift of Death,* trans. D. Willis. Chicago: University of Chicago Press.

———. 1997. *Politics of Friendship,* trans. G. Collins. New York: Verso.

Dif, Malika. 2002. *Être musulmane aujourd'hui.* Lyon: Tawhid.

Dobbelaere, Karel. 1999. Towards an Integrated Perspective of the Processes Related to the Descriptive Concept of Secularization. *Sociology of Religion* 60 (3): 229–247.

Doomernik, Jeron. 1995. The Institutionalisation of Turkish Islam in Germany and the Netherlands: A Comparison. *Ethnic and Racial Studies* 18 (1): 46–63.

Dornhof, Sarah. 2012. Rationalities of Dialogue. *Current Sociology* 60 (3): 382–398.

Durkheim, Emile. 1995. *The Elementary Forms of Religious Life.* New York: Free Press.

Dworkin, Ronald. 1978. *Taking Rights Seriously.* Cambridge, MA: Harvard University Press.

Eddaouda, Souad. 2008. Implementing Islamic Feminism: The Case of Moroccan Family Code Reform. In *Islamic Feminism: Current Perspectives,* ed. A. Kynsilehto, 37–46. Tampere, Finland: Tampere Peace Research Institute.

Eickelman, Dale, and James Piscatori. 1996. *Muslim Politics.* Princeton, NJ: Princeton University Press.

El-Guindi, Fadwa. 1999. *Veil: Modesty, Privacy and Resistance.* Oxford, UK: Berg.

El-Shabassy, Eva. 1998. *Die Frau im Islam.* Garching: Informationszentrale Dar-us-Salam.

El-Tayeb, Fatima. 2011. *European Others.* Minneapolis: University of Minnesota Press.

Euben, Peter. 2001. The Polis, Globalization, and the Politics of Place. In *Democracy and Vision: Sheldon Wolin and the Vicissitudes of the Political,* ed. A. Botwinick and W. E. Connolly, 256–289. Princeton, NJ: Princeton University Press.

Evens, T.M.S. 2008. *Anthropology as Ethics: Nondualism and the Conduct of Sacrifice.* New York: Berghahn Books.

Ewing, Katherine Pratt. 2008. *Stolen Honor: Stigmatizing Muslim Men in Berlin.* Stanford, CA: Stanford University Press.

———. 2010. The Misrecognition of a Modern Islamist Organization: Germany Faces "Fundamentalism." In *Rethinking Islamic Studies,* ed. C. Ernst and R. Martin, 52–71. Columbia: University of South Carolina Press.

Fabian, Johannes. 1983. *Time and the Other: How Anthropology Makes Its Object.* New York: Columbia University Press.

Fadil, Nadia. 2008. Submitting to God, Submitting to the Self: Secular and Religious Trajectories of Second-Generation Maghrebi in Belgium. Unpublished Dissertation, Katholieke Universiteit Leuven, Belgium.

———. 2009. Managing Affects and Sensibilities: The Case of Not-Handshaking and Not-Fasting. *Social Anthropology* 17 (4): 439–454.

———. 2011a. Not-/Unveiling as an Ethical Practice. *Feminist Review* 98 (1): 83–109.

———. 2011b. Rediscovering the "Everyday Muslim": Notes on an Epistemological Battle Ground. Unpublished paper presented at the international workshop "Islam in Europe: The Emergence of the 'Muslim Question' in Europe: Reflections on the Governmental and Epistemological Regulation of Islam in Europe." Center for the Study of Religion, University of Berkeley, November 21.

———. Fakhry, Majid. 1994. *Ethical Theories in Islam.* Leiden, UK: Brill.

Fanon, Frantz. 2004. *The Wretched of the Earth*, translated from French by Richard Philcox; introductions by Jean-Paul Sartre and Homi K. Bhabha. New York: Grove Press.

———. (1959) 1965. *A Dying Colonialism. Freedom for Algeria*. New York: Grove Press.

Fassin, Didier, ed. 2012. *A Companion to Moral Anthropology*. Malden, MA: Wiley-Blackwell.

Faubion, James D. 2001. Toward an Anthropology of Ethics: Foucault and the Pedagogies of Autopoiesis. *Representations* 74: 83–104.

———. 2011. *An Anthropology of Ethics*. Cambridge, UK: Cambridge University Press.

Featherstone, Mike, ed. 1990. *Global Culture: Nationalism, Globalization and Modernity*. Vol. 2. London: SAGE.

Felski, R. 2002. Telling Time in Feminist Theory. *Tulsa Studies in Women's Literature* 21 (1): 21–27.

Fernando, Mayanthi. 2009. Exceptional Citizens: Secular Muslim Women and the Politics of Difference in France. *Social Anthropology* 17 (4): 379–392.

———. 2010. Reconfiguring Freedom: Muslim Piety and the Limits of Secular Law and Public Discourse in France. *American Ethnologist* 37 (1): 19–35.

Ferrari, Silvio. 2006. The Secularity of the State and the Shaping of Muslim Representative Organizations. In *European Muslims and the Secular State*, ed. Network of Comparative Rerearch on Islam and Muslims in Europe, 14–34. Surrey, UK: Ashgate.

Fetzer, Joel S., and J. Christopher Soper. 2005. *Muslims and the State in Britain, France, and Germany*. Cambridge, UK: Cambridge University Press.

Fortier, Anne-Marie. 2006. The Politics of Scaling, Timing and Embodying: Rethinking the "New Europe." *Mobilities* 1 (3): 313–331.

———. 2010. Proximity by Design? Affective Citizenship and the Management of Unease. *Citizenship Studies* 14 (1): 17–30.

Foucault, Michel. 1977. *Discipline and Punish: The Birth of the Prison*. New York: Random House.

———. 1980. *Power/Knowledge: Selected Interviews and Other Writings, 1972–1977*. New York: Vintage Books.

———. 1985. *The Use of Pleasure: The History of Sexuality*. Vol. 2: The Use of Pleasure. New York: Pantheon Press.

———. 1997a. The Ethics of the Concern for Self as a Practice of Freedom. In *Ethics: Subjectivity and Truth*, ed. P. Rabinow, 281–301. New York: New Press.

———. 1997b. On the Genealogies of Ethics: An Overview of Work in Progress. In *Ethics: Subjectivity and Truth*, ed. P. Rabinow, 253–280. New York: New Press.

———. 1997c. Technologies of the Self. In *Ethics: Subjectivity and Truth*, ed. P. Rabinow, 223–251. New York: New Press.

———. 1997d. The Social Triumph of the Sexual Will. In *Ethics: Subjectivity and Truth*, ed. P. Rabinow, 157–162. New York: New Press.

———. 2000. Confronting Governments: Human Rights. In *Essential Works of Foucault 1954–1984*. Vol. 3: *Power*, ed. D. Faubion, 474–476. New York: New School.

———. 2001. *Fairless Speech*. Los Angeles: Semio-text(e).

———. 2003. *Society Must Be Defended: Lectures at the Collège de France, 1975–1976.* New York: Picador.

Fraser, Nancy. 1997. *Justice Interruptus: Critical Reflections on the "Postsocialist" Condition.* New York: Routledge.

Freeman, Elizabeth. 2010. *Time Binds: Queer Temporalities, Queer Histories.* Durham, NC: Duke University Press.

Frégosi, Franck. 1996. Les problèmes liés à l'organisation de la religion musulmane en France. *Revue de Droit Canonique* 46 (2): 28–48.

———. 1998. *La formation des cadres religieux musulmans en France: approches socio-juridiques.* Paris: L'Harmattan.

———. 2004. L'Imam, le conférencier et le jurisconsulte: retour sur trois figures contemporaines du champ religieux islamique en France. *Archives de Sciences Sociales des Religions*: 131–146.

Gadamer, Hans-Georg. 1979. The Problem of Historical Consciousness. In *Interpretive Social Science: A Reader,* ed. P. Rabinow and W. M. Sullivan, 103–160. Berkeley: University of California Press.

———. (1975) 2004. *Truth and Method.* London: Continuum.

Gade, Anna M. 2004. *Perfection Makes Practice: Learning, Emotion, and the Recited Qur'an in Indonesia.* Honolulu: University of Hawaii Press.

Galembert, Claire de. 2005. La gestion publique de l'islam en France et en Allemagne. Les modèles nationaux à l'épreuve. In *Les codes de la différence: race, origine, religion: France, Allemagne, États-Unis,* ed. R. Kastoryano, 175–202. Paris: SciencesPo.

Gardner, Howard. 1999. *Intelligence Reframed: Multiple Intelligences for the 21st Century.* New York: Basic Books.

Gaspard, Françoise, and Farhad Khosrokhavar. 1995. *Le foulard et la République.* Paris: La Découverte.

Gasper, Michael. 2001. 'Abdallah al-Nadim, Islamic Reform, and "Ignorant" Peasants: State-Building in Egypt? In *Muslim Traditions and Techniques of Power,* ed. A. Salvatore, 75–92. Münster: Lit Verlag.

Geisser, Vincent. 2003. *La nouvelle islamophobie.* Paris: La Découverte.

Geschiere, Peter 2009. *The Perils of Belonging: Autochthony, Citizenship, and Exclusion in Africa.* Chicago: University of Chicago Press.

Gilligan, Carol. 1982. *In a Different Voice: Psychological Theory and Women's Development.* Cambridge, MA: Harvard University Press.

Gilroy, Paul. 2005. *Postcolonial Melancholia.* New York: Columbia University Press.

Giroux, Henry, and Peter McLaren. 1991. Radical Pedagogy as Cultural Politics: Beyond the Discourse of Critique and Anti-Utopianism. In *Theory/Pedagogy/Politics: Texts for Change,* ed. D. Morton and M. Zavarzadeh, 152–186. Champaign: University of Illinois Press.

Gökariksel, Banu. 2012. The Intimate Politics of Secularism and the Headscarf: The Mall, the Neighborhood, and the Public Square in Istanbul. *Gender, Place and Culture* 19 (1): 1–20.

Goldberg, Ellis. 1991. Smashing Idols and the State: The Protestant Ethic and Egyptian Sunni Radicalism. *Society for Comparative Study of Society and History* 31: 3–35.

Goldberg, David Theo. 2006. Racial Europeanization. *Ethnic and Racial Studies* 29 (2): 331–364.

Göle, Nilüfer. 1996. *The Forbidden Modern: Civilization and Veiling.* Ann Arbor: University of Michigan Press.

———. 2001. La deuxième phase de l'islamisme, l'expérience turque. In *La différence culturelle. Une reformulation des débats,* ed. M. Wieviorka and J. Ohana, 62–69. Paris: Balland.

———. 2002. Islam in Public: New Visibilities and New Imaginaries. *Public Culture* 14 (1): 173–190.

———. 2005. *Interpénétrations. L'islam et l'Europe.* Paris: Galaade Éditions.

———. ed. 2013a. *Islam and Public Controversy in Europe.* Global Connections series. Surrey, UK: Ashgate.

———. 2013b. Introduction: Islamic Controversies in the Making of European Public Spheres. In *Islam and Public Controversy in Europe,* ed. N. Göle, 3–20. Surrey, UK: Ashgate.

Gonzales-Quijano, Yves. 1991. Les livres islamiques: histoires ou mythes? *Peuples méditerranéens* 56–57: 283–292.

Gould, Carol S. 1994. A Puzzle About the Possibility of Aristotelian Enkrateia. *Phronesis* 39 (2): 174–186.

Grewal, Inderpal. 2006. "Security Moms" in the Early Twentieth-Century United States: The Gender of Security in Neoliberalism. *Women's Studies Quarterly* 34 (1/2): 25–39.

Grunebaum, G. E. von. (1951) 1976. *Muhammadan Festivals.* London: Curson Press.

Guénif-Souilamas, Nacira. 2006. The Other French Exception: Virtuous Racism and the War of the Sexes in Postcolonial France. *French Politics, Culture & Society* 24 (3): 23–41.

Guiné, Anouk, and Francisco J. M. Fuentes. 2007. Engendering Redistribution, Recognition, and Representation: The Case of Female Genital Mutilation (FGM) in the United Kingdom and France. *Politics & Society* 35 (3): 477–519.

Habermas, Jürgen. 1991. *The Structural Transformation of the Public Sphere: An Inquiry into a Category of Bourgeois Society.* Cambridge, MA: MIT Press.

———. 2003. Intolerance and Discrimination. *International Journal of Constitutional Law* 1 (1): 2–12.

———. 2005. Equal Treatment of Cultures and the Limits of Postmodern Liberalism. *Journal of Political Philosophy* 13 (1): 1–28.

———. 2006. Religion in the Public Sphere. *European Journal of Philosophy* 14 (1): 1–25.

———. 2008. Notes on Post-Secular Society. *New Perspectives Quarterly* 25 (4): 17–29.

Hadot, Pierre. 1992. Reflections on the Notion of "the Cultivation of the Self." In *Michel Foucault: Philosopher,* ed. T. J. Armstrong, 225–232. London: Harvester.

Haenni, Patrick. 2002. Au-delà du repli identitaire . . . Les nouveaux prêcheurs égyptiens et la modernisation paradoxale de l'islam. *Religioscope,* November. http://religio-scope.com/pdf/precheurs.pdf (accessed May 3, 2006).

Hallaq, Wael B. 1995. Ijtihad. In *The Oxford Encyclopedia of the Modern Islamic World*, ed. J. Esposito, 171–181. Oxford, UK: Oxford University Press.

Hammer, Juliane. 2008. Identity, Authority, and Activism: American Muslim Women Approach the Qurān. *Muslim World* 98 (4): 443–464.

———. 2010. Performing Gender Justice: The 2005 Woman-Led Prayer in New York. *Contemporary Islam* 4 (1): 91–116.

———. 2012. *American Muslim Women, Religious Authority, and Activism: More than a Prayer*. Austin: University of Texas Press.

Hartmann, Martin, and Axel Honneth. 2006. Paradoxes of Capitalism. *Constellations* 13 (1): 41–58.

Hassan, Mona. 2011. Women Preaching for the Secular State: Official Female Preachers (*Bayan Vaizler*) in Contemporary Turkey. *International Journal of Middle East Studies* 43: 451–473.

Hassini, Mohamed. 1997. *L'École: une chance pour les filles de parents maghrébins*. Paris: L'Harmattan.

Heckmann, Friedrich, and Dominique Schnapper. 2003. *The Integration of Immigrants in European Societies: National Differences and the Trends of Convergence*. Stuttgart: Lucius and Lucius.

Held, David. 2010. *Cosmopolitanism: Ideals and Realities*. Cambridge, UK: Polity Press.

Held, Virginia. 2006. *The Ethics of Care: Personal, Political, and Global*. New York: Oxford University Press.

Helly, Denise. 2006. Diaspora: History of an Idea. In *Muslim Diaspora: Gender, Culture and Identity*, ed. Haideh Moghissi, 3–22. London: Routledge.

Henkel, Heiko. 2005. "Between Belief and Unbelief Lies the Performance of Salat": Meaning and Efficacy of a Muslim Ritual. *Journal of the Royal Anthropological Institute* 11: 487–507.

Hervieu-Léger, Danièle. 1999. *Le pélerin et le converti. La religion en mouvement*. Paris: Champs Flammarion.

Hirschkind, Charles. 2001a. Civic Virtue and Religious Reason: An Islamic Counterpublic. *Cultural Anthropology* 16 (1): 3–34.

———. 2006 *The Ethical Soundscape: Cassette Sermons and Islamic Counterpublics*. New York: Columbia University Press.

———. 2012. Experiments in Devotion Online: The YouTube Khutba. *International Journal of Middle East Studies* 44 (1):5–21.

Hodgson, Douglas. 2003. *Individual Duty within a Human Rights Discourse*. Surrey, UK: Ashgate.

Hoffman, Valerie J. 1985. An Islamic Activist: Zaynab al-Ghazali. In *Women and the Family in the Middle East: New Voices of Change*, ed. E. W. Fernea, 233–254. Austin: University of Texas Press.

Hollywood, Amy. 2004. Gender, Agency, and the Divine in Religious Historiography. *Journal of Religion* 84 (4): 514–528.

Honneth, Axel. 1995. *The Struggle for Recognition: The Moral Grammar of Social Struggles*. Cambridge, UK: Polity Press.

Howell, Signe, ed. 1997. *The Ethnography of Moralities.* London: Routledge.

Hoy, David C. 2004. *Critical Resistance: From Poststructuralism to Post-Critique.* Cambridge, MA: MIT Press.

Ismael, Salwa. 2004. Being Muslim: Islam, Islamism and Identity Politics. *Government and Opposition* 39 (4): 614–631.

Ismail, Benjamin. 2010. Ban the Burqa? France Votes Yes. *Middle East Quarterly* 17 (4): 47–55.

Ismaïli, Miloud. 2003. *Comment se concentrer dans la prière.* Paris: Les Jumeaux.

———. 2005. *Comment augmenter sa foi.* Paris: Les Jumeaux.

Jacobsen, Christine M. 2011. *Islamic Traditions and Muslim Youth in Norway.* Leiden: Brill.

Johnston, David. 2004. A Turn in the Epistemology and Hermeneutics of Twentieth Century usul al-fiqh. *Islamic Law and Society* 11 (2): 233-282.

Jonker, Gerdien. 2002. *Eine Wellenlänge zu Gott: der "Verband der Islamischen Kulturzentren" in Europa.* Bielefeld: transcript Verlag.

———. 2003. Islamic Knowledge Through a Woman's Lens: Education, Power and Belief. *Social Compass* 50: 35–46.

———. 2005. The Mevlana Mosque in Berlin-Kreuzberg: An Unsolved Conflict. *Journal of Ethnic and Migration Studies* 31 (6): 1067–1081.

Joppke, Christian. 2009. *Veil.* Cambridge, UK: Polity Press.

Jouili, Jeanette S. 2009. Negotiating Secular Boundaries: Pious Micro-Practices of Muslim Women in French and German Public Spheres. *Social Anthropology* 17 (4): 445–470.

———. 2011. Beyond Emancipation: Subjectivities and Ethics among Women in Europe's Islamic Revival Communities. *Feminist Review* 98: 47–64.

———. 2014. Refining the Ummah in the Shadow of the Republic: Islamic Performing Arts and New Islamic Audio-Visual Landscapes in France. *Anthropological Quarterly* 87: (4): 1079-1104.

Jouili, Jeanette, and Melanie Kamp. 2014. Islamic Education in Germany: The "Institut für Internationale Pädagogik und Didaktik" and the "Zentrum für Islamische Frauenförderung und Forschung." In *Islamic Movements of Europe,* ed. F. Peter and O. Rafael, 287–291. London: I. B. Tauris.

Jouili, Jeanette, and Nikola Tietze. 2008. L'émergence d'intellectuel(les) de l'Islam en Allemagne: entre discipline politique et herméneutique féministe. *Revue des Mondes Musulmans et de la Méditerranée* 123 (1): 77–92

Kant, Immanuel. 1998. *Religion within the Boundaries of Mere Reason and Other Writings,* ed. and trans. A. Wood and G. Di Giovanni. Cambridge, UK: Cambridge University Press.

Karakaşoğlu-Aydin, Yasemin. 2000. *Muslimische Religiosität und Erziehungsvorstellungen. Eine empirische Untersuchung zu Orientierungen bei türkischen Lehramts- und Pädagogik-Studentinnen in Deutschland.* Frankfurt am Main: IKO-Verlag für Interkulturelle Kommunikation.

Karam, Azza M. 1998. *Women, Islamisms and the State: Contemporary Feminisms in Egypt.* London: Macmillan Press.

Kashani-Sabet, Firoozeh. 2006. The Politics of Reproduction: Maternalism and Women's Hygiene in Iran, 1896–1941. *International Journal of Middle East Studies* 38 (1): 1–29.

Kastoryano, Riva. 1996. *La France, l'Allemagne et leurs immigrés. Négocier l'identité.* Paris: Armand Colin.

Keane, Webb. 2003. Self-Interpretation, Agency, and the Objects of Anthropology: Reflections on a Genealogy. *Comparative Studies in Society and History* 45 (2): 222–248.

———. 2005. The Hazards of New Clothes: What Signs Make Possible. In *The Art Of Clothing: A Pacific Experience*, ed. S. Küchler and W. Graeme, 1–16. London: UCL Press.

———. 2007. *Christian Moderns: Freedom and Fetish in the Mission Encounter.* Berkeley: University of California Press.

———. 2008. The Evidence of the Senses and the Materiality of Religion. *Journal of the Royal Anthropological Institute* 14 (1): 110–127.

———. 2009. Modes of Objectification in Educational Experience. *Linguistics and Education* 19 (3): 312–318.

Keaton, Tricia Danielle. 2006. *Muslim Girls and the Other France: Race, Identity Politics, and Social Exclusion.* Bloomington: Indiana University Press.

Kepel, Gilles 1987. *Les banlieues de l'islam. Naissance d'une religion en France.* Paris: Seuil.

———. 1994. *A l'Ouest d'Allah.* Paris: Seuil.

Khaled, Amrou. 2005. *La purification des coeurs.* Beyrouth: Arab Scientific Publishers.

Killian, Caitlin. 2006. *North African Women in France: Gender, Culture, and Identity.* Stanford, CA: Stanford University Press.

Kittay, Eva Feder. 1999. *Love's Labor: Essays on Women, Equality and Dependency.* London: Routledge.

Klinkhammer, Gritt. 2000. *Moderne Formen islamischer Lebensführung. Eine qualitativ-empirische Untersuchung zur Religiosität sunnitisch geprägter Türkinnen der zweiten Generation in Deutschland.* Marburg: diagonal-Verlag.

König, Karin. 1989. *Tschador, Ehre und Kulturkonflikt. Veränderungsprozesse türkischer Frauen und Mädchen durch die Emigration und ihre soziokulturellen Folgen.* Frankfurt am Main: IKO-Verlag für Interkulturelle Kommunikation.

König, Matthias 2005. Politics and Religion in European Nation-States: Institutional Varieties and Contemporary Transformations. In *Religion and Politics: Cultural Perspectives*, eds. D. Suber and B. Giesen, 291–315. Leiden: Brill.

———. 2007. Europeanising the Governance of Religious Diversity: An Institutionalist Account of Muslim Struggles for Public Recognition. *Journal of Ethnic and Migration Studies*, 33 (6): 911–932.

Koonz, Claudia. 1987. *Mothers in the Fatherland: Women, the Family, and Nazi Politics.* New York: St. Martin's Press.

Kosman, Lois A. 1980. Being Properly Affected: Virtues and Feelings. In *Essays on Aristotle's Ethics*, ed. A. Oksenberg Rorty, 103–116. Berkeley: University of California Press.

Kymlicka, Will. 2001. Politics in the Vernacular: Nationalism, Multiculturalism, and Citizenship. Oxford, UK: Oxford University Press.

Kynsilehto, Anitta. 2008. Introductory Notes. In *Islamic Feminism: Current Perspectives*, ed. A. Kynsilehto, 9–14. Tampere, Finland: Tampere Peace Research Institute.

Lacoste-Dujardin, Camille. 1992. *Yasmina et les autres, de Nanterre et d'ailleurs. Filles de parents maghrébins en France*. Paris: La Découverte.

Laidlaw, James. 1995. *Riches and Renunciation: Religion, Economy, and Society among the Jains*. Oxford, UK: Oxford University Press.

———. 2002. For an Anthropology of Ethics and Freedom. *Journal of the Royal Anthropological Institute* 8: 311–332.

Lambek, Michael. 1993. *Knowledge and Practice in Mayotte: Local Discourses of Islam, Sorcery, and Spirit Possession*. Toronto: University of Toronto Press.

———. 2000. The Anthropology of Religion and the Quarrel between Poetry and Philosophy. *Current Anthropology* 41 (3): 309–320.

———. 2002a. *The Weight of the Past: Living with History in Mahajanga, Madagascar*. New York: Palgrave Macmillan.

———. 2002b. Nuriaty, the Saint and the Sultan. Virtuous Subject and Subjective Virtuoso of the Postmodern Colony. In *Postcolonial Subjectivities in Africa*, ed. R. Werbner, 25–43. London: Zed Books.

———. 2008. Value and virtue. *Anthropological Theory* 8 (2): 133–157.

———. 2010. *Ordinary Ethics: Anthropology, Language, and Action*. New York: Fordham University Press.

———. 2011. Reflections on Hermeneutics and Translocality. ZMO Working Paper no. 4. Berlin: Zentrum Moderner Orient.

Lapidus, Ira M. 1984. Knowledge, Virtue, and Action: The Classical Muslim Conception of Adab and the Nature of Religious Fulfilment in Islam. In *Moral Conduct and Authority: The Place of Adab in South Asian Islam*, ed. B. D. Metcalf, 38–61. Berkeley: University of California Press.

Lash, Scott. 1990. *The Sociology of Postmodernism, London and New York*. London: Routledge.

Lave, Jean. 1991. Situating Learning in Communities of Practice. *Perspectives on Socially Shared Cognition* 63: 63–82.

Lee, Robert D. 1997. *Overcoming Tradition and Modernity: The Search for Islamic Authenticity*. Boulder, CO: Westview Press.

Lefebvre, Henri. *The production of space*, transl. Donald Nicholson-Smith. Oxford: Blackwell, 1991.

Leggewie, Claus, Angela Joost, and Stefan Rech. 2002. *Der Weg zur Moschee: eine Handreichung für die Praxis*. Bad Homburg: Herbert Quandt-Stiftung.

Lenclud, Gérard. 1990. Vues de l'esprit, art de l'autre. L'ethnologie et les croyances en pays de savoir. *Terrain* 14: 5–19.

Lentin, Alana. 2008. Europe and the Silence about Race. *European Journal of Social Theory* 11 (4): 487–503.

Lentin, Alana, and Gavan Titley. 2011. *The Crisis of Multiculturalism: Racism in a Neoliberal Age*. London: Zed Books.

Levinas, Emmanuel. 1990. *Nine Talmudic Readings*, trans. A. Aranowicz. Bloomington: Indiana University Press.

———. 1998. *Entre Nous: Essays on Thinking-of-the-Other.* New York: Columbia University Press.

Lewis, Reina. 2007. Veils and Sales: Muslims and the Spaces of Postcolonial Fashion Retail. *Fashion Theory: The Journal of Dress, Body and Culture* 11: 423–441.

Lipovetsky, Gilles. 1994. *The Empire of Fashion: Dressing Modern Democracy.* Princeton, NJ: Princeton University Press.

Lithman, Yngve 2010. The Holistic Ambition: Social Cohesion and the Culturalization of Citizenship. *Ethnicities* 10 (4): 488–502.

Lübben, Ivesa. 2006. Gamal al-Banna: Gerechtigkeit für alle. In *Der Islam am Wendepunkt. Liberale und konservative Reformer einer Weltreligion,* eds. K. Amirpur and L. Ammann, 164–172. Freiburg: Herder Verlag.

Lynch, Kathleen, John Baker, and Maureen Lyons, eds. 2009. *Affective Equality: Love, Care and Injustice.* London: Palgrave Macmillan.

Mabro, Judy. 1991. *Veiled Half-Truths: Western Travellers' Perceptions of Middle Eastern Women.* London: I. B. Tauris.

MacIntyre, Alasdair. (1981) 2007. *After Virtue: A Study in Moral Theory.* London: Duckworth.

———. 1988. *Whose Justice? Which Rationality?* London: Duckworth.

MacLeod, Arlene Elowe. 1991. *Accommodating Protest: Working Women, the New Veiling, and Change in Cairo.* New York: Columbia University Press.

Mahdi, Tahar. n.d. *Le témoignage de la femme n'est en rien inférieur à celui de l'homme.* http://oumma.com/article.php3?id_article=663 (accessed June 25, 2006).

Mahmood, Saba. 2001. Feminist Theory, Embodiment, and the Docile Agent: Some Reflections on the Egyptian Islamic Revival. *Cultural Anthropology* 6 (2): 202–236.

———. 2005. *Politics of Piety: The Islamic Revival and the Feminist Subject.* Princeton, NJ: Princeton University Press.

———. 2013. Religious Reason and Secular Affect: An Incommensurable Divide? In *Is Critique Secular? Blasphemy, Injury, and Free Speech,* by T. Asad, W. Brown, J. Butler, and S. Mahmood, 64–100. New York: Fordham University Press.

Mandel, Ruth. 2008. *Cosmopolitan Anxieties: Turkish Challenges to Citizenship and Belonging in Germany.* Durham, NC: Duke University Press.

Mannitz, Sabine, and Werner Schiffauer. 2004. Taxonomies of Cultural Difference: Constructions of Otherness. In *Civil Enculturation: Nation-State, School and Ethnic Difference in The Netherlands, Britain, Germany and France,* ed. W. Schiffauer, G. Baumann, R. Kastoryano, and S. Vertovec, 60–87. Oxford, UK: Berghahn.

March, Andrew F. 2007. Reading Tariq Ramadan: Political Liberalism, Islam, and "Overlapping Consensus." *Ethics & International Affairs* 21 (4): 399–413.

———. 2010. The Post-Legal Ethics of Tariq Ramadan: Persuasion and Performance in *Radical Reform: Islamic Ethics and Liberation. Middle East Law and Governance* 2 (2): 253–273.

———. 2011. Law as a Vanishing Mediator in the Theological Ethics of Tariq Ramadan. *European Journal of Political Theory* 10 (2): 177–201.

Marfleet, Peter. 2000. Globalization, Islam and the Indigenization of Knowledge. In *Sit-*

uating Globalization: Views from Egypt, ed. C. Nelson and S. Rouse, 15–51. Bielefeld: transcript Verlag.

Mas, Ruth. 2006. Compelling the Muslim Subject: Memory as Post-Colonial Violence and the Public Performativity of "Secular/Cultural Islam." *Muslim World* 96 (4): 585–616.

———. 2011. On the Apocalyptic Tones of Islam in Secular Time. In *Secularism and Religion Making,* ed. A. Mandair and M. Dressler, 87–103. Oxford, UK: Oxford University Press.

Massumi, Brian 2002. *Parables for the Virtual: Movement, Affect, Sensation.* Durham, NC: Duke University Press.

Masud. (1977) 1995. Khalid. *Shatibi's Philosophy of Islamic Law.* Kuala Lumpur: Islamic Book Trust.

Masuzawa, Tomoko. 2005. *The Invention of World Religions: or, How European Universalism Was Preserved in the Language of Pluralism.* Chicago: University of Chicago Press.

Mattingly, Cheryl. 2012. Two Virtue Ethics and the Anthropology of Morality. *Anthropological Theory* 12 (2): 161–184.

Maussen, Marcel. 2007. Islamic Presence and Mosque Establishment in France: Colonialism, Arrangements for Guestworkers and Citizenship. *Journal of Ethnic and Migration Studies* 33 (6): 981–1002.

McLarney, Ellen. 2015. *Soft Force: Women in Egypt's Islamic Awakening.* Princeton, NJ: Princeton University Press.

McLarney, Ellen, and Banu Gökariksel. 2010. Muslim Women, Consumer Capitalism, and the Islamic Culture Industry. *Journal of Middle East Women's Studies* 6 (3): 1–18.

McNay, Lois. 1999. Subject, Psyche and Agency: The Work of Judith Butler. *Theory, Culture & Society* 16 (2): 175–193.

———. 2003. Agency, Anticipation and Indeterminacy in Feminist Theory. *Feminist Theory* 4 (2): 139–148.

———. 2008. *Against Recognition.* Cambridge, UK: Polity Press.

———. 2009. Self as Enterprise: Dilemmas of Control and Resistance in Foucault's The Birth of Biopolitics. *Theory, Culture & Society* 26 (6): 55–77.

Melchert, Christopher. 2004. Whether to Keep Women out of the Mosque: A Survey of Medieval Islamic Law. In *Authority, Privacy and Public Order in Islam,* ed. B. Michalak-Pikulska and A. Pikulski, 59–69. Leuven: Peeters.

Mendel, Milos. 1995. The Concept of "ad-Da'wa al-Islamiya": Toward a Discussion of the Islamist Reformist Religio-Political Terminology. *Archiv Orientalni* 63: 268–304.

Mendus, Susan. 1995. Human Rights in Political Theory. *Political Studies* 43: 11–25.

Merad, Ali. 1967. *Le réformisme musulman en Algérie de 1925 à 1940: essai d'histoire religieuse et sociale.* Paris: Mouton.

———. 1973. Islah. In *Encyclopedia of Islam.* New Edition. Vol. 4, Leiden: Brill, 141–171.

Mercer, Kobena. 1990. Black art and the burden of representation. *Third Text* 4 (10): 61–78.

Merlan, Francesca. 2010. Ordinary Ethics and Changing Cosmologies: Exemplification from North Australia. In *Ordinary Ethics: Anthropology, Language, and Action,* ed. M. Lambek, 207–224. New York: Fordham University Press.

Messick, Brinkley. 1996. Media Muftis: Radio Fatwas in Yemen. In *Islamic Legal Inter-*

pretation: Muftis and Their Fatwas, ed. B. Messick, M. K. Masud, and D. Powers, 310–320. Cambridge, MA: Harvard University Press.

Mir-Hosseini, Ziba. 1999. *Islam and Gender: The Religious Debate in Contemporary Iran.* Princeton, NJ: Princeton University Press.

———. 2006. Muslim Women's Quest for Equality: Between Islamic Law and Feminism. *Critical Inquiry* 32 (4): 629–645.

Mitchell, Richard. (1969) 1993. *The Society of the Muslim Brothers.* Oxford, UK: Oxford University Press.

Mittermaier, Amira. 2010. *Dreams That Matter: Egyptian Landscapes of the Imagination.* Berkeley: University of California Press.

———. 2012. Dreams from Elsewhere: Muslim Subjectivities beyond the Trope of Self-Cultivation. *Journal of the Royal Anthropological Institute* 18 (2): 247–265.

Modood, Tariq. 2003. Muslims and the Politics of Difference. *Political Quarterly* 74 (1): 100–115.

Moghadam, Valentine M. 2002. Islamic Feminism and Its Discontents: Toward a Resolution of the Debate. *Signs* 27 (4): 1135–1171.

Mohanty, Chandra Talpade. 1991. Under Western Eyes: Feminist Scholarship and Colonial Discourses. In *Third World Women and the Politics of Feminism,* ed. A. Russo, C. T. Mohanty, and L. Torres, 61–88. Bloomington: Indiana University Press.

Mohsen-Finan, Khadija. 2002. Tariq Ramadan: Voice of a New Religiousness. In *Intercultural Relations and Religious Authorities: Muslims in the European Union,* ed. W.A.R. Shadid and P. S. van Koningsveld, 208–214. Leuven: Peeters.

Monnot, Guy. 1995. Salat. In *Encyclopedia of Islam.* New Edition. Vol. 8. Leiden: Brill, 925–33.

Moors, Annelies. 2007. Fashionable Muslims: Notions of Self, Religion, and Society in Sana. *Fashion Theory: The Journal of Dress, Body and Culture* 11: 319–346.

———. 2009. The Dutch and the Face-Veil: The Politics of Discomfort. *Social Anthropology* 17 (4): 393–408.

Moors, Annelies, and Emma Tarlo. 2007. Introduction: Muslim Fashion. *Fashion Theory: The Journal of Dress, Body and Culture* 11 (2/3, Special Issue): 133–141.

Moosa, Ebrahim. 2000. The Dilemma of Islamic Rights Schemes. *Journal of Law and Religion* 15 (1/2): 182–215.

———. 2005. *Ghazali and the Poetics of Imagination.* Chapel Hill: University of North Carolina Press.

Morey, Peter, and Amina Yaqin. 2011. *Framing Muslims: Stereotyping and Representation After 9/11.* Cambridge, MA: Harvard University Press.

Morgan-Foster, Jason. 2005. Third Generation Rights: What Islamic Law Can Teach the International Human Rights Movement. *Yale Human Rights & Development Law Journal* 8: 67–116.

Morin, Edgar. 1990. "Le trou noir de la laïcité." Le débat 58: 38–41. http://palimpsestes.fr/quinquennat/2012/octobre/sem27oct/morin_laicite.pdf (accessed July 15, 2008).

Murata, Sachiko. 1992. *The Tao of Islam: A Sourcebook on Gender Relationships in Islam.* Albany: State University of New York Press.

Muslim Brotherhood. 1994. *The Role of Women in Islamic Society According to the Muslim Brotherhood.* London: International Islamic Forum.

Najmabadi, Afsaneh. 1998. Crafting the Educated Housewife in Iran. In *Remaking Women: Feminism and Modernity in the Middle East,* ed. L. Abu-Lughod, 91–125. Princeton, NJ: Princeton University Press.

Nancy, Jean-Luc. 2000. *Being Singular Plural.* Stanford: Stanford University Press.

Nasr, Seyyed H. 2002. *The Heart of Islam: Enduring Values for Humanity.* New York: HarperCollins.

Navaro-Yashin, Yael. 2002. The Market for Identities: Secularism, Islamism, Commodities. In *Fragments of Culture: The Everyday of Modern Turkey,* ed. D. Kandiyoti and A. Saktanber, 221–253. London: I. B. Tauris.

Nedelsky, Jennifer. 1989. Reconceiving Autonomy." *Yale Journal of Law & Feminism* 1 (1): 7–36.

Noddings, Nel. 1984. *Caring: A Feminine Approach to Ethics and Moral Education.* Berkeley: University of California Press.

Nökel, Sigrid. 2002. *Die Töchter der Gastarbeiter und der Islam. Zur Soziologie alltagsweltlicher Annerkennungspolitiken. Eine Fallstudie.* Bielefeld: transcript Verlag.

Nussbaum, Martha. 1986. *The Fragility of Goodness: Luck and Ethics in Greek Tragedy and Philosophy.* Cambridge, UK: Cambridge University Press.

———. 1997. *Cultivating Humanity: A Classical Defense of Reform in Liberal Education.* Cambridge, MA: Harvard University Press.

Öncü, Ayşe. 2006. Becoming "Secular Muslims": Yaşar Nuri Öztürk as a Super-Subject on Turkish Television. In *Religion, Media, and the Public Sphere,* ed. B. Meyer and A. Moors, 227–250. Bloomington: Indiana University Press.

Opwis, Felicitas. 2005. Maslaha in Contemporary Islamic Legal Theory. *Islamic Law and Society* 12 (2): 182–223.

Özdalga, Elisabeth. 2003. Following in the Footsteps of Fethullah Gülen: Three Women Teachers Tell Their Stories. In *Turkish Islam and the Secular State: The Gülen Movement,* ed. H. Yavuz and J. Esposito, 85–114. Syracuse, NY: Syracuse University Press.

Parkins, Ilya. 2010. Fashion as Methodology: Rewriting the Time of Women's Modernity. *Time & Society* 19 (1): 98–119.

Partridge, Damani J. 2012. *Hypersexuality and Headscarves: Race, Sex, and Citizenship in the New Germany.* Bloomington: Indiana University Press.

Parvez, Fareen Z. 2011. Debating the Burqa in France: The Antipolitics of Islamic Revival. *Qualitative Sociology* 34 (2): 287–312.

Pepicelli, Renata. 2008. Islamic Feminism: Identities and Positionalities. In *Islamic Feminism: Current Perspectives,* ed. A. Kynsilehto, 91–101. Tampere, Finland: Tampere Peace Research Institute.

Peter, Frank. 2006a. Individualization and Religious Authority in Western European Islam. *Islam and Christian-Muslim Relations* 17 (1): 105–118.

———. 2006b. Islamism, Islamic Reformism and the Public Stigmatization of Muslims: A Study of Muslim Discourses in France. *Oriente Moderno* 25 (3): 443–460.

———. 2010a. Welcoming Muslims into the Nation: Tolerance, Politics and Integration in Germany. In *Muslims in the West after 9/11: Religion, Politics and Law,* ed. J. Césari, 119–144. London: Routledge.

———. 2010b. Die Union des Organisations Islamiques de France und die Tradition der Muslimbrüder im Zeitalter der Integrationspolitik. In *Islam in Europa: Religiöses Leben heute,* ed. D. Reetz, 145–170. Münster: Waxmann.

Ramadan, Tariq. 1995. *Islam, le face à face des civilisations. Quel projet pour quelle modernité?* Lyon: Tawhid.

———. 2004. *Western Muslims and the Future of Islam.* Oxford, UK: Oxford University Press.

———. 2006. Muslims, the Pope and European Identity. *New Perspectives Quarterly* 23 (4): 14–18.

Ramm, Christoph. 2010. The Muslim Makers: How Germany "Islamizes" Turkish Immigrants. *Interventions: International Journal of Postcolonial Studies* 12 (2): 183–197.

Rana, Junaid. 2011. *Terrifying Muslims: Race and Labor in the South Asian Diaspora.* Durham, NC: Duke University Press.

Rawls, John. 1971. *A Theory of Justice.* Cambridge, MA: Harvard University Press.

Rida, Rashid. (1928) 1984. *Yusr al-islam wa usul al-tashri' al-'amm (The Ease of Islam and the Foundation of General Legislation).* Cairo: Maktabat al-Salam.

Riesner, Silke. 1990. *Junge türkische Frauen der zweiten Generation in der Bundesrepublik Deutschland. Eine Analyse von Lebensentwürfen anhand lebensgeschichtlich orientierter Interviews.* Frankfurt am Main: IKO-Verlag für Interkulturelle Kommunikation.

Roald, Anne Sofie. 2001. *Women in Islam. The Western Experience.* London: Routledge.

Robbins, Joel. 2004. *Becoming Sinners: Christianity and Moral Torment in a Papua New Guinea Society.* Berkeley: University of California Press.

———. 2007. Causality, Ethics, and the Near Future. *American Ethnologist* 34 (3): 433–436.

Roest Crollius, Ary R. 1978. Mission and Morality: Al-amr bi-l-ma'ruf as Expression of the Communitarian and Missonary Dimensions of Qur'anic Ethics. *Studia Missionalia* 27: 257–284.

Rose, Nikolas. 1999. *Powers of Freedom: Reframing Political Thought.* Cambridge, UK: Cambridge University Press.

Rosenow-Williams, Kerstin. 2012. *Organizing Muslims and Integrating Islam in Germany: New Developments in the 21st Century.* Leiden: Brill.

Rosenthal, Franz. 1970. *Knowledge Triumphant.* Leiden: Brill.

Rostock, Petra, and Sabine Berghahn. 2008. The Ambivalent Role of Gender in Redefining the German Nation. *Ethnicities* 8 (3): 345–364.

Rottmann, Susan B., and Myra Marx Ferree. 2008. Citizenship and Intersectionality: German Feminist Debates About Headscarf and Antidiscrimination Laws. *Social Politics: International Studies in Gender, State and Society* 15: 481–513.

Rouse, Carolyn M. 2004. *Engaged Surrender: African American Women and Islam.* Berkeley: University of California Press.

Roy, Olivier. 2004. *Globalized Islam: The Search for a New Ummah.* New York: Columbia University Press.

Safran, William. 1990. Ethnic Diasporas in Industrial Societies: A Comparative Study of the Political Implications of the "Homeland" Myth. In *Les Étrangers dans la Ville*, ed. I. Barouh-Simon and P.-J. Simon, 163–193. Paris: L'Harmattan.

Saktanber, Ayşe. 2002. "We Pray Like You Have Fun": New Islamic Youth in Turkey Between Intellectualism and Popular Culture. In *Fragments of Culture: The Everyday of Modern Turkey*, ed. D. Kandiyoti and A. Saktanber, 254–276. New Brunswick, NJ: Rutgers University Press.

Salime, Zakia. 2011. *Between Feminism and Islam: Human Rights and Sharia Law in Morocco*. Minneapolis: University of Minnesota Press.

Salvatore, Armando. 1998. Staging Virtue: The Disembodiment of Self-Correctness and the Making of Islam as Public Norm. In *Islam—Motor or Challenge of Modernity*, ed. G. Stauth, 87–120. Yearbook of the Sociology of Islam. Hamburg: Lit Verlag.

———. 2007. *The Public Sphere: Liberal Modernity, Catholicism, Islam*. New York: Palgrave Macmillan.

———. 2009. Qaradawi's Maslaha: From Ideologue of the Islamic Awakening to Sponsor of Transnational Public Islam. In *The Global Mufti: The Phenomenon of Yusuf al-Qaradawi*, eds. J. Skovgaard-Petersen and B. Gräf, 239–250. New York: Columbia University Press.

Samb, Amadou Makhtar. 2005. *De la confiance en Dieu*. Paris: al-Bustane.

Sandel, Michael. 1982. *Liberalism and the Limits of Justice*. Cambridge, UK: Cambridge University Press.

Schielke, Samuli. 2009. Being Good in Ramadan: Ambivalence, Fragmentation, and the Moral Self in the Lives of Young Egyptians. *Journal of the Royal Anthropological Institute* 15 (1): 24–40.

———. 2010. *Second Thoughts about the Anthropology of Islam, or How to Make Sense of Grand Schemes in Everyday Life*. ZMO Working Paper no. 2. Berlin: Zentrum Moderner Orient.

Schiffauer, Werner. 2000. *Die Gottesmänner. Türkische Islamisten in Deutschland*. Frankfurt am Main: Suhrkamp.

———. 2006. Enemies Within the Gates: The Debate about the Citizenship of Muslims in Germany. In *Multiculturalism, Muslims and Citizenship: A European Approach*, ed. A. Triandifyllidou, T. Modood, and R. Zapata-Barrero, 94–116. New York: Routledge.

———. 2010. *Nach dem Islamismus. Eine Ethnographie der Islamischen Gemeinschaft Milli Görüş*. Frankfurt am Main: Suhrkamp.

Schiffer, Sabine. 2005. *Die Darstellung des Islam in der Presse. Sprache, Bilder, Suggestionen. Eine Auswahl von Techniken und Beispielen*. Erlangen: Ergon.

Scott, David. 1999. *Refashioning Futures: Criticism after Postcoloniality*. Princeton, NJ: Princeton University Press.

———. 2004. *Conscripts of Modernity: The Tragedy of Colonial Enlightenment*. Durham, NC: Duke University Press.

Scott, Joan W. 1996. *Only Paradoxes to Offer: French Feminists and the Rights of Man*. Cambridge, MA: Harvard University Press.

———. 2005. Symptomatic Politics: The Banning of Islamic Head Scarves in French Public Schools. *French Politics, Culture & Society* 23 (3): 106–127.

———. 2007. *The Politics of the Veil.* Princeton, NJ: Princeton University Press.

Selby, Jennifer A. 2012. *Questioning French Secularism: Gender Politics and Islam in a Parisian Suburb.* New York: Palgrave Macmillan.

Shakry, Omnia. 1998. Schooled Mothers and Structured Play: Child Rearing in Turn-of-the-Century Egypt. In *Remaking Women: Feminism and Modernity in the Middle East,* ed. L. Abu-Lughod. Princeton, NJ: Princeton University Press.

Sheffer, Gabriel. 2003. *Diaspora Politics.* Cambridge, UK: Cambridge University Press.

Silvers, Laury, and Ahmed Elewa. 2011. "I Am One of the People": A Survey and Analysis of Legal Arguments on Woman-Led Prayer in Islam. *Journal of Law and Religion* 26 (1): 141–171.

Silverstein, Paul A. 2004. *Algeria in France: Transpolitics, Race, and Nation.* Bloomington: Indiana University Press.

———. 2005. Immigrant Racialization and the New Savage Slot: Race, Migration, and Immigration in the New Europe. *Annual Revue of Anthropology* 34: 363–384.

Simmel, Georg. 1997. *Simmel on Culture.* London: Sage.

Smith, Neil. 1992. Geography, Difference, and the Politics of Scale. In *Postmodernism and the Social Sciences,* ed. J. Doherty, E. Graham, and M. Malek, 57–79. London: Palgrave Macmillan.

Smith, William. 2007. Cosmopolitan Citizenship: Virtue, Irony and Worldliness. *European Journal of Social Theory* 10 (1): 37–52.

Sounaye, Abdoulaye. 2011. "Go Find the Second Half of Your Faith with These Women!" Women Fashioning Islam in Contemporary Niger. *Muslim World* 101 (3): 539–554.

Spielhaus, Riem. 2011. Making Islam Relevant: Female Authority and Representation of Islam in Germany. In *Women, Leadership, and Mosques: Changes in Contemporary Islamic Authority,* ed. M. Bano and H. Kalmbach, 437–456. Leiden: Brill.

Staeheli, Lynn, Eleonore Kofman, and Linda Peake. 2004. *Mapping Women, Making Politics: Feminist Perspectives on Political Geography.* London: Routledge.

Stallybrass, Peter. 1993. "Worn Worlds: Clothes, Mourning, and the Life of Things." *The Yale Review* 81 (2): 35–50.

Starrett, Gregory. 1995. The Hexis of Interpretation: Islam and the Body in the Egyptian Popular School. *American Anthropologist* 22: 953–969.

Stowasser, Barbara Freyer. 1987. Religious Ideology, Women, and the Family: The Islamic Paradigm. In *The Islamic Impulse,* ed. B. F. Stowasser, 262–296. Washington, DC: Center for Contemporary Arab Studies.

———. 1994. *Women in the Qur'an, Traditions and Interpretation.* Oxford, UK: Oxford University Press.

Suniers, Thiel. 2004. Argumentative Strategies. In *Civil Enculturation: Nation-State, School and Ethnic Difference in The Netherlands, Britain, Germany and France,* ed. W. Schiffauer, 210–241. Oxford, UK: Berghahn.

Tarlo, Emma. 2007. Islamic Cosmopolitanism: The Sartorial Biographies of Three Muslim Women in London. *Fashion Theory: The Journal of Dress, Body and Culture* 11: 143–172.

———. 2010. *Visibly Muslim: Fashion, Politics, Faith.* Oxford, UK: Berg.

Taylor, Charles. 1985. *Philosophy and the Human Sciences*. Cambridge, UK: Cambridge University Press.

———. 1989. *Sources of the Self: The Making of the Modern Identity*. Cambridge, MA: Harvard University Press.

———. 1991. *The Ethics of Authenticity*. Cambridge, MA: Harvard University Press.

———. 1994. Justice after Virtue. In *After MacIntyre: Critical Perspectives on the Work of Alasdair MacIntyre*, ed. S. Mendus and J. Horton, 16–43. Cambridge, UK: Polity Press.

———. 2003. *Modern Social Imaginaries*. Durham, NC: Duke University Press.

Tezcan, Levent 2012. *Das muslimische Subjekt: Verfangen im Dialog der Deutschen Islam Konferenz*. Konstanz: Konstanz University Press.

Tietze, Nikola. 2002. *Jeunes musulmans de France et d'Allemagne*. Paris: L'Harmattan.

Todd, Emmanuel. 1994. *Le destin des immigrés, assimilation et ségrégation dans les démocraties occidentales*. Paris: Seuil.

Tribalat, Michèle. 1995. *Faire France. Une enquête sur les immigrés et leurs enfants*. Paris: La Découverte.

Tronto, Joan. 1993. *Moral Boundaries: A Political Argument for an Ethics of Care*. New York: Routledge.

Turner, Bryan S. 2000. Liberal Citizenship and Cosmopolitan Virtue. In *Citizenship and Democracy in a Global Era*, ed. A. Vandenberg, 18–32. London: Palgrave Macmillan.

———. 2001. Cosmopolitan Virtue: On Religion in a Global Age. *European Journal of Social Theory* 4 (2): 131–152.

———. 2002. Cosmopolitan Virtue, Globalization and Patriotism. *Theory, Culture & Society* 19 (1–2): 45–63.

Tyler, Carole Anne. 1994. Passing: Narcissism, Identity and Difference. *Differences* 6: 212–248.

Vatuk, Sylvia. 2008. Islamic Feminism in India: Indian Muslim Women Activists and the Reform of Muslim Personal Law. *Modern Asian Studies* 42 (2/3): 489–518.

Venel, Nancy. 1999. *Musulmanes françaises. Des pratiquantes voilées à l'université*. Paris: L'Harmattan.

Verkaaik, Oskar. 2010. The Cachet Dilemma: Ritual and Agency in New Dutch Nationalism. *American Ethnologist* 37 (1): 69–82.

Vinken, Barbara. 2001. *Die deutsche Mutter. Der lange Schatten eines Mythos*. Zürich: Piper.

———. 2005. *Fashion Zeitgeist: Trends and Cycles in the Fashion System*. Oxford, UK: Berg.

Wadud, Amina. 1999. *Qur'an and Woman: Rereading the Sacred Text from a Woman's Perspective*. Oxford, UK: Oxford University Press.

Waldron, Jeremy. 1987. *Nonsense upon Stilts: Bentham, Burke and Marx on the Rights of Man*. York, UK: Methuen.

Walzer, R. 1979. Akhlak. In *Encyclopedia of Islam*. Vol 1., 325-29. Leiden: Brill.

Wan Daud, Wan M. N. 1989. *The Concept of Knowledge in Islam and Its Implications for Education in a Developing Country*. London: Mansell.

Warner, Michael. 2002. Publics and Counterpublics. *Public Culture* 14 (1): 49–90.

Warnier, Jean-Pierre. 1999. *Construire la culture matérielle: L'Homme qui pensait avec ses doigts.* Paris: Presses Universitaires de France.

———. 2001. A Praxeological Approach to Subjectivation in a Material World. *Journal of Material Culture* 6 (1): 15–24.

Weber, Beverly. 2004. Cloth on Her Head, Constitution in Hand: Germany's Headscarf Debates and the Cultural Politics of Difference. *German Politics & Society* 22 (3): 33–64.

Weber, Max. (1930) 1996. *The Protestant Ethic and the Spirit of Capitalism.* Los Angeles: Roxbury.

Weeks, Kathy. 2009. "Hours for What We Will": Work, Family, and the Movement for Shorter Hours. *Feminist Studies* 35: 101–127.

Weibel, Nadine. 2000. *Par-delà le voile. Femmes d'Islam en Europe.* Paris: Complexe.

Werbner, Pnina. 1999. Political Motherhood and the Feminisation of Citizenship: Women's Activisms and the Transformation of the Public Sphere. In *Women Citizenship and Difference,* ed. N. Yuval-Davis and P. Werbner, 221–245. London: Zed Books.

———. 2005. Islamophobia: Incitement to Religious Hatred—Legislating for a New Fear? *Anthropology Today* 21 (1): 5–9.

———. 2007. Veiled Interventions in Pure Space: Honour, Shame and Embodied Struggles Among Muslims in Britain and France. *Theory, Culture & Society* 24 (2): 161–186.

———. 2009. Revisiting the UK Muslim Diasporic Public Sphere at a Time of Terror: From Local (Benign) Invisible Spaces to Seditious Conspiratorial Spaces and the "Failure of Multiculturalism" Discourse. *South Asian Diaspora* 1 (1): 19–45.

White, Jenny. 2002. The Islamist Paradox. In *Fragments of Culture: The Everyday of Modern Turkey,* ed. by D. Kandiyoti and A. Saktanber, 191–217. London: I. B. Tauris.

Winter, Bronwyn. 2008. *Hijab and the Republic: Uncovering the French Headscarf Debate.* Syracuse, NY: Syracuse University Press.

Wolin, Sheldon, 1985. Revolutionary Action Today. In *Post-Analytic Philosophy,* eds. J. Rajchman and C. West, 244–258. New York: Columbia University Press.

Yeğenoğlu, Meyda. 1998. *Colonial Fantasies: Towards a Feminist Reading of Orientalism.* Cambridge, UK: Cambridge University Press.

Young, Iris Marion. 1990. *Justice and the Politics of Difference.* Princeton, NJ: Princeton University Press.

Yükleyen, Ahmet. 2012. *Localizing Islam in Europe: Turkish Islamic Communities in Germany and the Netherlands.* Syracuse, NY: Syracuse University Press.

Yurdakul, Gokce. 2009. *From Guest Workers into Muslims: The Transformation of Turkish Immigrant Associations in Germany.* Newcastle upon Tyne: Cambridge Scholars.

Zaman, Muhammad Qasim. 2004. The ʿUlama of Contemporary Islam and Their Conceptions of the Common Good. In *Public Islam and the Common Good,* ed. A. Salvatore and D. F. Eickelman, 129–155. Brill: Leiden.

Zentrum Islamischer Frauenforschung (ZIF). 2005. *Ein einziges Wort und seine große Wirkung—Eine hermeneutische Betrachtungsweise zum Qur'an Sure 4, Vers 34, mit Blick auf das Geschlechterverhältnis im Islam.* Köln: ZIF Verlag.

Zigon, Jarrett. 2008. *Morality: An Anthropological Perspective.* Oxford, UK: Berg.

INDEX